D1617326

NEW APPROACHES IN SOCIOLOGY
STUDIES IN SOCIAL INEQUALITY, SOCIAL CHANGE, AND SOCIAL JUSTICE

Edited by
Nancy A. Naples
University of Connecticut

A ROUTLEDGE SERIES

NEW APPROACHES IN SOCIOLOGY
STUDIES IN SOCIAL INEQUALITY, SOCIAL CHANGE, AND SOCIAL JUSTICE
NANCY A. NAPLES, *General Editor*

THE SOCIAL ORGANIZATION OF POLICY
*An Institutional Ethnography of
UN Forest Deliberations*
Lauren E. Eastwood

THE STRUGGLE OVER GAY, LESBIAN, AND
BISEXUAL RIGHTS
Facing Off in Cincinnati
Kimberly B. Dugan

PARENTING FOR THE STATE
*An Ethnographic Analysis of
Non-Profit Foster Care*
Teresa Toguchi Swartz

TALKING BACK TO PSYCHIATRY
*The Psychiatric Consumer/Survivor/
Ex-Patient Movement*
Linda J. Morrison

CONTEXTUALIZING HOMELESSNESS
*Critical Theory, Homelessness, and
Federal Policy Addressing the Homeless*
Ken Kyle

LINKING ACTIVISM
*Ecology, Social Justice, and Education
for Social Change*
Morgan Gardner

Linking Activism
Ecology, Social Justice, and Education for Social Change

Morgan Gardner

Routledge
New York & London

Published in 2005 by
Routledge
Taylor & Francis Group
270 Madison Avenue
New York, NY 10016

Published in Great Britain by
Routledge
Taylor & Francis Group
2 Park Square
Milton Park, Abingdon
Oxon OX14 4RN

Printed in the United States of America on acid-free paper
10 9 8 7 6 5 4 3 2 1

International Standard Book Number-10: 0-415-97459-3 (Hardcover)
International Standard Book Number-13: 978-0-415-97459-2 (Hardcover)
Library of Congress Card Number 2005011677

Library of Congress Cataloging-In-Publication Data

Gardner, Morgan.
    Linking activism : ecology, social justice, and education for social change / Morgan Gardner.
        p. cm. -- (New approaches in sociology)
    Includes bibliographical references and index.
    ISBN 0-415-97459-3
    1. Social values. 2. Social action. 3. Environmental justice. 4. Social justice. 5. Collective behavior. I. Title. II. Series.

HM681.G37 2005
303.3'72--dc22   2005011677

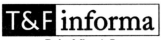

Taylor & Francis Group
is the Academic Division of T&F Informa plc.

Visit the Taylor & Francis Web site at
http://www.taylorandfrancis.com

and the Routledge Web site at
http://www.routledge-ny.com

To
Mikaela Mary Joy
who lives life's connections in wonderment

Contents

Acknowledgments

My warm thanks are extended to family, friends, and colleagues who have given in direct and indirect ways to this project. Thanks to Michelle Meyer who has given invaluable forms of care, encouragement, and feedback since the inception of this work. Thanks to friends and colleagues Kathleen Cooper, Sobia Shaikh, Diana Gustafson, Nancy Quinn, and Si Transken for their insights, listening, and counsel at different stages of this project. I am also indebted to Margrit Eichler, Ardra Cole, and Budd Hall for their encouragement and review of my work. I am deeply appreciative to each activist who participated in this study for the sharing of their experiences and insights. My thanks to Frank Williams for his research assistance support; Alfred Dyck for his work on Figure 1 contained in this book; and Roberta Hammett for helping me navigate resources. To family members Mary Gardner, Mikeala Clark Gardner, Stephen Clark, and Hugh Clark thank you for your care, encouragement, and love of learning—all qualities which have enriched my work on this project. Thanks to both long time and recent friends who are here for the richness of the journey—Catherine, Sobia, Alf, Mary Lou, Alan, Rita, Clar, Bobbi, Ursula, and the Green Amazons. Thanks to Memorial University and to my colleagues in the Faculty of Education who provide a vibrant place to pursue research, scholarship, and teaching.

Chapter One

Envisioning Linking Activism: Agency and Self in the Creation of Ecologically Healthy and Socially Just Communities

Journal note: Looking back I realize I witnessed the links between social justice and environmental protection from a young age. As a child I remember noticing that the air was dirtier in the poor parts of town. I recall a family friend's husband sick and dying with a lung disease from years of working unprotected in the mines. I saw First Nations communities living adjacent to waste dumps. And I have seen many homeless men, women, and children sleeping in filthy urban streets. These experiences haunted me as a child, and as I grew older they became buried inside me, as if, in some respects, they never existed. And in a way, this was true, because the societal culture around me was not recognizing or acting on these forms of social and ecological oppression. The dominant culture around me treated these injustices as if they were invisible.

I didn't begin to truly confront my own collusion with these forms of socially constructed invisibility until my early twenties when I became involved in environmental advocacy. I started catching myself in one instance, and then in another, unwittingly living my activism in ways which isolated rather than linked social justice and environmental practice. I began realizing that many of my activist assumptions, standpoints, and practices needed re-examination. From the outside, this awareness of fragmentation challenged me to open myself to the complex dimensions and layers of social change work. For instance, I began asking, how would workers and communities impacted by environmental reforms be dealt with justly? Do our environmental efforts resonate with minoritized individuals? As activists, are we aware of the ways our social locationality frames our environmental work? What blocks environmental activists from asking certain kinds of socially related questions?

From the inside, I began experiencing the desire to gather and integrate different values, experiences, and positionalities within me. While the nature-lover, the strategist, and rabble-rouser in me were well utilized in my environmental work, my feminist, spiritual, and social justice values needed to influence my agency more strongly. I began making feminist analyses of environmental problems and solutions visible in my activism. I started advocating for consensus decision-making in environmental decision-making forums. I struggled to embody a holistic approach to environmental change-making—an approach centered on both social justice and ecological health so that one form of oppression or concern would not be pitted against another.

In retrospect, I realized that in order to honor the webs of our social-ecological connections I needed to embrace the opportunity for transformative change, both in myself, and in the world around me.

There are many reasons for investigating social change makers' attempts to work in more integrative and holistic ways. Perhaps the most crucial reason stems from the notion that if we want to live in ecologically healthy *and* socially just communities, we need solutions that integrate rather than separate these concerns. Anecdotal reports and empirical studies are demonstrating that we are not only in the current environmental challenge together, we are also in it differently. Gender, race, class, ethnicity, geographical location, and other forms of social locationality intersect with our natural environments (Faber, 1998c; Bryant, 1995; Shiva, 1989, 1991, 1997). Systemic oppressions position some individuals in disproportionately more highly polluted areas than others (Szasz, 1994; Hofrichter, 1993; Faber 1998c). Social injustices, moreover, isolate some individuals from accessing "public" environmental protections and progress (Dowie, 1996; Faber 1998c; Bryant, 1995; Hofrichter, 1993). These realities demonstrate that advocates of environmental protection need to confront not only complex ecosystems but also complex social inequalities which intersect these landscapes. Athanasiou (1996) describes this attention to social justice realities as an unavoidable shift within the movement for environmental change:

> [T]he "social issues" are everywhere seeping up through the floor of old-school environmentalism. The need for "justice" and "equality" haunts the green movement. Those who seek to avoid it, to advocate "nature protection" in any simple manner, seem atavistic even to themselves. Ten

years ago, only a few isolated radicals saw the Third World's crushing international debt as a green issue. Today, it is well known as a key link in the fiscal chains strangling the world's ecosystems. Likewise, land reform, women's rights, world trade, consumerism, technology, poverty, and immigration are widely recognized as environmental issues. There is a common sense of a new holism in which the ambit of green politics expands to include the entire cultural and institutional nexus of environmental degradation, to become a "social ecology" more fully realized than any even suspected during the long chill of the Cold War (p. 9).

More than just "seeping up through the floor of old-school environmentalism," this need for "a new holism," to which Athanasiou refers, is challenging all forms of environmental advocacy. In working to bridge the social-cultural and political-economic divisions which isolate social and ecological work, the practice of this "new holism" is likely to be more than any of us bargained for. This is particularly apparent given the context of reductionist ideologies and practices of dominant Western cultures.

This work examines attempts toward more holistic environmental change-making through the study of 30 activists striving to address social justice issues within the context of their environmental advocacy. I refer to this blended social-ecological justice practice as "linking activism," although I also use the terms integrative, holistic, or social justice-ecological practice to refer to this activist work. I have done this intentionally, in part, because it is a struggle to find the right words to talk about more complex forms of agency; and in part, because I want to disrupt assumptions that broadly defined change practices benefit from being positioned in a single construct. Like its diversity of forms, linking activism will also benefit, I believe, from a diversity of terms to articulate its meanings.

Activist stories demonstrate a weaving of social justice issues across varied contexts and environmental commitments. In asking activists to narrate their linking efforts, we see, for instance, varied forms of social injustice (e.g., sexism, racism, poverty) and a broad range of environmental concerns (e.g., forestry, water quality, waste, transportation). In a similar vein, activist accounts are situated in a wide range of contexts, including from local sites to international arenas, from rural communities to urban centers, from large environmental organizations to small grassroots groups, from locations both inside and outside the environmental movement. It is this multi-dimensionality of linking activist practice that is explored in this work.

There is a paucity of research which examines how activists involved in environmental protection conceptualize social justice issues within their work, and moreover, how these activists work to address these justice issues. Additionally, as researchers, we have little knowledge of the span of activists' linking experiences, and thereby also lack insight into how these experiences are reframing or transforming their environmental practice. Most studies of activism continue to prioritize either an environmental or social justice focus. Additionally, literature which examines environmental inequities tends to investigate *a* specific set of connections, (such as the connection between gender or race and the environment), or else examines environmental inequities within a specific case study account. Presently, Canadian research examining environmental change-makers' social justice practice is limited; and again, these studies do not focus on the multi-dimensionality of activists' linking work.

This research seeks to understand integrative practice through the range of activists' different linking involvements. This approach is valuable both at practical and theoretical levels. Few activists involved in environmental change have the opportunity to concentrate exclusively on one ecological issue. Funding structures of nonprofit environmental groups and the array of environmental challenges facing communities often dictate that activists become adept at juggling many environmental issues within a given social context. This demonstrates the need to understand linking activism from a perspective of breadth so that the actual dimensions of activist practice can be revealed and a more accurate theoretical discourse concerning activists' realities can be offered.

In an era of neo-liberal governments and global economic forces, environmental and social justice movements are increasingly challenged to tackle the structures underpinning social inequality and environmental degradation. As Naples (2002) succinctly states:

> Community-based social change efforts seem all too limited when placed up against the structures of inequality that shape the wider political and economic context. Global processes of economic restructuring are undermining unionization, job security, sustainability of communities and the environment, and social supports, especially those provided through the so-called welfare state (p. 3).

Similarly, we are increasingly recognizing that societal problems reside in a web of broader intersecting relationships that defy fragmented solutions. Global educators Pike and Selby (1988) express this point well:

> Problems cannot be understood within a simple cause(s) and effect(s) framework. They are locked into a dynamic, interwoven and multi-layered web in which interaction and relationship are the principal features. Hence, a major environmental problem may well impact upon and be impacted upon by, for instance, a raw materials shortage, an

energy crisis, rising unemployment, a longstanding issue of wealth maldistribution and a famine crisis, each of which will be simultaneously impacting upon each other at a range of levels, personal to global. It follows that we cannot hope to compartmentalize solution strategies without running the risk of our actions being ultimately counter-productive (p. 23).

These realities activate the need to work across the borders and boundaries that reside in our communities and larger surrounding contexts, calling to the forefront the ripeness of more holistic forms of social change agency. That being said, some actors, in contrast, are further ignited to adopt narrow forms of agency. Many environmental campaigns continue to be isolated from their social contexts, devoting tireless effort to advance narrowly defined ecological goals. Ultimately, these kinds of initiatives lead to questions of the effectiveness and longevity of piecemeal change. Similarly, most holistic forms of activism pose their own set of challenges for practitioners and researchers to explore.

In this work, linking activism is investigated through the following research questions: What range of social justice issues do activists confront in their environmental work? What factors influence their efforts? What structures and processes impede their efforts? What strategies do they develop to confront social injustices? How do activists communicate their more complex agency? And, how does linking work inform our notions of self and identity? These questions are meant to elucidate some of the politics and practice of linking activism. Additionally, these questions provide access to the diverse ways activists are conceptualizing and responding to social justice challenges.

On the one hand, responses to these questions reveal narratives of activists' frustration with the separation of ecological and social justices issues within environmental organizations, government institutions, social movements, and other social contexts. On the other hand, these questions elicit stories of activists being creatively engaged and empowered in their linking efforts. In utilizing questions that can access these tensions, visibility is given to the ways activists shape as well as become shaped by their multi-layered contexts.

CHALLENGES TO LINKING ACTIVISM IN DOMINANT AND ACTIVIST CULTURES

If one lives in a culture steeped in segmentation it is challenging to live and act holistically. Dominant Western paradigms constantly give us messages to live and act in fragmented ways. Patriarchy, colonialism, capitalism, anthropocentrism, and other systems of domination disconnect us from others and ourselves. Mind, body, and spirit are continually viewed in separation; logical reason tends to preside over intuition and emotion; the separation of public and private spheres continues to be perceived as normative; humans are viewed as superior to the natural world; as a group, men continue to be privy to more societal power than women; minoritized cultural groups are dealt less societal influence than Caucasian groups; and individuals are viewed as more separate than connected to one another. Referring to this ideology of separation, feminist theorist Jordan (1995) states, for instance:

> [T]he separate-self paradigm would suggest that separation and disconnection is the primary state of affairs ("We are born alone; we die alone"). According to this view, from a place of essential aloneness, we at best reach out to relate to or use "objects" who can meet our needs or provide some passing solace in this lonely journey (p. 1).

Critiques of dominating ideologies have been made from countless social locations—feminist, anti-racist, First Nations, environmental, labor unionist, and anti-poverty groups/movements to name a few.[1] These movements are reclaiming values, experiences, and identifications marginalized by dominant cultures; and new visions of self, society, and agency are being voiced. The contributions of these countercultures to integrative notions of self and agency cannot be underestimated. In vital ways, movements of race, class, and gender, for instance, are empowering aspects of ourselves which are restricted by mainstream cultural beliefs, assumptions, and priorities. At the same time, however, anti-oppressive activisms also contribute to fragmentation. Often, in their impassioned focus on empowering an aspect of who we are (e.g., gender), more holistic articulations of ourselves and contexts get marginalized. There is still much effort needed across progressive social movements to work within the greater complexities and multi-dimensionality of people's lives. For instance, speaking to the "appositional paradigm" for social change utilized in the feminist movement, Flinders (1998) has stated:

> One of the reasons the [feminist] movement has not attracted the large numbers of women it should have, or held all it *has* attracted—is the appositional paradigm that we've inherited from patriarchy itself—the winner-take-all model that assumes a champion and a challenger, one who is victorious, and one who is vanquished. Women feel themselves to be too profoundly connected with men—as wives, mothers, daughters, coworkers even—to embrace that model for anything resembling a sustained campaign. Our loyalties to one another can be strong, but

not so strong as to overshadow those other connections altogether (pp. 182–183).

Mainstream American environmental movements have also lacked support from many community sectors because of their lack of attention to broader social issues (Hofrichter, 1993; Faber, 1998; Dowie, 1996). Actors within the U.S. environmental justice movement have led this critique, as have activists within the larger feminist, anti-racist, anti-poverty, and labor unionist movements.

The seductiveness of reductionist politics and practice is encouraged by dominant ideologies. And, just as anti-oppressive movements may resist reductionist practice, they may also slide into collusion with this fragmentation because of its pervasiveness. In fact, these pressures to segment our lives into compartments can be overwhelming to the point where such divisions feel sewn into our contexts and our notions of who we are. As Griffin states (1995):

> [This] shift in a way of thought [to less reductionistic notions] requires more than simple knowledge or intellectual understanding. . . . This dividedness is rooted deeply, in childhood memory, in a sense of self, as if written into the body. . . . All the dualities that structure the social order also become powerful ways of ordering experience. . . . All this, the very boundaries and definitions of one's life, are attached by countless threads of culture to an old epistemology. To sever them would seem like erasing the very facts of one's own existence. To change how one sees the world is to change the self (p. 40).

Contesting these fractures, numerous social theorists are proposing more integrative frameworks for understanding social oppression. For instance, Dei (1996) uses the concept of a lens in advocating integrative anti-racism; Warren (1994) proposes a quilt model of understanding oppressions; Plumwood (1994) refers to the web; Razack (1998) theorizes an inter-locking blocks of oppression model; and Hill Collins (1998) uses the construct of intersectionality (although she critiques this as well). However, these valuable conceptualizations do not span the breadth of social-ecological connections, which is something this research will help to accomplish. For a good overview of these authors with respect to their views on an integrative anti-oppressive perspective see Shaikh (2000).

There is also growth of integrative practices developing in anti-oppressive movements, particularly with respect to anti-globalization efforts. For instance, just as we heard Naples (2002) identify the breadth of inequities connected to global economic forces, she also asserts the real presence of activisms challenging these structures. She states:

> However, political activism designed to challenge the expansion of global inequality has generated worldwide attention, as evident in protests against the World Trade Organization, the World Bank, and the International Monetary Fund in Seattle; Washington, D.C.; Toronto, and many non-Western locales that receive little if any media attention. Furthermore, community actions on behalf of progressive agendas remain salient features of local encounters with the state, with corporations, with employers, and with racist and sexist forces pervading many spheres of social life (p. 1).

These examples demonstrate the necessity and value of integrative approaches. This research contributes to the growth of this important area of study.

DEFINING CONCEPTS

"You don't see something until you have the right metaphor to perceive it."
—Thomas Kuhn

This research is clearly allied with the efforts depicted by the environmental justice movement in the United States. The term "environmental justice," however, is not used as the conceptual frame for activists' efforts described in this study. This is for a number of reasons. First, the term environmental justice was not generally known or used by Canadian/Ontario activists in the environmental movement sector at the time of this investigation. Second, specific historical and political economic factors (e.g., the civil rights movement and the lack of publicly funded social programs, such as medicare) shaped the development of the environmental justice movement in the United States and its use of the term environmental justice. These factors are not representative of the Canadian experience. As a result, I felt that the casual appropriation of this term to the Canadian context was inappropriate. In a similar vein, the majority of activists in this research worked within the existing Canadian environmental movement and possessed the privileges of being white, formally educated, and having modest to middle-income economic means. This does not reflect the majority of activists in the U.S. environmental justice movement. These actors position themselves outside of the mainstream American environmental movement and as having to face systemic injustices because of their race and/or class. Additionally, as a concept with specifically located meanings, environmental justice does not provide a conceptual frame that can be freely shaped by the experiences of activists involved in this research.

The concept of linking activism articulated in this research shares many strong "family resemblances" to the concept of environmental justice, while also offering its own unique strengths and attributes. Terms such as link, connect, integrate, bridge, and synthesize are radical concepts which need to become increasingly prominent in the lexicon of social change discourse. These terms bring to the forefront the value of focusing on "an agency of interconnections" within our progressive social change movements. When we begin to ask ourselves, "How are we linking or integrating?" as often as we currently ask, "What is the problem and how can we stop this?," social change as we know it will take on new levels of meaning and impact for ourselves and our communities. There are crucial steps that can be taken to nurture this agency of interconnections. One step involves utilizing a term like linking activism, which makes this priority of connections explicit. Another step involves the re-telling or re-storying of activists' work through the lens of their efforts to connect across social and ecological issues. This research is focused on both of these important steps.

LINKING ACTIVISM

As previously noted, the concept of linking activism has been developed to make visible the experiences of 30 activists in their efforts to address social justice issues within their environmental work. More specifically, three central challenges are reflective of linking work. The first is the challenge of understanding and tackling the inequitable distribution of environmental risks/costs and benefits between privileged and marginalized social groups. Bullard (1993c) puts it bluntly:

> Why do some communities get "dumped on" while others escape? Why are environmental regulations vigorously enforced in some communities and not in others? Why are some workers protected from environmental threats to their health while others (such as migrant farm workers) are still being poisoned? How can environmental justice be incorporated into the campaign for environmental protection? (p. 15)

In contesting the trading off of one form of oppression for another, linking activism engages the second challenge of becoming aligned to the multiple sectors of a community. Here community sectors such as housing, health, labor, and community economic development become relevant players within activists' understanding of their environmental work. Activist Pam Tau Lee echoes this need to bridge these divisions, stating the importance of being:

> able to bring together different issues that used to be separate. If you're talking about lead and where people live, it used to be a housing struggle,

if you're talking about poisoning on the job it used to be a labor struggle, people sick from TB or occupational exposure used to be separate
health issues, so environmental justice is able to bring together all of
these different issues to create one movement that can really address
what actually causes all of these phenomena to happen and gets to the
root of the problems (as quoted in Di Chiro, 1998, p. 106).

In the desire to address the root structures which create social inequality
and ecological strife, to which Pam Tau Lee alludes, linking activism
engages the third challenge of advocating fundamental social change.
Shirley, an activist I interviewed, articulates this goal in her desire to get "to
the heart of things." She asserts:

I see [linking activism] as the issue that really gets to the heart of things
and asks us, how are we going to live so that we can all live together in
peace? How can we develop and create a community that we want to
live in on a local level? I see it as an issue that broadens the environmental movement, to embrace people of color, poor people, women. I
see it as more inclusionary. . . . People can feel for seals, this is a moth-
erly response. It is about seeing yourself in a community, as part of the
puzzle in struggling for a sustainable, peaceful, equitable community.
This is more complicated activism. It is more directed towards democracy and making it a broader movement with workers, mothers, the
unemployed, you name it.

In this research the portrayal of linking activism is characterized around
these powerful and intersecting themes.

MULTI- OR COMPLEXLY-ALIGNED IDENTITIES

"Gandhi's real genius was simply that . . . he was utterly inept at com-
partmentalizing life."   —Carol Lee Flinders

"As a lover of life I cannot keep out of any field of life. . . . As a lover of
life, how can I separate any part from the whole?"—Vimala Thakar

Many would argue that activism is not a category of employment or work,
but is instead, a form of calling to social change agency which is continually
being connected to our values, locationalities, and experiences in a powerful
way. Illuminating this dialectic interplay between identity and social change
is central to our understanding of more integrative or holistic activisms. With
respect to the inattention to "identity" in environmental change research,
Payne (2000) argues, "In the absence of forceful insights into how personal
identities are formed, destabilized, re-sought, contradicted or maintained

'for the environment' (or being neutral to, or 'against' the environment!), questions will persist about the strategies, efficacy and, ultimately, purposes of environmental education" (p. 69). In relation to this dynamic between identity and social change, there are many questions that need our reflection. How is self and identity understood in this shifting, complex world? How do social and ecological contexts shape conceptions of activism? How can fragmented and narrow portrayals of self and activism be contested? How can activists "use" their multi-faceted identities to strengthen integrative change (i.e., ecologically viable and socially just)? And, how can the complexities of self support the navigation of complex environments?

In this book I argue that linking activism highlights the notion of what I am calling "multi- or complexly- aligned" identities or selves. Within this conceptual frame I am drawing from postmodern notions of identity which reject "the modernist assumption that the self exists in some essential form that remains unchanged as it passes through experience" (Davis et. al., 2000, p. 170) thereby implying "a conscious, knowing, unified, rational subject" (Weedon, 1987, p. 21). Davis et. al. (2000) summarize these modernist conceptions, stating:

> Modernist conceptions of identity do not assert that the self is static. However, there tends to be an assumption of some "essential self," one that is unique to the individual and that remains constant across situations. . . . Although one's relationships, behaviors, and thoughts may vary dramatically across [the different] roles [we play in our lives], one's identity is not seen to vary or to be context-sensitive. Rather, such roles are seen as aspects of a multifaceted, but unified person. In brief, then, in modernist conceptions, the self is cast as isolated from other selves and insulated from the physical world (pp. 166–167).

Postmodern conceptions of self contend, in contrast, that "in the complexity of being human, identities are increasingly uncertain, fluid and often destabilized" (Payne, 2000, p. 70) and thereby, as Weedon (1987) writes, "subjectivity [can be seen] as a site of disunity and conflict" (p. 21). Here identity is seen as a continual narrative construction emerging out of the complex interplay and conceptualization of our personal-social worlds. Describing this postmodern notion of self, Davis et al. (2000) state:

> One's sense of self, it is suggested, unfolds continuously through the recursive and reiterative processes of representing and interpreting one's identity in relation to (and in distinction from) other forms—persons, objects, events, and so on. . . . From a postmodern perspective, one's sense of self is always fluid and shifting. . . . [T]he self is the product of communal

relations and is thus always being produced . . . one's sense of personal identity is understood to emerge from one's involvements in signifying systems and practices—and, in some ways, to be contained in these systems and practices. The stories that one tells and is told, the objects that one cherishes and scorns, the activities that one supports and avoids—these are the sites of self identity/identification (pp. 169–170).

In taking up this postmodern frame, activists' "linking" identities become viewed as continually emergent and as intimately constructed in relation to their layered social contexts. My use of the concept "multi or complexity-aligned identity" is meant to highlight this view. It is also being used to explore three narratives of identity expression which emerged in activists' linking stories. First, linking activism draws attention to the interplay of activists' narratives of personal and social change. Second, linking work makes visible activists' narrative claims to multiple social locationalities and alliances. Third, linking practice gives view to conceptualizations of self which are rooted in deepening and expanding notions of relationality with self, others, and nature; ways in which activists locate themselves in this breadth of interconnectedness are also revealed.

THE DYNAMIC BETWEEN PERSONAL AND SOCIAL CHANGE

Perhaps more than other activisms, linking activism brings to the forefront the challenge as Mahatma Gandhi has stated, to "be the change you wish to see in the world." In striving to span different issues and priorities to support ecological and social justice change, the individual is challenged to embody deepened capacities of connection and integration. In taking up this challenge, activist practice becomes focused not just on the activist's *doing* or *outer process* but also on his or her *being* and its *inner process*. This dynamic interplay between the inner and outer process is articulated by Pike and Selby (1999) in their statement:

> While the journey outwards leads [individuals] to discover the world in which they live, the journey inwards heightens their understanding of themselves and of their potential. Both journeys constitute a necessary preparation for personal fulfillment and social responsibility in an interdependent and rapidly changing world. In conducive conditions, both journeys can be undertaken simultaneously (p. 14).

In acknowledging the importance of these simultaneously journeys, several narrative themes relevant to linking activist work emerge. One theme involves the recognition that balancing our inner and outer lives can be difficult. In the whirlwind of struggle against structures of inequity, and the accompanying challenges of limited resources most activists and their groups face, it can be hard to maintain focus on the intrapersonal journey. A second theme, which further elucidates Ghandi's statement, is that without dismantling our internalized oppression, success in transforming patriarchy and other forms of human and non-human domination will be short-lived. This premise is shared by many feminist activists such as hooks (1990, 2000), Macy and Brown (1998), Macy (1991, 2000), Flinders (1998), and Marino (1997). Speaking of this need to challenge internalized oppressions, even as we become continually ensnared by them, Marino (1997) states, for instance, "My experience has been that I continually reproduce oppressive and coercive habits because I am so deeply a creature of my context. Part of my task, then, becomes actively acknowledging, articulating, disrupting those habits" (p.121).

A third theme which is raised when exploring the interplay of personal and social change is the dominant ideologies of the individual. Kohn (1990), for instance, argues that dominant culture consistently frames humans in a negative light, focusing on instances of violence, deceit, and selfishness. The amount of media coverage given to advertising acts of violence as compared to acts of kindness is a good example of this point made by Kohn.

Activist cultures can get stuck in such mind-sets of negativity stemming from the exposures and experiences of justice work. Humans have been viewed as mere parasites or rapists by some activists because of humanities exploitive attitude and treatment of the planet. Activists can lose sight of human acts of beauty and kindness due to their awareness and proximity to such forms of oppression and exploitation. And yet the point can also be made, that in failing to challenge blanket negativity towards the human species, our ability to see the potential for social change can be lost, making activist work ultimately pointless. Kohn's (1990) belief that people possess the need to express goodness towards others is one that I share. He states:

> My argument . . . is not that aggression and competition, selfishness and egocentricity, do not exist. Obviously they do, . . . But the dominant sounds in this culture are grumbles of cynicism about human nature . . . human beings are also decent, able to feel others' pain and prepared to try to relieve it. . . . that concern for the well-being of others often cannot be reduced to self-interest, that social structures predicated on human selfishness have no claim to inevitability—or even prudence (Kohn, 1990, p. 4).

The dynamic between activists' inner sense of hope and despair towards the possibility of outer change (our capacity and will as a human culture to create ecologically sustainable and socially just communities) was a narrative theme in many activists' linking stories. While activists' inner processes impeded aspects or instances of integrative practice, stories of how their inner lives empowered their linking work were also narrated. In staying alive to the messy interplay of their inner and outer journeys, activists engaged more complexly-aligned identities.

GIVING VIEW TO THE BREADTH OF SOCIAL LOCATIONALITY AND ALLIANCE

In working to bridge social and ecological terrains, the activists presented here drew on complex rivers of selves—selves that are multi-dimensional, multi-identitied, and multi-aligned. Activists' resistance to narrow conceptualizations of their agency exemplified one expression of their claim to multi-aligned selves. Socially constructed divisions separating aspects of self, such as between environmentalist and feminist; mother and worker; mind and body; personal and political; local and global citizen; citizen and consumer; aesthetic and pragmatic become contested and reconfigured in linking work. Examples of activists' more complexly-aligned identities include, for instance, Serren and Rick who link their labor unionist backgrounds with their ecological concerns and values; Yuga who connects his African and Canadian identities to environmental discourse; and Helen who expresses her simultaneous commitment to ecological, First Nations, feminist, and community economic sensitivities.

The terms "multi or complexly-aligned identity" have been used to acknowledge activists' multiple locationalities, and to make visible the challenges and opportunities of engaging this complex self in one's agency. Flinders (1998) portrays some of the challenge of aligning across our identities. Her description of striving to reconcile her feminism with her spirituality is insightful and applicable to the connection of ecological and social justice identities. She states:

> [M]y feminism and my spirituality have always been closely connected, laying claim on me at the same level. I'd taken up meditation out of a driving and, yet, *aching* need for self-knowledge and meaning. My feminism had arisen out of that same well of feelings, and in many regards the life I'd chosen had satisfied it (p. 53).

Further referring to this connection, Flinders (1998) asserts, "I was sure that feminism and spirituality ('real' feminism and 'real' spirituality, meaning, of course, my own versions of each) were compatible. At least that. But I was a long way from understanding how these two strong tugs in myself could be aligned—how I could start filling in that blank space on the map" (p. 54). Implicit in Flinders' (1998) description of her struggle are also the opportunities that alignment offer. MacFarlane (1999) provides one example of such opportunity. Specifically, he refers to Monte Hummel's success in balancing forest protection and community viability in a heated battle between southern Ontario environmentalists and many northern Ontario communities. Mac-Farlane (1999) argues that it was Hummel's ability to engage his identities as a high profile city environmentalist and kid who grew up in northern Ontario, that supported his efforts to find integrative solutions to this heated conflict. Referring to the "Lands for Life" political battle, MacFarlane (1999) states, "[t]hat Hummel can inhabit this unlikely cusp between divergent points of view" (p. 93). MacFarlane (1999) then goes on to indicate that Hummel:

> watched with considerable dismay as the Lands for Life process opened the wound between north and south. (Some angry northern editorialists went so far as to propose separation.) At the same time, he realizes that his position between these two worlds is one of his strengths. He points out that while he is perfectly at home in the boardrooms and media studios of downtown Toronto, he was raised in the north, and so has enormous sympathy for traditional hunters, and for fisherman, and for northerners who complain that they are ignored or misunderstood by their more affluent neighbours to the south (p. 93).

In this research I argue that in understanding and utilizing the complexities of our identities, we are better equipped to navigate the complexities of our social-political and ecological contexts. The concept of "identity deployment" is useful in unpacking this contention. "*Identity for deployment*" is defined by Bernstein (1997) "as expressing identity such that the terrain of conflict becomes the individual person so that the values, categories, and practices of the individuals become subject to debate" (p. 537). In bringing their complexly or multi-aligned identities to their linking activist efforts, activists engaged in a form of identity deployment. That is to say, they used as a site of political struggle, or in Bernstein's terms "deployed," aspects of their social identity within their environmental advocacy as a way to push for, not just environmental change, but *socially just* environmental change. Linking activists attempt to get across a complex message of there being *multiple* concerns (of social locationality and environment) to attend to simultaneously. Their political message is that an environmental problem is not only an ecological one, but also includes, for instance, issues and inequities related to gender, race, class, and other forms of social locationality. In deploying their identity as a woman or African-Canadian, for instance, in their political efforts, they are highlighting the linkages between social inequalities and the environment.

In consciously deploying a greater breadth of their social identity within their political activism, linking activists give visibility to the greater complexity of social contexts within which environmental problems reside. As this book explores, this is no easy task. Canadian mainstream environmental discourse and governmental environmental decision-making continues to deny, ignore, and/or minimize forms of environmental racism, classism, sexism, and other forms of social marginalization. The political strategy of which issue (i.e., ecological *or* social justice) or which combination of issues (e.g., environment *and* gender *and* race) to push into the terrain of political debate and protest is a messy and shifting context-dependent challenge facing linking activists. As Bernstein (1997) argues, "identity deployment in the political realm will depend on the structure and relations among movement organizations, the extent of political access, and the types of opposition" (p. 541). In striving to address social justice issues within the context of their environmental change work, linking activists are faced with such challenging deliberations. The concept of multi or complexly-aligned identities is meant to bring view to this complexity of self and the varied possibilities of its representation with their political agency—a practice which can be seen as a form of identity deployment.

SHIFTING UNDERSTANDINGS OF SELF: EXPANDING AND DEEPENING NOTIONS OF RELATIONALITY

Activist expressions of multi-aligned identities connect to shifting understandings of our world and selves. Notions of self are being articulated which diminish the separation between "self" and "other" and emphasize the human capacity to be connecting thinkers, feelers, and actors. The Buddhist notion that all living forms are sacred and interconnected has entered the postmodern sciences and social sciences. The earth has become Gaia, a complex, living, self-regulating organism. Humanity has become a web of interdependent relationships crossing all geographical borders (Capra, 1996; Briggs & Peat, 1999; Pike & Selby, 1999; Noske, 1997). Metaphors of relationality, interconnectedness, and holism are pushing against the mechanistic, individualistic, and reductionist metaphors of the Modern age. Feminism and ecology; chaos and non-linear systems theories; transpersonal and postmodern philosophies are challenging classical science and industrial economic worldviews. Peavy (1998) encapsulates this shift in the following statement:

In a very general sense, we are leaving a paradigm of fixed causes, laws, and explanations where the universe and everything in it was construed in more-or-less mechanical terms. We are entering into a paradigm of flux, in which certainties have evaporated and there are multiple views on virtually everything, even the most basic scientific entities. . . . This means that our basic frames for understanding both the physical and human world are transforming from a perspective which reduces material and living entities into ever smaller parts and classifications to a perspective which integrates all things into patterns and configurations or networks of meaning and communication. We are beginning to have a more holistic or ecological frame for understanding ourselves, others and the world (p. 34).

For instance, within the deep ecology movement, theorists have articulated the concept of the "ecological self" referring to ways we *are* the natural world (Naess, 1989; Macy 1991; Macy & Brown, 1998; Seed, Macy, Flemming, & Naess, 1988). Macy (1991) portrays this notion of the "ecological self" in her call to see "*world as lover* instead of a stage set for our moral battles or a prison to escape, the world is beheld as a most intimate and gratifying partner" (p. 8). She continues, "Just as lovers seek for union, we are apt, when we fall in love with our world, to fall into oneness with it as well. . . . The tree that will grow from the seed, that art thou; the running water, that art thou, and the sun in the sky, and all that is, that art thou" (p. 11). Similarly, feminist theorists are articulating broader notions of the capacity for human connectedness and relationality (Jordan 1995, 1997; Belenky, Clinchy, Goldberger, & Tarule, 1986; Miller & Scholnick, 2000; Gilligan, 1982; Miller & Stiver, 1997; Goldberger, Tarule, Clinchy, & Belenky, 1996; Gilligan, Lyons, & Hammer, 1990; Surrey 1985). These feminist works challenge Western notions of "self" rooted in separation, competition, and the unbridled devotion to autonomy. Surrey (1985) articulates the concept of "self-in-relation" to reflect the strong level of relationality she found in female relationships. Similarly, Jordan describes "a relational model of psychological development," stating:

In a relational model of psychological development, disconnection from others is viewed as one of the primary sources of human suffering. . . . We suggest that people gain a central sense of meaning, well-being, and worth through engagement in growth-enhancing relationships; we further suggest that an active interest in being connected and movement toward increasing connection are at the core of human development (Miller, 1988). . . . In speaking about relational being, I am suggesting that there is primary energy that flows towards others, toward joining with others in an expansive sense of interconnectedness (Jordan, 1995, p. 1).

As Gomes and Kanner (1995) articulate, it is the joining of these varied forms of relationality that is needed. Naess' "ecological self" may be extended to include human-to-human interconnectedness, and Jordan's (1995) and Surrey's (1985) concepts of relationship expanded to include the "more-than-human world." In this regard, Gomes and Kanner (1995) state:

> Like most psychological theories, the self-in-relation model has, thus far, focused largely on relationships among people. But it could easily be extended beyond the human realm to include an ecopsychological perspective. To quote Catherine Keller again, by defining "relationship" more inclusively, we can create "places of inner and outer freedom in which new forms of connection can take place. Liberated from relational bondage, we range through an unlimited array of relations—not just to other persons, but to ideas and feelings, to the earth, the body, and the untold contents of the present moment (p. 118).

Linking activism draws on these relational notions of self, offering a window to view individuals' increasing engagement with the whole of their personhood (mental, emotional, social, physical, spiritual, aesthetic) and contexts (from local to planetary) as they strive for ecological viability and social justice. In this multi-dimensioned journey, activists are engaging a kind of transformative learning process. O' Sullivan, Morrell, and O'Connor (2002) offer one description of what this may look like:

> Transformative learning involves experiencing a deep, structural shift in the basic premises of thought, feelings, and actions. It is a shift of consciousness that dramatically and permanently alters our way of being in the world. Such a shift involves our understanding of ourselves and our self-locations; our relationships with other humans and with the natural world; our understanding of relations of power in interlocking structures of class, race and gender; our body-awareness, our visions of alternative approaches to living; and our sense of possibilities for social justice and peace and personal joy (p. xvii).

This kind of transformative journey facilitated by linking practice comprises another layer of meaning to the concept multi-aligned identities used in this research.

THE PROCESS OF CONDUCTING THIS STUDY

This study was conducted within a feminist qualitative paradigm. Within this framework, understandings of activists' linking experiences were developed by attending to three levels of comprehension. These included the hermeneutic and critical interpretative epistemological approaches. Narrative method also informed this work.

Hermeneutics is interested in uncovering the meaning people give to their experiences. It is engaged in understanding experience from the experiencer's vantage point, or as Elbow states, "the act of affirming or entering into someone's thinking or perceiving" (quoted in Connelly & Clandidin, 1990, p. 3). It is through the active process of dialogic reflection that the researcher makes meaning or understands a person's experience. This exchange takes place in the discourse between researcher and research participant as well as between the researcher (and/or participant) and the text itself (transcript). Furthermore, the understanding or interpreting of human experience is rooted in the relevant social and historical contexts (Gadamer, 1975, 1976). The hermeneutic process of dialogic reflection supported activists and myself to explore the complexities of their (linking) activism and the meanings they gave to these experiences.

A critical interpretative layer of comprehension was also utilized in this study to move beyond the interpretation of individual activists' experiences and situations. Lather (1992) describes critical inquiry as one that "takes into account how our lives are mediated by systems of inequity such as classism, racism, and sexism" (p. 87). Sullivan (1990) regards a critical framework as one that goes beyond hermeneutic interpretation "to elucidate and criticize those features of a human situation which frustrate intentional agency (i.e., projects)" (p. 123). The present study gives attention to issues of power inequity and the need for social change, thereby drawing from the following tenets of critical research: 1) the assumption that knowledge is socially and politically constructed; 2) an assertion that understanding needs to be informed by a critical analysis of structures and processes of power; 3) an assertion that while people possess agency in their lives, they also face social conditions which impede their agency; and 4) an assertion that research should advance justice and challenge marginalization and oppression (See Denzin, 1989; Gitlin, Siegel, & Boru, 1989; Harding, 1987a; Lather, 1992; Sullivan, 1990).

Through the application of these broad critical assertions, a further set of assumptions emerge which are specific to this study. They include: a) environmental problems are rooted in issues of social power and control over resources; b) ecological degradation and human injustices are often rooted in common structural inequalities within society; c) ecological degradation and social injustice should not be resolved in a manner that pits one against the other, but should be dealt with simultaneously with the goal of mutual emancipation and empowerment; d) activists engaged in environmental change have a role and responsibility to address social inequities which are connected to their issue(s) of ecological concern; and e) activists' linking efforts need to be understood both within the context of the constraints (e.g., structural barriers) they face and within the agency they possess to resist and maneuver these challenges.

That "we live storied lives" (Carter, 1993, p. 7) and that "stories have the power to direct and change our lives" (Noddings, 1991, p. 157) are additional precepts I brought to this study. Unpacking these assumptions entails an acknowledgement that narrative provides a way of representing experience through the creation of stories (Connelly & Clandidin, 1990); and strives to reflect the complexity and integrity of individuals' experiences through the creation of stories (Connelly & Clandidin, 1990). Traditional data analyses can lend themselves to simple reductionistic representations removing from view the complexities (multi-faceted lives) and movements (lives and stories as never-ending works-in-progress) that exist in the lives of research participants. Narratives, in contrast, ground themselves in the richness of human experience and in the desire to portray these experiences holistically.

Narrative representational forms, moreover, provide modes of communication that are "comprehensible, memorable, and shareable" (Olson, 1990, pp. 100–101), and which can, furthermore, be tools of potential personal and social transformation. Writing in a style and manner that is accessible, engaging, and powerful to varied audiences (i.e., citizens, activists, and the academic community) is an important priority I brought to this research. These foci informed my interviews and knowledge construction process with activists.

The Interview and Information Gathering Process

While the activists in this study were engaged in and committed to environmental change, many did not refer to themselves as environmentalists but identified themselves by names such as community activist, social justice activist, activist, feminist, human being, environmental health activist, First Nations woman, anti-racist, ecofeminist, or other identification which situated their environmental concerns within a broader and larger sphere of social identification and cultural critique. Of the 30 Ontario activists interviewed, more than half would consider themselves as having been connected to the environmental movement community at the time of our interview. Craig, Kathleen, Brennain, Doug, Rick, Jack, Marge, Carol, Jane, Helen, and Irene are examples of such activists. Many activists also experienced their relationship with the environmental movement from within the context of the feminist (e.g., Dorothy, Shirley, Si, Helen), First Nations (e.g., Dwayne, Gail) community health (e.g., Nita, Michelle), peace/anti-nuclear (e.g., Brennain, Irene, Dorothy, Michelle), labor (e.g., Rick, Serren), new immigrant or anti-racist (e.g., Yuga, Sue, Marge) social justice sectors/movements. As shown above, numerous activists identified with multiple sectors or movements.

With the goal of establishing a varied and multi-dimensional conversation about linking work, attention was paid to the expression of different social justice-ecological linkages (e.g., environment and gender, environment and race, environment and class), geographical locations (e.g., northern and southern regions of Ontario, rural and urban areas), and environmental organizational characteristics (e.g., size (large/small), financial structure (staff run/volunteer driven), scope (local/regional/provincially-based) and mandate).

Approximately two thirds of those interviewed were women. Approximately one third of activists spoke of growing up in working-class households. At the time of our interviews, most activists made a living wage, several activists were living below the poverty line, and a handful earned wages in the higher middle-income brackets. I interviewed men and women who identified themselves as Canadian, Anglo-Saxon, Caucasian, First Nations, Jewish, African, Malaysian, Black, New Immigrant, Canadian East Indian, white, and Immigrant background. Approximately two thirds of those interviewed were Caucasian.

Some of the educational backgrounds of the activists interviewed include undergraduate and/or graduate degrees in biology, education, environmental sciences, environmental education, physiotherapy, chemical engineering, naturopathy, policy analysis, law, sociology, and business.

All 30 activists were interviewed for this study. Seven pilot interviews were conducted in 1994 followed by an additional 23 interviews conducted in 1996. The interviews were semi-structured and were between one and three hours in length, the average length being two hours. Questions were framed to allow activists to shape their understanding of the ways they connected social justice within their environmental work. During the interviews activists were asked, for instance, to describe an initiative where they were linking environmental and social justice concerns; or to describe ways they were addressing social justice issues within their environmental work. I attempted to ask questions in ways which drew activists into, rather than away from, their linking experiences and stories (Chase, 1995). I asked questions such as: "What was your experience of this initiative? How did that feel? Can you tell me what else happened during this initiative?" Once activists had been given time to relay and explore their linking experiences, time was taken to explore issues that were hinted at or not raised by an activist during the interview. For instance, if issues of gender and environment had not been raised, I inquired whether this linkage was meaningful to the activist, and if so, how? Interviews were tape-recorded and transcribed. In this book, activists have been identified by either their first name or by a pseudonym.

Documents comprised another source of information collected. Activists were asked to share any materials that would further illustrate their linking work and involvements and complement their interview data. I received materials from approximately one quarter of the activists. These materials varied. Activists shared newsletters, magazine and newspaper articles, pamphlets or other written public education and awareness materials, minutes of meetings, letters, and academic journal articles.

Throughout this study I maintained a research journal of my thoughts, emotions, and reflections related to this work. I have included some of these journal entries in this book as a way to keep the reader aware of my personal process and connections to this study. This has been done in conjunction with the expanding movements of feminist and qualitative research inquiry which both place the researcher squarely and consciously into the research process (Greed, 1990; Hunt, 1987, 1992; Kirby & McKenna, 1989; Moustakas, 1990; Reason & Marshall, 1987; Seidman, 1991).

Understanding and Relaying Activists' Linking Experiences

The interviews with activists created a vast amount of research material to understand, synthesize, and integrate. As Glesne and Peshkin (1992) indicate:

> Data analysis involves organizing what you have seen, heard, and read so that you can make sense of what you have learned. Working with the data, you create explanations, pose hypotheses, develop theories, and link your story to other stories. To do so, you must categorize, synthesize, search for patterns, and interpret the data you have collected (p. 127).

My analysis process continued, growing and developing throughout the data collection, note taking, and writing process. In effect, these research phases overlapped, intermingled, started, stopped, and started again like a continual spiral dance. It was a dynamic which kept shifting between gradation of chaos and order. Throughout this process was the recurrent interplay of movement and complementarity between: 1)the hermeneutic and critical interpretative; 2) the whole and the particular of activists' experiences; 3) the collective and the individual (activists as a collective group and as individuals); 4) the intuitive/emotive/creative and the analytical/ intellectual /structured; 5) the context (or scene) and plot (or action) of activists' stories; 6) the inner and the outer domains of activists' linking work (e.g., between inner fears and outer social/structural constraints); and 7) the strengths and limitations/gaps of activists' linking practice.

Within this tapestry of assessment, specific analysis strategies were utilized including "sitting" with activists' experiences, carrying on a dialogue with their stories, as well as summarizing, sorting, arranging, categorizing, and searching for themes and patterns (Glesne & Peshkin, 1992; Kirby & McKenna, 1989; Reinharz, 1992; Strauss, 1987). Detailed and abbreviated summaries of each transcript were written. Folders of themes and sub-themes were created and continually expanded. I devised outlines and maps of the material, and themes were continually reorganized, renamed, and reassessed throughout this process. Given the scope of investigation, and the number of activists interviewed, there were many valuable directions which could have served as the focus of this text. Stepping back from the plethora of analyses, I asked myself four main questions: What key rhythms did I hear when I submerged myself in activists' voices as a collective group? What areas of linking activism did I feel most passionate about? Which aspects of linking work needed to be depicted and discussed to foster academic and social movement dialogue and reflection on this area? And most importantly, what collective narrative of linking activism was waiting to be told that was honest and empowering? As Rappaport (1995) states, "The goals of empowerment are enhanced when people discover or create and give voice to, a collective narrative that sustains their own personal life story in positive ways. This process is reciprocal, such that many individuals, in turn, create, change, and sustain the group narrative" (p. 796). These questions guided the chapters written for this book.

In brief, this is a story of weaving—of gathering threads across activists' linking accounts into a tale which portrays some of the images and issues of linking activist practice. Specifically, this book juggles areas of theoretical/philosophical review and critique with a narrative form. Balancing the tension between an analytical-theoretical voice (with its linear, abstract qualities) and a narrative voice (which seeks to portray the contextual richness of activists' experiences) has been challenging. As the reader you will feel this tension at times. This tension is, however, a useful pedagogical tool. Linking activism is a journey of navigating tensions—a journey of balancing and transforming socially constructed dichotomies within us and around us. In witnessing my own struggle to balance theoretical and narrative forms, the reader is given another means to experience the messiness of linking activist

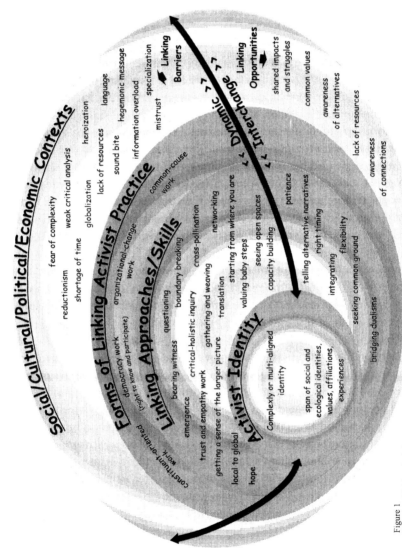

Figure 1
Mapping Linking Activism

work. An overview depicting some of the varied layers and themes of linking activism is shown in Figure 1.

CHAPTER OUTLINE

Chapter Two provides a literature review of the intersection of environmental problems to issues of sexism, racism, classism, and other forms of social injustice. Referencing empirical evidence and anecdotal reports, this chapter makes the point that we are not only in this environmental challenge together, we are also in it differently. The narration of environmental discriminations provides a strong foundation for the exploration of linking activism in this book.

Why don't we hear more stories of activists addressing social justice issues in their environmental work? Chapter Three discusses three ways linking experiences are marginalized in environmental accounts. Here single-issue narratives, site-specific case studies, and hero-based narratives are explored. Using activists' accounts, this chapter discusses the limitations of existing environmental narratives and advocates the need for a greater diversity of narrative frameworks.

The theme of giving voice is the focus of Chapter Four. In many respects, linking activists are faced with the challenge of being messengers of complex narratives. They need to weave different social and ecological threads into connected patterns of meaningful relationship, becoming verbal tapestry makers. This chapter explores activists' efforts to be linking messengers and examines societal forces which impede their efforts. Some of the barriers explored include the prevalence of the communication sound bite and the limits of language. I argue that in making these barriers explicit, activists are better prepared to navigate these challenges successfully.

Chapter Five focuses on two types of social justice struggle portrayed by activists—the right to know environmental information and the right to participate in government environmental decision-making processes. Nine forms of power inequity between citizens and government/corporate sectors are explored. The lack of a level playing field within government forums and the attack on citizens' right to information are two forms of inequity discussed. Strengths and limits of activists' linking work in these areas are explored.

How do environmental organizations support or restrict social justice efforts? Chapter Six examines activists' efforts to strengthen the social justice mandate of environmental organizations. Here categories of activists' organizational critique are outlined, including, for instance, the lack of membership diversity, the lack of outreach to socially disempowered communities, and the failure to consult impacted groups on environmental protection proposals. Barriers impeding environmental organizations from addressing social injustices are discussed, such as time and resource constraints. Activists' successful attempts to engage linking work from environmental organizations are also outlined.

The perspectives of marginalized constituencies have motivated many activists' environmental involvements. Chapter Seven explores activists' efforts within, for instance, First Nations, feminist, labor, and new immigrant constituencies. Seven themes of this form of "constituency-oriented" linking practice are discussed. Another form of linking practice is outlined in Chapter Eight. This chapter recounts activists' efforts to build relationships of alliance between environmental and social justice sectors. Common root causes of social and ecological problems are explored and the need for societal transformation is voiced. Challenges, opportunities, and rewards of this common cause work, as expressed by activists, are recounted.

Chapters Nine and Ten examine capacities/approaches/skills of linking activist practice. Chapter Nine explores the themes of bearing witness, questioning, critical-holistic reflection and demythologizing within activists' practice. Chapter Ten discusses the significance of translation, trust building, hope and emergence within activist accounts. It is argued that these capacities/approaches/skills need accentuating because 1) they foster awareness of social justice-ecological linkages; 2) they assist navigation towards more integrative change; and 3) they are valuable tools of communication. Chapter Eleven discusses insights and connections across chapters and revisits the value of the concepts linking activism and complexly or multi-aligned identities. Specific attention is given to the relationship between forms of linking practice and to areas of future investigation.

Part One
Linking Environmental Protection and Social Justice—Issues of Theory and Discourse

Chapter Two

We Are Not Only in It Together, We Are Also in It Differently: Ecological Burden and Social Location

Journal Note: I was sitting in the hairdresser's waiting for my wee-daughter's hair to be cut. It was not a hair salon but more of down-and-out, no-nonsense hair cutting shop. A woman in her late-60s was getting her hair cut. Her son (her chauffeur it seems) was waiting. The man stood out because his hands were wrapped in thick bandages. The hairdresser asked him what happened to his hands. He proceeded to reply that the chemicals at work burn his hands. "Don't you wear protective gloves?," asked the hairdresser. "Yes," replied the man, "but the chemicals eat through my gloves anyway." Unwrapping his bandages, horribly raw and irritated skin could be seen everywhere. His hands were an ugly patchwork of scars and seething wounds.

As the conversation continued we learned that he worked for just over minimum wage in a non-unionized job in the east end of town. His boss believes his skin condition is the result of sweat combined with an allergic reaction to the latex gloves. The hairdresser told him he should quit his job and that his boss was "full of shit." The man replied he couldn't afford to lose his job. Re-wrapping his hands the man paid for his mother's hair cut and together they walked out the door.

The pain and injustice I witnessed in this encounter brought home to me the power of Black American activist Dollie Burwell's words:

> I believe that environmental justice is a human right. Even though I live in a poor community where that land is cheap and the population is 85 percent black, I'm just as entitled to clean air and water. I'm just as

29

entitled to be free from industry's pollutants and toxic waste incinerators sited in my community as those people who live near the country
club. Their right to life is no greater than my right, their children no
more deserving of human life than my children, who are poor and have
to live in Warren County (as quoted in Guzman, 1996, p. 195).

Within Western societal contexts social impacts and benefits are not shared
equally among members of society, and this includes environmental
impacts and benefits. Small (2000) makes these realities vivid, stating:

> Automobile fuel economy is an environmental issue. But when an Inuit
> fisherman has to import frozen seal meat because he cannot take it safely
> from a bay fouled by an oil spill resulting from the rush to meet soaring
> demand for gasoline, that is a justice issue. Recycling is an environmental
> issue. But when an African-American develops lung cancer from breath-
> ing fumes emitted from an incinerator in her neighbourhood that burns
> recyclable trash, that is a justice issue. The greenhouse effect is an environ-
> mental issue. But when a Pacific islander discovers that the rising sea level
> resulting from profligate energy use in the developed world will obliterate
> her low-lying nation within decades, that is a justice issue. Organic food is
> an environmental issue. But when a Guatemalan banana worker becomes
> sterile from pesticide exposure, that is a justice issue (p. 1).

Faber (1998b) powerfully articulates some of the sociopolitical dynamics
underpinning the injustices, stating:

> The weight of the ecological burden upon a community is dependent
> upon the balance of power and level of struggle between capital, the
> state, and social movements responding to the needs and political
> demands of the populace. And in the United States, it is (as it always
> has been) the least politically powerful segments of peoples of color,
> industrial laborers, the underemployed and the working poor (espe-
> cially women), rural farmers and farm workers, and undocumented
> immigrants that are being damaged to the greatest extent by the ecolog-
> ical crisis. This is not to say that the white middle class is not also being
> significantly harmed by industrial pollution and other abusive corpo-
> rate practices, because it too is impacted. But in contrast to the salaried
> and professional classes, who can often buy themselves access to eco-
> logical amenities and a cleaner environment, there is significantly less
> investment of social capital (spending for education, job training, hous-
> ing, wages and benefits, health care, and so forth) for the maintenance
> of the working poor. Therefore, it costs capital and the state much less
> to displace environmental health problems onto people who lack health
> care insurance, possess lower incomes and property values, and as
> unskilled and semiskilled laborers are more easily replaced if they

become sick or die. In this sense, environmental inequalities in all forms, whether they be class, race, gender, or geographically based, are socially constructed features grounded in the systemic logic of capitalist accumulation (pp. 4–5).

A linking activism is an activism that pays attention to these distribution inequalities, acknowledging that we are not only in the environmental challenge together but also differently. This chapter looks at some of the ways marginalized constituencies[1] and communities are being disproportionately impacted by environmental degradation and pollution because they, for instance:

1) face structural inequalities and power inequities within society which affect their lives;
2) are targeted by hegemonic interests because they are less powerful and are given lower value;
3) possess fewer options or resources to counteract the effects of pollution than others; and
4) fall between the cracks in terms of receiving effective environmental information.

In this chapter negative environmental exposures are explored in relation to issues of gender, race, class, age, and geographical location.

INTRODUCTION

Environmental discriminations have smoldered beneath public consciousness and mainstream attention for decades. For instance, Field (1998) states that current studies documenting the disproportionate impact of environmental degradation on poor and minorities communities "confirm what Friedrich Engels observed about 1840s Manchester: that dirty air, dirty water, and dirty industries are invariably located in poor neighbourhoods far removed from middle-class suburbs" (p. 81). Occasionally, vivid crises of environmental injustice startled public consciousness. These crises are often framed as odd or occasional misfortunes. However, during the span of the last ten to fifteen years, social inequities have become more steadily intertwined with environmental degradation, making it harder to keep these linkages from the public eye. The social inequities of ecological deterioration are increasingly jarring our communities and the array of social-political forces that reside in these landscapes. Environmental injustices are being shown to be symptoms of larger systemic problems which are challenging the basic building blocks of hegemonic interests and values.

Traditional social movements and new social movements (NSMs)[2] are having to expand their discourse and practice to address the complexity of our intertwined social-ecological challenges. Environmental organizations, for example, have been confronted with the need to diversify their membership, to provide specific outreach to vulnerable and marginalized communities, and to critically assess their activist practice (Bullard, 1993a; Dowie, 1996; Gottlieb, 1993; Moore & Head, 1993; Taylor, 1993). Labor unions are being challenged to push for cleaner technologies (Adkin, 1998; Brophy, 1999; Environmental and Occupational Working Groups, 2000; Kazis & Grossman, 1991; Legault et al., 1998; Milani, 2000; Rice & Weinberg, 1994). Feminists are expanding the women's movement to address environmental concerns and their connection to issues of sexism (Diamond & Orenstein, 1990; Lynn, 1999; Plant, 1989; Warren, 1997). Health agencies are being faced with demands to address issues of environmental health (Armstrong, 1999; Batt, 1999; Chivian, McCally, Hu, & Haines, 1994; Miller, 1995). Anti-poverty organizations need to consider the ramifications of environmental policies and decision-making, such as the privatization of water on the poor. Housing advocacy organizations need to make connections between the lack of affordable housing and the lack of environmentally sustainable building codes and practices which perpetuate the building of homes only for the rich and upwardly mobile. Moreover, anti-racist organizations need to confront environmental health problems caused by substandard housing where many minoritized citizens, such as new immigrants without economic means, live. Community social workers must give attention to clients' environmental problems, not just to their social challenges. These are all key sites where environmental inequities and injustices exist and need to be addressed.

Events contributing to this awakening of social justice-ecological linkages in the United States and Canada include the Brundtland Report's call for "sustainable development" and the United Nations conference on Environment and Development in Rio de Janiero in 1992,[3] the reaction to toxic waste in Love Canal,[4] the rise of ecological feminism and the Fourth World Conference on Women, Equality, Development and Peace in Beijing in 1995[5], the creation of a Movement for Environmental Justice in the United States,[6] the heated discourse pitting jobs versus the environment,[7] and the continual struggle for justice by First Nations peoples in Canada and the United States. Together these forces are pushing issues of gender, race, class, labor, health, democracy, geographical location, and North-South world power relations into the arena of environmental debate and concern. Their message is clear: we are not simply in this environmental challenge and solution together, we are also in it differently.

Empirical evidence indicates that many of those who are disadvantaged within current socio-political-economic systems are disproportionately affected by environmental pollution and ecological degradation. Some of the most powerful evidence of environmental discriminations is being documented around the issues of hazardous waste, pesticides, and toxic chemicals. These studies have been primarily initiated in the United States stemming from the pressure and reverberations from the Movement of Environmental Justice. In Canada, there has been a paucity of primary research of this kind undertaken. Anecdotal evidence of environmental injustices has been narrated, informally and formally, but has yet to be compiled to illustrate the overall empirical significance of these inequities. These linkages are part of a lived and common sense knowing which are repeatedly devalued by the scientific community of bureaucracies and decision-makers.

EXAMINING FORMS OF INJUSTICE WITHIN ENVIRONMENTAL CONCERNS: RACE AND ETHNICITY

Robert Bullard describes environmental racism as "any policy, practice, or directive that, intentionally or unintentionally, differentially impacts or disadvantages individuals, groups, or communities based on race or color" (as quoted in Gibbs, 1997, p. 250). He also states that "Despite the many federal laws, mandates, and directives by the federal government to eliminate discrimination in housing, education, and employment, government rarely addresses discriminatory environmental practices" (Bullard, 1993b, p. 25). Articulating some of the sites of environmental racism within institutional contexts, he indicates, "Institutional racism influences local land use, enforcement of environmental regulations, industrial facility siting, economic vulnerability, and where people of color live, work, and play. Environmental racism is just as real as the racism that exists in housing, employment and education" (Bullard, 1993a, p. 25). Evidence that environmental burdens are not equally distributed across race and class has been documented, for instance, in examining locations of hazardous waste sites, in measuring disparate pollution levels in different localities, and in comparing health ailments among differently socially located children and adults (see Collin & Harris, 1993; Dowie, 1996; Hofrichter, 1993; Bryant, 1995; Gibbs, 1997; Szasz, 1994; United Church of Christ Commission for Racial Justice, 1987).

The 1987 report Toxic Waste and Race in the United States: A National Report on the Racial and Socioeconomic Characteristics of Communities with

Hazardous-Waste Sites revealed a national pattern of race constituting the most significant indicator to influence the location of commercial hazardous waste sites. According to this report, three out of every five African and Hispanic Americans resided in communities with uncontrolled toxic waste sites (United Church of Christ Commission for Racial Justice, 1987). Research in the United States has also found that many African-American, Hispanic, Asian, Pacific Islander, and First Nations communities confront higher levels of air pollution, and groundwater and soil contamination (Goldman, 1993; Wernette & Nieves, 1992). For instance, Goldman (1993) reported that Latino residents are approximately 90 percent more likely to live in areas that fail to meet EPA air quality standards; the figure for African Americans was 40 percent (Goldman, 1993).

Environmentally related health ailments have also been found to be higher in these communities. For instance, African American children suffer greater lead contamination, lead-related health effects, and have more asthma, cites Field (1998) who states, "African American children have the greatest impairments from asthma and the most frequent hospitalizations. Death rates from asthma are far greater for African Americans that whites. . . . and among inner-city low-income African American children the rate [of lead blood levels] approaches an astounding 70 percent" (p. 84). Adult cancer rates, pesticide-related ailments, reproductive disorders, miscarriages, and respiratory illnesses have also been shown to be higher than in white communities (Chivian et al., 1994; Hofrichter, 1993; Moore & Head, 1993; Novotny, 1998, p. 139). Faber (1998b) states health problems are higher for those living near toxic waste sites, citing that:

> [T]he National Research Council has found a disturbing pattern of ele-
> vated health problems, including heart disease, spontaneous abortions
> and genial malformations, and death rates, while infants and children
> are found to suffer a higher incidence of cardiac abnormalities,
> leukemia, kidney-urinary tract infections, seizures, learning disabilities,
> hyperactivity, skin disorders, reduced weight, central nervous system
> damage, and Hodgkin's disease (p. 28).

In Canada, environmental racism was said to have affected Halifax's decision to situate a landfill near the black community of Beechville, Nova Scotia. This decision was viewed by many as another assault of racism that black Canadians have endured since first settling in Nova Scotia over 150 years ago. For example, MacKinnon (1998) states:

> Beechville has raw memories of white ambition for development being
> foisted on them. Over history, they've been forced to relocate twice;

each time to scrubbier land further away from Halifax. Even the rocky non-arable property around them now has been ogled by developers, and gradually the community has shrunk away, now sandwiched between two industrial parks and surrounded by a knot of highways. Those who have stayed feel it's just a matter of time before Halifax's encroaching growth swallows them up. . . . The people of Beechville are haunted by the memory of Africville—a black community in Halifax that was quite literally made to disappear, reduced now to a squatter's trailer in a park. Africville was where the blacks lived; where the city felt free to locate its abattoir, its incinerator. And most offensive of all—the city's open garbage dump right next door. As the years passed, the oceanfront land Africville occupied became valuable—the dump was closed and the black people forcibly moved too, as their homes were bulldozed. That was 30 years ago, but the bitterness lingers (p. 3).

Systemic racism is further layered in the unequal reaction minoritized communities have received in response to some of these concerns. Rather than receiving top priority in efforts to prevent, remediate, and clean up the effects of this disproportionate impact, the opposite has occurred. U.S. air quality enforcement laws are applied less in these minoritized communities than in white ones. In one U.S study, while white populations received 78.7 percent enforcement of Clean Air Act cases, black residents received 14.2 percent and Hispanic populations 8.2 percent (Lavelle & Coyle, 1992; Lavelle & Coyle, 1993). Polluters in minoritized communities have paid fewer fines. Minoritized communities have received lower priority in toxic site cleanup programs and have endured longer waiting times and less thorough remediation than white communities. Presenting the central results from a 1992 study conducted by the *National Law Journal* which analyzed U.S. lawsuits over a seven-year period, Lavelle and Coyle (1993) outline "how the federal government's policies of dealing with polluters during the past decade have contributed to the racial imbalance" (p. 136). Some of the statistics reported by Lavelle and Coyle (1993, p. 137) include:

- 500 percent higher penalties given to polluters in white as compared to minoritized populations
- 20 percent longer waiting periods encountered by minoritized as compared to white areas to get placed on a hazards-waste cleanup list
- 22 percent more orders given to use treatment cleanup methods in white areas with hazardous waste, whereas in minoritized areas containment was chosen 7 percent more frequently

Shirley, an environmental health activist interviewed for this research, argues that differential response times to environmental crises are also seen in Canada. She cites the fire at a recycling plant in an Ontario community where two hundred tonnes of toxic PVCs (polyvinyl chloride) went up in flames. The community situated adjacent to the recycling company has been described as being a predominately working-class, ethnically diverse neighborhood—with limited political clout. She states:

> [The actions of this company] was a sure indication that [environmental discrimination] is a problem here in Canada, too. In the United States environmental justice has often been about regulation, the differing regulations, the differing zones. "Who gets a good response when they complain [and who doesn't]?" "Who gets action?" [The community near the plant] had been complaining [about all kinds of company infractions]—mercury exposure, minor fires, low security, not meeting fire regulations, and then the big fire took place. If it was an important community that had political clout [these infractions] would not have been allowed to continue. If the owners had lived near the plant and had been personally threatened this situation would not have been tolerated.

Ann, another activist I interviewed, confirms these views from the first-hand experience of her and her family. A resident of the affected neighborhood, she is convinced that had the children of public health and municipal officials been exposed to the fire an evacuation order would have been swiftly enacted. Instead, for Ann and her community the evacuation order was delayed. She also declared that such a huge potential environmental hazard would never exist in an upper-income area. Because English is a second-language for many residents in this largely blue-collar neighborhood Ann believes that the company assumed, "No one in the community would say, boo." Similarly, getting accountability from government and the company (in terms of environmental remediation, damages, health, and psychological impacts) has continued to be an uphill fight for those in the affected community. Patronizing attitudes of officials towards community residents created another layer of challenge these citizens had to tackle.

First Nations Experience of Environmental Racism

Canadian First Nations peoples have endured a long history of oppression from the imposition of colonial powers. Environmental racism has been a central component of this subjugation, which continues today in the polluting and degrading of First Nation communities—in the air, water, and land that is their homeland. Despite First Nations' legally entrenched rights under constitutional law as Canada's original people and their struggle for self-governance, First Nations communities face environmental contamination from dominant powers. White colonialist industries' and governments' economic models and development practices are racist as they fail to adequately consider their implications on First Nations peoples. Alarmingly, there are numerous examples of the results of environmental racism faced by First Nations people, including:

1) the high levels of PCBs in breast milk of Inuit women living in the Arctic;
2) the construction of James Bay dams in Quebec which flooded native territory;
3) the low-level flight testing of military planes over Innu territory disrupting wildlife and native communities with noise pollution;
4) the uranium mines in First Nations communities poisoning land and water;
5) mercury from pulp and paper mills poisoning water and fish in First Nations communities living downstream, such as in Grassy Narrows near Dryden, Ontario;
6) the health impacts for the Walpole Island First Nations community living downstream from Sarnia chemical and automotive industries; and
7) the struggle over the proposed Voisey's Bay nickel mine on Innu territory.

Importantly, First Nations struggles against the pollution and disruption of their land are not isolated from the other layers of injustice faced by these communities. Interconnecting issues such as cultural expropriation, poverty, pending land claim resolutions, and residential schools demonstrate the breath of their struggle and highlight the centrality of understanding environmental justice within this larger context. Given their unique history, rights, and place in Canada, First Nations people are also distinct from all other cultural groups, making their political fight against environmental racism different from other minoritized groups in Canada.

With the growing force of the Environmental Justice Movement in the United States since the 1980s, race and ethnicity have become central characteristics within the U.S. landscape of environmental change. While the links between environment and race/culture are being forged within some Canadian communities, there is not this history of insurgence in Canada. In part, motivated by the United State's empirical findings of environmental racism, Canadian environmental groups are slowly (re)-examining historical and present-day patterns of environmental degradation and the benefits of environmental protection, in terms of race, ethnicity, and culture.

In Canadian discourse, socioeconomic status has been given greater attention in connection with issues of environmental injustice than race or ethnicity, with the exception of Canada's First Nations communities. Clearly, however, low socioeconomic status exposes many minoritized and immigrant communities to environmental burdens in Canada which may be disproportionately affecting their lives.

SOCIOECONOMIC STATUS AND ENVIRONMENTAL DISCRIMINATION

At least eight indicators suggest that individuals and communities of lower socioeconomic status can face disproportionately higher degrees of environmental harm (Shrybman, 1987; Bryant, 1995, Hofrichter, 1993):

1) polluting companies targeting the siting of their industries and waste in lower-income areas;
2) individuals with lower incomes are more likely to live in substandard housing and/or closer to hazardous locations such as industrial areas;
3) lower-income individuals/communities can face exposure from the multiple pathways of environmental hazards (e.g., in their homes as well as from their outdoor and work environments);
4) lower-income families lack economic resources to shield themselves from hazardous exposures (e.g., through actions such as the purchase of bottled water or air cleaners);
5) health vulnerabilities related to lower-income status such as poor nutrition and high stress exacerbate environmental health impacts;
6) a lack of educational outreach to lower-income individuals/communities regarding environmental health risks and measures specifically designed to address these impacts;
7) lower-income individuals/communities often confront multiple layers of historical and systemic injustice and therefore face greater challenges in changing the realities and circumstances of their lives; and
8) the internalization of oppression can position vulnerable populations to expect and demand less safety and justice for themselves.

Toronto's South Riverdale community featured in the *New Internationalist* magazine provides one such snapshot of environmental discrimination based on lower socioeconomic status in Canada. Depicted as a neighborhood "characteristic of the world's poor urban communities," this section of the city faced the impacts of lead contamination from the adjacent Canada Metal Company. According to Labonte (1986) the company chose to "set up shop 60 years ago . . . for the same reasons industry usually locates in poorer neighbourhoods: cheap land and residents so eager to work they won't complain about a factory in their backyard" (p. 20). Field (1998) traces the rise of this economic status-geographical inequity, historically, to the creation of the industrial town/city during the industrial revolution. He states:

> Typically, the commercial core was first encircled by a band of industrial activity, surrounded by worker housing and finally, at the outer core, more wealthy residences, thus creating the "concentric circle" model of urban development. In the industrial city, the workers, who were often recent immigrants, were most likely to live closest to industrial activity and bore the brunt of industrial pollution (p. 89).

It is not just geographical proximity to industrial activity that can expose less economically advantaged individuals and communities. Often situated in alignment to the trail or path of pollution, lower-income residents are affected by wind and water current directions. Steingraber's (1997) book, *Living Downstream: An Ecologist Looks at Cancer and the Environment* is a powerful personal and empirical narrative of pollution's trail and its associated health impacts, such as cancer. Land-use policies instituted by political and economic decision-makers often serve to make poorer citizens more vulnerable to the path of toxic exposures. Housing values are cheaper in areas situated in the wind or water path of industrial pollution.

The interweaving of geographical location, power imbalances, and environmental injustices has been played out between Ontario's northern and southern regions. The lack of remediation of northern mines and the proposals to site southern Ontario nuclear waste and garbage in the north are examples of environmental injustices faced by northern Ontarians. Brennain, an activist in northern Ontario, articulately describes these imbalances:

> There are 6,000 abandoned mine sites across north-eastern Ontario. Probably at least half of them would be deemed hazardous. This does not even make it onto the political map. The biggest polluters in Ontario are the mining companies. The provincial and federal governments have considered mining issues as marginal issues.

This and the fact that nuclear waste is proposed for burial somewhere in a sparsely populated area of northern Ontario, I think it is the most classic case of environmental injustice. Or tons of Toronto garbage, a million tons a year that is to be shipped to an abandoned iron ore mine in Kirkland Lake where 95 percent of people are on record to being opposed. The Toronto garbage is the most immediate and classic example of that kind of environmental injustice . . . environmental classism or environmental geographical location—"ism," or urbanism. . . . It is very discouraging. It certainly confirms anything anyone might want to say or think or feel because the north-south disparity is absolutely confirmed by this, because this is the south just fucking the north. This is the south putting their garbage in our front yards, in our drinking water.

The waving of financial incentives at economically vulnerable communities and regions to get them to house hazardous waste has been deemed a clear issue of environmental injustice by many (Bullard, 1993a; Faber, 1998c; Szasz, 1994). Such incentives are steeped in the trading off of short-term financial gain for long-term community and ecological health, security, and self-reliance. Such proposals often create intense community conflict and division as some community members vie for prospective jobs and others concentrate on long-term health. Irene, an activist interviewed for this research who was involved for ten years in the Nuclear Waste Hearing in Ontario, witnessed the community turmoil in the proposed siting of nuclear waste. She states:

> The question of siting and siting process were central through the hearings and has been a key issue and concern for us. We have seen this in the siting of another nuclear waste dump process. Namely, that it is incredibly destructive for communities faced with the proposition of accepting or rejecting a nuclear waste site. . . . The social psychological impact on the community is great, often leading to the utter destruction of community fabric caused by these proposals. . . . The fights within those communities between those who wanted the economic development and cash as opposed to those people who did not want a nuclear waste dump near their town tore those communities apart. Differences of opinion broke families and relationships apart because people fought about it viciously. Town councils were thrown out over the proposal, elections would go by and entire councils would disappear over this issue. It was very disruptive.

Equally problematic is the fact that these kinds of negative psychological community impacts are not recognized with classical epidemiology measures used by health officials in assessing health impacts. Therefore, they go unrecognized (Novotny, 1998).

Lack of economic means and political clout handicap communities' ability to stop or contain proposed and existing hazardous industrial facilities. One 1984 U.S. study, called the "Cerrell Report," found that while "All socioeconomic groupings tend to resent [the] nearby siting of major [hazardous waste] facilities. . . . middle and upper socioeconomic strata possess better resources to effectuate their opposition" (Dowie, 1996, p. 142–143). Further citing this report, the variables of age, community size, education level, job type, political leaning, and economic ideology are discussed in terms of likelihood to resist hazardous disposal:

> [T]hose least likely to resist are disproportionately middle aged or older; live in communities of less than 10,000 population; have a high school education or less, low incomes, and blue-collar jobs; and are not concerned with issues." Also said to be characteristic of the nonresistant group are people in "nature exploitative occupations—farming, ranching or mining"—those who are "not property owners or whose property is of modest value," and the "religious and politically conservative—people with a free market orientation, who don't lean toward a socialist-welfare state" (Dowie, 1996, p. 143).

Current economic frameworks further intensify these environmental injustices. In becoming globalized, capitalism has created a logic for governments and companies to lower ecological and social standards so that there exist as few barriers as possible for companies to prosper and compete economically across borders (Athanasiou, 1996; Brecher et al., 2000; Faber & O'Connor, 1993; Henderson, 1999; McQuaig, 1998; Milani, 2000). As a result, companies are sending their waste across borders to regions or countries where environmental standards are less stringent and are moving their facilities to areas with lower health, safety, and environmental standards and lower wage rates. At a provincial level, offshoots of this economic paradigm can be seen within Ontario. Cuts to social programs and environmental deregulation measures implemented by the Conservative government from the mid-1990s to 2003 increased social and ecological burdens for marginalized groups. Cooper (1998) describes some of the inequities of the environmental burdens stemming from environmental deregulation:

> The impacts of environmental de-regulation will be disproportionately felt by the poor, non-English speaking minorities, people on fixed incomes, Native people, and regions of the province that have long been disadvantaged, particularly the North. Pollution and polluting industries have affected such segments of Ontario society more than others. The barriers of poverty, language, distance, lack of time, and resources, will be made worse by a loss of legal tools to protect the

environment and the loss of citizens' rights to obtain information and participate in environmental decision-making (p. 80).

More specifically, she continues to state:

> For example, with the removal of rational land use planning controls, the poor or those on fixed incomes will be hit hardest by reduced public transit and increased property taxes and/or user fees that must pay for the well-known inefficiencies of urban sprawl. Industry self-regulation of mining and forestry will perpetuate and indeed accelerate the pattern of northern "boom and bust" development. The historical drain of northern resource wealth may create some short-term gain but long-term sustainability of jobs and northern-based, value-added industries is a more remote idea than ever. The clear bias towards unregulated resource extraction in the North will also increase conflicts over Native rights and continue to marginalize Native people from control over the management of natural resources (Cooper, 1998, p. 80).

The kinds of negative impacts outlined by Cooper (1998), including reduced accessibility, higher costs, and loss of community control, can be further linked to health problems stemming from the reduction of environmental protection measures.

Poverty and Environmental Health Problems

As outlined by Miller (1995), exposures to contaminated environments threaten human health:

> The accumulation of persistent toxic substances in our air, water and food supply has been increasingly recognized as posing a major threat to human health. Since persistent toxic substances remain in the biophysical environment for long periods of time and become widely dispersed, and since many of these substances bioconcentrate in plants and animals, including humans, that comprise the food chain, the ecosystem is unable to break down many of these substances (International Joint Commission, 1992). The fact that some persistent toxic chemicals are not naturally occurring chemicals for which metabolic pathways for detoxification have been developed also poses a barrier to their absorption in the ecosystem; indeed, many of these chemicals have been developed precisely because they are not readily metabolized and detoxified. The presence of toxic substances in the ecosystem has been linked to a number of adverse health effects, including cancer in animals and humans (p. 29).

Economic vulnerability lessens the ability to shield oneself from environmental health exposures. Bottled water, indoor air cleaners, organic foods and access to alternative health care are not affordable to many living on low incomes. Similarly, possessing less economic means often makes moving to another community, job, or home unrealistic options. Opposing environmental health threats from a position of societal marginality is often arduous due to the multiple layers of discrimination needing confrontation and the psychological disempowerment that can often result from facing forms of social oppression. Lawyers of the Canadian Environmental Law Association (CELA) are recognizing this connection between poverty and environmental health risks and are taking on cases which challenge these injustices. For instance, CELA lawyers have fought on behalf of:

1) low income single mothers whose homes had been built on an abandoned waste site, causing problems of toxicity, and unsafe and unhealthy homes;

2) a poor family prosecuting a pesticide company because the family's pre-school son suffered health impacts from being drenched in pesticide;

3) low income farmers whose marginal agricultural operations have been virtually destroyed by pollution of their water supplies;

4) poor citizens' groups organizing for cleanups of contaminants that have polluted entire residential neighborhoods;

5) a blind senior living on a small rural property whose well had been de-watered by a local quarrying operation in violation of its operation license (Swenarchuk, 1997).

Indoor Home Environments and Environments in the Paid Workplace

Indoor environments are another aspect of potential environmental health risk, as toxins are released not only outdoors but also inside our buildings. Mould, pesticide spraying, poor ventilation, off-gassing from VOCs (volatile organic compounds) in carpets, paint, cleaning solvents, plastic toys, and sewage backup are some of the environmental health risks faced within indoor environments (Cooper et al., 2000; Alcasid, Chaudhuri, Miller, & Petrie, 1997). Again, there can be an inequity of exposure between marginalized and more advantaged groups. Within lower-cost and poorly maintained housing, exposure to these health risks is often higher and left ignored. Many new immigrants, women and children, the elderly, and persons living with disabilities are faced with poor or inadequate housing conditions. As women are often the predominate primary caregivers of children in their families, they face greater hours of exposures to household toxins as compared to men.

Many minoritized and economically marginalized men and women also face awful health risks in the workplace. Garment workers, immigrant farm workers, and those in countless other low-paying chemical and resource-based industrial jobs are exposed to hazardous working conditions and suffer the affects of health and safety violations via pesticide and other toxic chemical exposures (Appendini, 1999; Chavez, 1993; Krauss, 1993; Levenstein & Wooding, 1998; Martinez-Salazar, 1999; Moses, 1993; Noble, 1993; Paleczny, 2000; Wright & Bullard, 1993). In her study of pesticide use in the U.S. agricultural industry, Moses (1993) depicts the health risk stemming from pesticide exposure and the mediation of these risks by class, race, and ethnicity. She states:

> The most insidious hazard [in agricultural work] is pesticide exposure. Almost all commercial crops are heavily and repeatedly sprayed with pesticides, and the great majority are toxic chemicals that pose acute and chronic health problems to exposed workers. . . . over one billion pounds of insecticides, herbicides, and fungicides are applied annually. . . . The environmental threat to farmworkers is not just rooted in class exploitation: it is also firmly grounded in a racist occupational segregation that powerfully shapes the nature of the farm labor force. The harvesting of perishable food crops in the United States is disproportionately performed by ethnic and racial minorities (pp. 161–162).

Sue, an activist interviewed in this research, gives another example of workplace environmental risks, and the layers of exposures that affect many immigrant women's lives. She describes her observation of immigrant women living in the northeast section of her community, where air pollution from the steel plant and other industries is the highest. In this area rents are cheaper but housing conditions are often poorer. Going into factories to teach English to immigrant women she has witnessed the low paying and the poor working conditions these women are subjected to—the toxic substances, the heat and often poor ventilation, and the physical strenuousness of their labor. Lacking political power and access to other supportive options for employment, these women suffer environmental injustices. Sue states:

> For a lot of immigrant women, many are ghettoized into low paying jobs. Many of the jobs are unsafe. I taught "English in the Workplace." I taught in a factory out in the east end of town. The factory was horrendous in terms of the physical environment. It smelled of glue all the time. It was very hot in the summer. There was no air conditioning. Women were doing repetitive work which was very hard on their bodies. They would get injuries to certain parts depending on the machine they were using. Some women had worked there for years doing the

same kind of work. They didn't get to see the whole process of what they were making. They suffered ghettoization, low pay, and unsafe working conditions. Some of these factories also pollute, they use materials that are environmentally unsound, but for a lot of immigrant women they have little choice. It's difficult too, in that, these environmental health issues can be seen as a white, middle-class issues. You have more privilege, you have more money, therefore, you have more time to see and want to address these concerns. If you try to bring up these issues to these women who are struggling in very low paid, ghettoized jobs it can be difficult and create tension. A lot of immigrant families are living in highly polluted areas of the city.

This rippling of adverse conditions across the multiple spheres of these women's lives described by Sue makes apparent connections between gender and environmental inequities.

WOMEN AND MEN

Women can be situated differently than men in our environmental challenge in a number of respects. First, because women face higher rates of poverty than men (Ricciutelli, Larkin, & O'Neill, 1998), and because poverty creates multi-layered vulnerabilities to being positioned in unhealthy physical environments, many women can be more adversely impacted by environmental degradation than men. Second, not all environmental insults necessarily affect men and women equally, or in the same way. The linkages between gender and environmental concerns need to be recognized. Breast cancer, infertility and reproductive disorders, and the contamination of women's breast milk are becoming conceptualized not just as health issues but as environmental health-related illnesses linked to women's exposure to industrial pollutants (Batt, 1999; Colborn, Dumanoski, & Myers, 1997; Steingraber, 1997). Framing these health problems solely in terms of women's genetic dispositions and/or lifestyle choices can be used to blame women and hide environmental factors, such as pollution, at the root of some illnesses. As environmental deterioration is increasingly felt and revealed in women's bodies, feminist and non-androcentric perspectives within environmental and health discourses become essential to women's health and empowerment. In addition, part of this feminist analysis would surely consider ways that men's breast and reproductive disorders (such as low sperm count) may be ignored since a patriarchal culture would see such ailments as unmanly and thereby leave these issues unpoliticized. While environmental health issues are *not* solely women's issues but everyone's issues, socially marginalized groups, such as women, and the concerns of some women more than others, need to have strong voice and participation in the defining and resolution of these issues.

Third, not only can women be affected differently (because of their physiology), or disproportionately (from higher poverty rates) by environmental degradation, environmental policy-making and solutions can reinforce and/or perpetrate women's oppression (Nelson, 1990). Environmental policy becomes gendered when responses to environmental problems involve the segregation, humiliation, silencing, control, or physical abuse of women (Nelson, 1990). In implementing fetal protection policies as a response to harmful environmental exposures on the job, women, Nelson (1990) states, remain disempowered:

> Protective/discriminatory/exclusionary policies are part and parcel of modern-day business-as-usual; that is; "the reproducers" or the "potentially pregnant" are classed as vulnerable and offered a kind of protection that usually only serves those trying to cover their liability. For example, in the workplace "Fetal protection policies" are the means by which employers take the focus off their own hazard production by offering to "protect the unborn" by removing pregnant (or wanting-to-be-pregnant) women from hazardous zones. In extreme cases, women have had themselves sterilized in order to keep their jobs and food on the table. More typically, practices include surveilling women's menstrual cycles or waiting for a woman to abort her pregnancy before placing her. Most reasonable people would agree that a choice between a hazardous workplace and demotion or unemployment is no choice at all (p. 178).

As Nelson (1990) argues, these policies fail to focus on instituting safe alternative substances within the production process. Because the goal of these policies is to reduce corporate liability (e.g., reducing lawsuits from birth defects) often women in childbearing years are not hired. Moreover, women at work who do become pregnant can face segregation from existing job sites or employment termination (Nelson, 1990). Here one form of oppression experienced by women (toxic exposures) is replaced by another (job instability/threat).

Western patriarchal conceptualizations of women as closer to nature than men is a fourth variable that positions women differently in the environmental challenge. This configured association has been used within Western patriarchal history as a tool to forge women's subjugation and devaluation. In this paradigm, women have been perceived to possess characteristics given to nature—wild, fallen, and dark, seen for instance in the labeling of women as possessing over-emotional natures—and like nature's objectification, women's nature too has been viewed within patriarchy as being in need of men's control, conquest, domination, and rational intellect (Dijkstra, 1986; Merchant, 1983). This connection of mutual devaluation of women and the earth has deeply pierced the human psyche. Both men (in their access to power) and women (in their internalized oppression) continue to silence, ridicule, and ignore many women who have sounded the alarms about environmental problems and the affects on human survival and wellness. Women who have complained of ill health effects, for instance, such as headaches and confusion (now associated with "sick building syndrome") in their workplace have been ridiculed and labeled as hysterical by their administrators who tell them their problems are imagined. Women activists making links between breast cancer and environmental toxins have been dismissed by government and health officials (Batt, 1999, 1994; Steingraber, 1997).

Societal power imbalances between men and women affect women's empowerment within the context of our environmental challenge. Men, and some men more than others, continue to possess disproportionate access to existing power and decision-making structures which are at the source of much of our ecological deterioration. This means that many women's voices are devalued in asserting their right to a just and healthy environment. Moreover, women continue to lack equal access to political and economic structures to foster such change.

Clearly, however, the structures of patriarchy fail not only women and the earth but also men. Men continue to be culturally socialized to narrow and restricting notions of "maleness" which deny their need for connection, co-operation, and nurturing. As a result, men can ignore or minimize their exposure to unsafe physical environments using well-worn scripts of being "tough guys." Men are often on the front lines of work in toxic industries, in the clean-up of toxic spills, and in war, with its arsenal of environmental health exposures from weapons men are ordered to arm. Moreover, both men and women suffer from a patriarchal structure whose values foster disconnection between the sexes and between humans and the earth. For this reason men and women need to collectively challenge patriarchal systems.

CHILDREN

Children's environmental health is becoming a crucial social justice link to environmental issues. Health risks and impacts from environmental toxins are being increasingly understood. Some studies reveal that children are more sensitive than adults to many pollutants (Colborn et al.,

1997; Cooper et al., 2000; Schwartz & Chance, 1999; Steingraber, 1997). Crucial window periods of brain, organ, and cell development in children make them more vulnerable to exposures, even exposures that were previously thought too small to be significant (Colborn et al., 1997; Cooper et al., 2000; Steingraber, 1997).

In contrast to adults, children breathe more rapidly and therefore have a higher air intake (by body rate ratio) of air pollutants (Cooper et al., 2000). Young children also face higher exposures due to their behavior of play on floors and in soil where toxins settle. Similarly, children, when walking or being pushed in strollers, are in closer proximity to car tail pipes from which toxic emissions spew (Cooper et al., 2000). These various forms of vulnerabilities are particularly disconcerting given that current Canadian environmental standards do not address these sensitivities. Levels set for "safe" human exposure to environmental toxins are based on the lifestyle and physiology of healthy adult males, not children (Cooper et al., 2000; Schwartz & Chance, 1999). Air quality standards in Ontario have been found to be five times higher than what is safe for children (OntAIRio Campaign, 1999). While this adult, androcentric approach to health risks from pollutants is changing, these changes will only influence the standards for new chemicals, leaving the slow process of reviewing existing standards for chemicals presently in use (Cooper et al., 2000).

SUMMARY REFLECTIONS

While we are all touched by the impacts of environmental deterioration regardless of our social positionings, we are not all affected equally. These inequalities are not coincidental. Historical, economic, and sociopolitical forces work to privilege some individuals, groups, communities while marginalizing and oppressing others. Recognition of such systemic social inequities needs to imbue environmental discourse and change-making practices. Environmental injustices force us to look more deeply at the causes and cures for environmental problems. These realities illustrate the need for a critical framework that makes visible the complex matrix of human and ecological oppressions and domination.

Equally important within this environmental discourse is the recognition that the social inequities and power imbalances manifest in people's lives (in the form of racism, classism, sexism, and other oppressions) are complex lived realities. Such injustices do not shape a person's life in a contained and tidy manner, imprinting one aspect of his/her life and not others. Giving voice to the plethora of impacts stemming from inequity, let alone their synergistic intersection, is a challenging task. However, within this challenge a large gap has been left largely unaddressed: namely, the often poor physical environments disadvantaged individuals face as a result of societal and institutional injustices. Also commonly lacking is the recognition that even when socially marginalized groups suffer the same pollution levels as more advantaged groups, the impacts can be greater as a result of the multiple stresses marginalization imposes (such as poor employment conditions, low wages, experiences of violence). Moreover, the research community has yet to get a handle on measuring the cumulative and interacting effects of different toxins on human health, for the reality is that people are exposed at multiple sites and at multiple levels. Such methodological challenges can impede acknowledgement of social justice-ecological links, as some argue the need to wait for the scientific community to provide the empirical evidence.

While not exhaustive, this chapter has illustrated that not all environmental burdens are shared equally. We are not only in it together but we are also in our environmental challenge differently. Empirical evidence demonstrating these environmental injustices is being increasingly gathered and documented in the United States. In Canada much of the literature relies on anecdotal evidence, highlighting the need for Canadian-based research. In our understanding and documentation of social justice-ecological links in Canada, the surface has only been scratched.

Countless questions and issues remain to be explored, such as: How do our "immigration and settlement" policies lead visible minorities to work in certain occupations, and are these occupations exposed to greater environmental risk? Should environmental pollutants be treated as a form of child abuse? How are current environmental injustices historically rooted? Do ethnic groups have equal access to local green spaces and other natural areas (e.g., provincial parks)? How will the repelling of public parks and green space impact the economically disadvantaged? What are the different models available to assist us in mapping the complexities of intersecting social-ecological oppressions in people's lives? What changes need to occur so that unintended negative impacts of policies and practices on marginalized groups are made visible and addressed?

In demonstrating ways we are not only in this ecological challenge together but also differently, the imperative of linking activism is clearly shown.

Chapter Three
Recounting Complex Stories: Limits and Possibilities of Narrative Frames

Journal note: What kinds of stories do we tell when describing our activism? Are there certain stories we feel encouraged to tell more than others? For instance, what stories do our activist movements support us to recount? And how do hegemonic forces work to bend and shape the stories we narrate? If Thomas King is correct, that "the truth about stories is that that's all we are" (2003, p. 2) these questions become very significant to activist work. In fact, many important questions come to mind, questions about language and meaning-making, and about the relationship between the stories we author and the social contexts within which we live. Responding to my queries from a poststructuralist view, Weedon (1987) states that "language is not the expression of unique individuality; it constructs the individual's subjectivity in ways which are socially specific" (p. 21).

Okanagan storyteller Jeannettee Armstrong, cited in King (2003), translates this poststructuralist view in a powerful and poignant manner, stating, "Through my language I understand that I am being spoken to, I'm not the one speaking. The words are coming from many tongues and mouths of Okanagan people and the land around them (p. 2). Stacey (1996), (as cited in Smith, 1997), reminds us of the political nature of storytelling stating, "Some people have more meaning-making power than others" (p. 6). So what kinds of stories are given credence and meaning-making power within dominant Western cultures? Smith (1997) refers to these stories as "pragmatic, time-tested, [and] value-laden" as well as "predictable, linear, "left-brain"[and] consumer-efficient" (p. 6). These reflections make me think about linking activism. Does Western culture have the words (i.e., language) to honor experiences of integrative agency? Do activists' linking experiences resonate with the kinds of socially constructed

*narrative forms described by Smith? Regardless of our answers, Smith
(1997) reminds us that, "to say . . . [that our stories are] 'socially constructed' doesn't mean . . . [they are] easy to modify or disregard" (p. 6).*

Some aspects of our lives have been written about more than others. Activists'
linking experiences are story themes that often remain untold. This paucity of
activist linking narratives was made apparent to me when I first began (over
15 years ago) looking within the U.S and Canadian environmental movement
literature. I sought stories of how activists striving to protect forests or stop a
company from polluting also struggled with community economic viability
and workers' job issues. I was interested in reading accounts of activists striving to get their environmental organization to build relationships with feminist, health, labor, First Nations, or anti-racist organizations, and to learn
what these experiences were like for them. I wanted to find narratives describing how activists were incorporating anti-racist ideologies and practices into
their environmental efforts. In broad terms, I was looking for environmental
narratives that made visible the range of social equity/justice landscapes
activists encounter across their span of ecological efforts. Working on provincial forestry issues would bring in one set of equity issues; advocating for
increased public transit in an ethnically diverse neighborhood would address a
different configuration of social equity issues. What I found, however, was a
lot of invisibility or cursory treatment of these integrative themes within the
environmental movement literature.

I had to ask myself, are activists involved in environmental change simply not engaged in these types of linking efforts? Are they not struggling with
social justice links in their work? While many may not be engaging these
issues, I knew from the experience of activists around me that some were. So
why are activists who *are* doing this work not having their experiences richly
narrated. One of the reasons for this gap stems from three narrative structures
used to tell activist stories. I have called these three frameworks *single-issue
narratives, site-specific case study narratives,* and *hero-based* or *heroization
narratives.* These story forms are problematic because they reduce and simplify issues in ways that ignore or restrict the narration of linking efforts.

Single-issue environmental narratives repeatedly ignore or give cursory mention to other issues they are connected to. These narratives view
activists' stories through an ecological lens. As a result, the interplay of
social justice issues is often undeveloped in these narratives even when
these are issues the activist is grappling with.

Site-specific case studies tend to embody a structure which highlights
the activist as the vehicle through which to tell the events of a story. Bound

to location, time, and issue, site-specific case studies rarely capture the span or variation of activists' linking involvements.

Hero-based narratives limit the visibility of less attractive aspects of activists' linking efforts. The portrayal of the activist (by writers) through idealization or "heroization" robs activists of key aspects of their complexity and humanity—aspects such as their internal contradictions and vulnerabilities. This humanness needs to be voiced if linking activist practice is to expand and mature across our social change movements. Many activists' linking experiences highlight this crucial human messiness.

As powerful tools of social change, stories carry seeds of movement that can germinate inside us, altering the contours and colors of our lives by providing us with new ways of seeing, feeling, and acting. Fulford (1999) speaks to the power of the story, stating:

> Storytelling is the mother of all literary arts, and anyone who reads must occasionally speculate on its enduring power. . . . Of all the ways we communicate with one another, the story has established itself as the most comfortable, the most versatile—and perhaps also the most challenging. Stories touch all of us, reaching across cultures and generations, accompanying humanity down the centuries (p. x).

Building on Fulford's (1999) assertion, we can see the legacy of story telling among indigenous people which richly demonstrates the enduring power of the story and its pervasive role in all aspects of community life (e.g., as method of communication, as means of teaching social rules, as strategy for problem solving).

Activists engaged in more integrative environmental work are living new narratives for researchers to explore. Story frames that limit these complex expressions of change making need to be recognized and narrative frames able to portray these themes also need utilization. This chapter examines some of the limitations of the single-issue, site-specific case study, and heroization narrative frames. The importance of a broad and diverse range of narrative frameworks to give voice to our social change work is also advocated.

LIMITS OF THE SINGLE-ISSUE NARRATIVE

While written environmental narratives highlight images of ecosystem complexity and diversity, often the intricacies of human injustice and the social implications intertwined in ecosystems are not developed in these texts. Similarly, other narratives focus exclusively on the human implications and costs of environmental pollution and include no tracings of the activists' relationship to the natural world. Such single-dimension narratives hide activists' concerns which span social and ecological contexts. This section examines examples of these environmental narratives and the ways they miss or gloss over social justice and equity connections.

Cursory treatment of social justice issues within environmental narratives can be seen when general position statements are noted without further elaboration. Environmental group position statements on First Nations land claims or jobs are two examples. Presenting a position statement as the expression of an activist's social equity concern is a "quick and dirty" way for authors to stay singularly focused on the ecological landscape. In Tindall and Begoray's (1993) case study of four environmental groups working to save Carmanah Valley in British Columbia, participants were asked to rank themselves as either "high" or "low" to the statements "Met with loggers" and "Worked with natives" as representing their social equity story.

Cursory treatment of activists' struggle with social equity issues is also seen in Wallace's (1993) narrative of Canadian forestry activist Colleen McCrory. Wallace's narrative includes strong undertones of McCrory's struggle with job and labor union issues within her forestry activism. We learn that McCrory connects loss of forestry worker jobs and deforestation to "mismanagement and automation" (p. 143) by the forest industry and to the lack of economic diversification into other industries such as tourism. We are also told McCrory tried to work out job strategies and work with labor unions, seeing the importance of building these connections. Beyond these brief linking practice statements the rest is left to the reader's imagination. What specific job strategies did McCrory work out? How has she always tried to work with labor unions? How much of her activism is devoted to this linking work with labor unions? Has her ecological analysis and strategy been changed by this union linking work? How have labor unions and her colleagues responded to these involvements? How has her linking work evolved over the years of her forestry activism? Activist narratives written within this framework leave the reader to seek outside the text to query about the greater social justice-ecological complexities and nuances grappled with by these activists.

Single-issue narratives keep readers' attention centrally located on the physical landscape, often with the aim of promoting an environmental protection agenda. Considering that our natural landscapes are continually denigrated and ignored in social-economic policies and behaviors, the use of specialized reductionist story frames to highlight environmental problems can appear strategically savvy. And yet, this tactic is problematic. Single-issue narratives of activists' environmental efforts support stereotypes of environmentalists as only caring for nature, not people. This unidimensional view has set a tone in many contexts whereby activists engaged in ecological efforts are deemed by many to have no right or obligation to comment on, or stand up to, social issues. The activist can thereby only express his or her ecological views. This caricature, propagated through the use of single-issue narratives, misrepresents countless activists who situate their activism within a broader scope of social change visions and commitments. Many activists entering the environmental movement in the 1960s came from the civil rights movement, the labor movement, or the women's movement. With this influx of activists, the environmental movement experienced a shift from its roots of ecological preservation and conservation to a broadened focus on more urban-based environmental concerns such as the impacts of air pollution on human health (Dowie, 1996). Gancher (1993) states, for example:

> [S]ome environmental activists came straight from the Peace Corps and the civil rights movement to groups such as Friends of the Earth and Greenpeace . . . The issue of ecology has always been associated with issues of social justice—if only because environmentalists could see oppressed nature and oppressed peoples were both victims of an exploitative form of capitalism. Poverty and pollution, racism and clear cutting are different aspects of the same social and natural dysfunctions (pp. xi-xii).

Similarly, Shabecoff (1993) echoes the social justice concerns of many environmental change-makers within the environmental movement:

> Many of the young activists who leaped into the crusade to save the environment shortly before or immediately after Earth Day and who now provide much of the leadership of the national environmental groups did so out of a broad sense of social justice rather than a specific interest in pollution or resource issues. Richard Ayres, a founder of the National Resources Defense Council and one of the many Yale University Law School graduates to become a professional environmentalist, explained that in the 1960s "there was a whole series of issues which people my age saw as part of one seamless web of need for social change—ending the war, better criminal justice system, dealing with poverty and protecting the environment, which was a new and emerging issue at the time" (p. 116).

These citations support me in proposing that many activists engaged in environmental change have linking aspirations and experiences to tell.

However, these accounts may be omitted from single-issue narratives because of a restricted focus on the ecological components (i.e., flora, tree species, level of acid rain) of an environmental issue. When this occurs, simplistic stereotypes of activists can be propagated. Single-issue narratives can also serve to make us acquiescent, "normalizing" a single-issue oriented activism. While this style of story telling may be familiar and comforting, its simplification draws us into reductionist analyses. This in turn restricts our social change understandings and growth, and reinforces existing paradigms of fragmentation which our activisms are trying to challenge. Single-issue narrative frameworks do not move us effectively towards a more holistic and integrative activist practice—endeavors which are at the root of linking activism.

THE NEED FOR MORE THAN THE SITE-SPECIFIC CASE STUDY

When social justice-ecological connections *are* narrated in activists' work, a predominant narrative form utilized is the site-specific case study. Here linking activists are depicted through their efforts on a specific initiative, usually centered on a set of particular local community events, to which they have mobilized a response. The narrative of Dollie Burwell and her fight for the removal of PCB-contaminated soil in her community of Warrenton, Mississippi, is an example. Written by Kaplan (1997), this story structure was used to articulate a new kind of activism variously referred to as environmental justice activism, anti-toxics activism or environmental health activism. In these activisms, issues of race, gender, and economic status, intertwined with human health issues, are portrayed as the central impetus for environmental change. Site-specific case studies, such as Kaplan's (1997), effectively demonstrate the historical, social, economic, and political forces that create and maintain environmental discrimination in marginalized communities. In this regard, the site-specific case connects environmental analyses to structures of social oppression thereby making linking practice visible. However, site-specific case studies are also problematic. What gets missed is the range of activists' linking involvement which span varied contexts. This section examines these limitations.

Activists' Span of Linking Involvements

Bound to a specific location, time, and issue, site-specific case studies miss aspects of linking work which do not fit into the efficient linearity of these storytelling frames. In contrast, many activists' linking work is best portrayed by a kind of richly woven narrative collage. Here, priority could be given to narrating varied forms of activists' intertwined ecological (e.g., toxics, land use, foresting, air quality) and social justice (e.g., labor union issues, First Nations rights, poverty, children's health) concerns. Furthermore, narrative tapestries or collages could be used to weave connections across the varied forms of linking practice found within and across activists' accounts.

The Need for More than the "Good Stories"

Site-specific case studies can not only be bound by the specifics of a particular time, place, and issue, they can also be bound by normative notions of what makes the telling of a "good story." Namely, these stories revolve around a clear sense of story development, discernment of beginning, middle and end, and tenor of appeal. Within these parameters, good linking stories would demonstrate clear links and be attractive to the mainstream media. "Good linking stories," moreover, would seek to cast the activist in a central leadership role, inspiring others to take action within a context of embattled struggle, while narrating the events that led to a concrete and positive outcome, such as winning a battle against an industrial polluter. Smith (1997) outlines the kinds of questions used by dominant Western cultures to determine a narrative's plausibility. These questions provide further description of "good story" characteristics being discussed. Smith relays:

> How coherent, consistent, or well-connected are the events being described? Do these accounts draw from commonly accepted cultural narratives, or do they seem unusual and odd. . . . Are events described sequentially so that there is a sense of movement through time, or are things mentioned more fluidly and haphazardly? Do narratives describe relevant features (who, what, where, when, etc.) in an explicit, economical, and selective way, or are they expressed in a vague, lengthy, roundabout fashion? (p. 6).

In my interviews with activists, some of their accounts fit the "good story" characteristics. They were concisely narrated stories that flowed smoothly and relayed successful outcomes. In a later chapter I recount, for instance, Jack's efforts at building dialogue with labor unions to phase out toxic chemicals. I refer to Dorothy's involvement in making a film which explores the links between breast cancer and environmental pollutants. I describe Craig's work as an environmental policy advisor for the Innu and Nita's work on environmental health issues in marginalized communities.

In contrast, other linking accounts by activists did not fit these "good story" characteristics. They were, instead, stories of small gestures and articulated hopes; encounters with confusion, disappointments, and humbling learning curves; stories of working outside the public eye without a tidy agenda or fixed start or end point. This section depicts some of these accounts and articulates their value in understanding linking activist work. Shirley, like many other activists I interviewed, took quiet steps and small actions to become better informed of another social justice sector or dimension. Shirley, for instance, sought to better understand First Nations culture and confront the ghosts she carried as a white person for the 500 years of travesties against Canada's original peoples. Reading, taking courses in Native studies, and spending time in First Nations communities allowed her to develop personal connections with First Nations people. These quiet forms of linking work were powerful in supporting her to move through her guilt and further strengthen the quality of her connection to First Nations issues within her activist work.

Other stories recounted activists' hopes for making social justice linkages. Kathleen, for instance, spoke of her desire, stemming from her sister's death from cancer, to initiate a project which would encourage family doctors to collect patient information that would assist in linking patient cancers to potential environmental health exposures, an experience cited in a later chapter. Serren depicts her wish to link to anti-poverty groups within a community-building and sustainable forestry initiative. Expressing her disappointment when preliminary inquiries revealed this wouldn't be possible, she states:

> Ideally, I was hoping we would be able to make connections with anti-poverty groups. It would have been really nice to pull in those elements of the community that give community economic development a different spin. When we started the project that was where we were first looking. However, the anti-poverty group in the area folded a year before we started the project. I would have liked to find out what anti-poverty groups were thinking so we could connect up with them on the work that we were doing on sustainable forestry. For instance, are there ways an [environmental] organization like ours can promote a co-operative value-added wood product manufacturing in the area that would support people who are out of work? I would have liked that dialogue to have started and to see if there was somewhere we could have taken it.

Honoring Serren's and Kathleen's linking hopes are important. Expressed desires to explore new questions and build new alliances are the seeds of potential future linking practice. However, intentions often get minimized, especially those not tangibly concretized. Narrating stories of these linking intentions can support movement towards linking practice.

Claiming as significant what others may conceptualize as a small or hardly noteworthy success, was another theme of activist linking accounts. Cecilia, for example, was able to recognize the power and importance of small linking acts. She narrated the sense of accomplishment she experienced at there being an environmental group in her community, given the tensions between jobs, health, and the environment in her northern single-industry town. She states:

> In our environmental organization just having an office downtown where people can stop and get information is a success. Just having that presence in what could potentially be a very hostile community towards the organization was a success. The fact that people are really beginning to call on our organization as a source of alternative information (and that they are not just believing what they read in the paper) is a success.

Similarly, Nita articulated the career success she felt from a linking experience that was unseen by her peers or colleagues, stating:

> No peer or colleague saw that performance of "Indoor Exposure," but it was an incredible success for me. It showed me that I had developed projects that were integrating and linking the issues. There was a coming together of different issues [such as health, environment, social justice]. There was a coming together of different people during that performance as the two groups represented different class realities and sets of reference points.

The "good story" frame would likely leave out Cecilia's and Nita's accounts just described because they are deemed "small" successes. And yet, their recognition of their own success is crucial to the practice of linking work. As an often challenging and risky form of activism, linking work relies on the strength and value activists can place on their efforts—on their ability to honor ways they are able to give agency to their complexly-aligned alliances and identities.

The "good story" format can also leave out dilemmas, learning curves and mistakes that are vital to acknowledge in linking work. Helen, for instance, shares her dilemma of trying to reconcile her support of bioregionalism and its principle of eating locally, with her sympathy for anti-racism and anti-discrimination principles which include importing foods that are native to other ethnicities but are not grown locally or available in Canada year round. Helen recounts:

> Regarding bioregional purchasing, I do not like to get imported fruits and vegetables in winter. Once in a while I do for a treat. But by and

large I do not eat a lot of salads and things in winter. A friend of mine
pointed out to me that if there weren't these fresh fruits and vegetables
that were imported and easily available, a lot of her friends, the immigrant men and women that she knows, would be even more uncomfort-
able and alienated and even more discriminated against in terms of
them not even being able to have their comfort foods or the normal
foods that they cook with. There's a problem if I'm saying "let's go
back to the days of turnips, apples, onions, carrots, potatoes." I am
automatically excluding half the population when I talk about food
self-sufficiency and bioregionalism in food. I have no idea what to do
with that. That is a stumper for me. So this friend of mine has made me
aware of some of the apparently irreconcilable differences between
bioregionalism and anti-racism and anti-discrimination.

In another example, one activist, a feminist herself, speaks of her failure to
take gender parity into account when in a position to support such a goal
within an environmental forum. Illustrating, rather than hiding the ways
we can "forget" our values and ignore social justice-ecological connections
can provide valuable insights to explore. Reflecting on why she initially
slipped into this omission, she shares:

> It is interesting, we just put in a suggested list to the government com-
> mittee for participants for a workshop. It was very interesting that the
> first list I drew up had two-thirds men to one-third women. I realized
> this in looking over it. [When] I went back to our list, [I saw that] it
> was very easy to bring it up to gender parity. I don't know why when I
> first drew it up I chose more men than women. When I did the first cut,
> I thought more men than women would be most interested and effec-
> tive. Only in the second cut when I looked at the list in terms of geogra-
> phy and gender was it easy enough to bring it up to gender parity.
> Maybe there is deep-seated reason why I did this.

In effect, activists' linking stories were not *just* composed of organizationally defined initiatives or traditionally defined success stories but were
also collections of small acts and moments, hopes, intentions, questions,
inner examinations, and unsolved challenges. Emphasis placed on "good
stories" within site-specific case studies can miss the rumblings of activists'
complexly-aligned experiences and identities which inform their linking aspirations and actions. The prevalent use of the site-specific case study raises
interesting questions about its popularity as a tool of framing our experiences. It is interesting to ask the question, what kinds of research, cultural,
and epistemological values tend to get affirmed within such a framework?
Alternatively, questions also need to be raised with respect to the priority of
linking work within environmental activism. Does linking work receive the

time, money, resources, concern, and attention in Ontario needed to bring about the intensive efforts that are often the focus of site-specific case study narratives?

LIMITS OF THE PORTRAYAL OF THE ACTIVIST AS HERO

The site-specific case study and the ways it is structured to tell a "good story" relates to the narration of the (linking) activist as "hero" within the social change struggle. Without doubt, the activists interviewed are inspiring for what they dare to envision and act upon in their community activism. They embody some of the best qualities of activist traditions—strength, knowledge, perseverance, commitment, resourcefulness, and altruism. They are pioneers and innovators of new ground both in their ideas and in their actions. Archetypal heroes portrayed across many cultures emanate such attributes. In fact, there is a growing amount of popularized literature that uses the metaphors of hero and archetype as a means to express the psychology of the individual (Bolen, 1984; Pearson, 1998). Clearly, the metaphor of the hero is culturally alive within Western society.

Given the challenges and importance of social change activism, and the inner strength needed to effect social change, it is not surprising that activists get framed as cultural heroes in many writers' accounts. Heroization of activists is a tendency within all stripes of activism, including those engaged in forms of linking activism. One of the most prominent linking activist heroes is Lois Gibbs. As Bantjes and Trussler (1999) state:

> Within the anti-toxics movement publications and academic literature, the figure of the housewife activist has begun to assume almost archetypal dimensions (Gottlieb, 1993: 207–10). There are a number of bona fide exemplars of this archetype, the most notable being Lois Gibbs, who organized the Love Canal Homeowner's Association and helped to bring the issue of the community health hazards of toxic waste disposal to public attention in North America in 1975 (p. 180).

Heroization tends to be more prevalent among American narrators who are situated within a cultural context which has viewed their history predominantly through the landscape of individual heroes. In part, this emphasis is born out of their strong values of rugged individualism (especially with masculine over tones), good guy-bad guy ideology, and an orientation toward the quick fix solution. In the use of heroization the struggle tends to become overly focused on an individual's acts and agency rather than on collective agency and the struggle for systemic change. Although clearly part of this socialized Western mind-set, Canadians' relative heroization restraint may stem from our cultural lineage of self-effacement. This being said, the landscape of the hero influences how we share, know, and hear our own and others' stories.

Heroization as Motivator and Protector

Activist hero images can motivate some people to engage in social change work. Activist heroizations can also give credence to alternative values and abilities in opposition to many of our historical and modern hegemonic hero models. Co-operation, democracy, citizenship, and justice are often held up within activist heroizations in contrast to hegemonic idealizations of power-over, competition, wealth, social status, and rationality. Examined from this angle, heroization can be constructive because it offers us different choices of values and priorities by which to lead a "successful" life. Activist heroizations can present images of persons offering or striving for a different paradigm.

Heroization of activists (by writers) also serves as a form of protection to both the activist and non-activist. Specifically, idealizing activists shelters them and their movement(s) from attack, and from the potential of detractors airing "dirty laundry" available to discredit them personally or politically. With the backlash against the environmental movement by wise use movements (Dowie, 1996; Gottlieb, 1993; Kazis & Grossman, 1991), this is a genuine concern. Gottlieb (1993) aptly describes wise use movements as "blatantly transparent pro-industry campaigns" used to "erode public support for certain environmentalist goals" (p. 316). These kinds of opponents have sought and fabricated ammunition to discredit and build an atmosphere of distrust around many environmental activists' social change efforts. In this respect, heroizations can serve as protective gear, a distancing mechanism from being crushed by overcharged or zealous targeted attacks. However, when criticisms of activists are accurate will a hero image be flexible enough to incorporate justified critique? Likely not.

Another problem with activist heroization consists of the fact that hero themes can be manipulated to detract from social change causes. A pattern of "divide and conquer" can be used to pit one activist against another. Implicit to hero worship is also the "one-god" model with the hero overcoming all obstacles on his or her own. This form of individualism promotes a false view of the realities of social change which demand collective effort.

Heroization as Intimidator

Heroization can also serve as a distancing mechanism for non-activist readers of these narratives, facilitating their rationalization of non-involvement.

Individuals can feel too intimidated and far removed from such hero images as the "Amazing Citizen" or "Stay at Home Mom who turns into Super Mom Activist," or "Activist who Chains Herself to an Old Growth Tree to Stop Chainsaws"—all images colored in daunting, all-consuming, tenacious commitment. Beneath these powerful images non-activist readers may feel less enabled to undertake such challenges even if they are sympathetic to and/or are affected by the issues being undertaken by these change-makers. Heroization and its superhuman face can serve unintentionally to dissuade or disempower community members who might otherwise consider more modest activist involvement, thereby undermining support for expanded social change efforts.

Activist Hero as Caricature

Without doubt, idealizations, like single-issue narratives, are oversimplifications that come with a price. They are caricatures as opposed to complex pictures of real people. Repeated caricatures often become stereotypes which, as Woodman (1982) argues, are "worn out vision[s]." She states, "a stereotype carries no luminosity, no living energy, no intensity of feeling. A stereotype is a worn out vision, a dead archetype, or perhaps even worse, a parody of it" (Woodman, 1982, p. 139). While such simplifications are problematic to all forms of activism, they are particularly untenable in the portrayal of linking activism. Notions of "legitimate" or "ideal" change-maker become even more complex within the broad and messy terrain of linking activism, and are likely futile. In effect, hero-based narratives limit our ability to perceive and understand the complex lived reality of our linking experiences and practices.

Two Strands of Activist Heroization

1. Pitting forms of activism against one another

Idealizing certain forms or characteristics of activism should be heeded with caution. Characteristics such as grassroots, personally impacted, direct action focused, volunteer, community-based, and mother/worker in the home are often idealized in eco-feminist, environmental justice, antitoxics and grassroots environmental literatures. While valuing the work of activists fitting such characteristics is deserved, these identifiers can be used to pit them against other supposedly less ideal representations of activism. Professionally paid activists, activists who work in large mainstream environmental organizations and activists who work within the system can be treated with automatic suspicion or reproach. These activists can get stereotyped as privileged activists who are far removed from any experience of environmental discrimination or who are insensitive to environmental injustice. Echoing several other activists, one paid activist working in a large environmental organization, expressed her frustration with such a response. Much of her activism, she stated, was devoted to supporting less advantaged groups and activists and to staying connected to local citizens and communities. Broad sweeping stereotypes of particular activist locations fail to acknowledge the complexly-aligned identities and affiliations many activists possess.

Bantjes & Trussler (1999) present a construct of "discursive innocence" or political naiveté which underpins many of these idealized activist attributes. Here the "ideal" activist is "not mobilized by an institutionalized political organization. Rather mobilization proceeded from the local and informal, to the national and institutional level" (p. 182). They go on to say:

> We argue that this emphasis speaks to a discursive context in the United States that is hostile to "professional" politics, and in particular to formal movement politics of the left. Narratives, such as those of Cathy Hinds, Lois Gibbs and others (Szasz, 1994: 90–92; Gottlieb, 1993: 207–10) have authenticating power within the American context. They operate by claiming a sort of "discursive innocence," while at the same time invoking a powerful set of normative oppositions within American discourse on "grass-roots" politics: experience versus ideology; "folk" versus professional politician; neighbourhood versus party; "local" and "homegrown" versus cosmopolitan; authentic versus artificial. To be grass roots is to speak the political truth with naivete and directness and with the authority of the people. (Bantjes & Trussler, 1999, pp. 182–183).

These dualities of activist attributes—experience versus ideology; folk versus professional politician; neighborhood versus party; local and homegrown versus cosmopolitan; authentic versus artificial, outlined by Bantjes & Trussler (1999), foster the heroization of some activists and not others. The problem is that effective linking activism defies these binary categorizations. For example, a Canadian study of anti-nuclear activists found that activists did not fit the construct of "discursive innocence" (Bantjes & Trussler, 1999). They came to their anti-toxics work from a place of prior political involvement and knowledge as opposed to political newness or inexperience. Are these activists then not "heroes" within our linking activist narrative? While some activists interviewed fit these preferred images, others did not. The integrity of their linking efforts could not be simplistically evaluated by the preferred cluster of activist attributes. Furthermore, depending on the context, activists moved in and out of preferred activist characteristics (sometimes paid professional, other times local volunteer; sometimes working within the system, sometimes not), a diversity that brought richness to their linking work.

2. *Turning problems into heroic strength*

Another "heroization" trick is to relay activist limitations, but to do so in a manner which only further serves their idealization. In other words, writers portray activists' weaknesses, messiness or dilemmas but frame the limitation in a way that makes them look even more heroic. For example, when referring to the enormous amount of time activists have given to a cause and its challenging impact on other aspects of their lives (e.g., their marriages or relationships with their kids), often the reader can be left feeling this personal sacrifice only further demonstrates their heroism. Here the reader receives an implicit message that "ideal" activists must sacrifice other important commitments. In such portrayals, critical questions, not "reframed" idealism, need to be given priority. What factors position activists to sacrifice their personal lives? Who benefits when activists do this? Who pays? Is sacrifice a secret rite of passage that is understood but not discussed or problematized? How does this intersect with hegemonic ideology?

Activist "Hero" or "Struggler"?

Heroization is problematic because genuine connections to others do not occur within a culture of hero-based narratives. The struggle to connect across social and individual diversity is at the center of the linking practice endeavor. Activists are faced with navigating differences across social movements and organizations; social locations and identity pegs; personalities and personal stories. In linking work, activists continually need to grapple with ways to expand the "us" and decrease the "them" (or "other") in attempts to strengthen connections between ecological and social justice communities. Linking activists need to acknowledge their complex humanity. Stepping on toes, acting insensitively, not knowing the answers, ambivalence, arrogance, feeling immobilized, and unwittingly colluding with oppressive systems are challenges that multiply within the complexities of linking practice. These challenges manifest an image of a linking struggler. Hero-based narratives do *not* highlight such areas of messy personal growth and challenge. In failing to make these aspects visible, hegemonic patterns are reproduced. Marino (1997) describes such an instance while engaged in a critical popular education project:

> Exactly what we did to make photostories was that we cleaned up the text. We took out the racism, we took out the sexism, we took out the classism. Ironically, we consciously linked this work to a critical perspective on the mass media, yet we still managed to turn out a whiter than white narrative—I mean they were very clean stories. Our personal silence around difference (in interpretation and experience) could be seen in a practice that inadvertently silenced conflict (pp. 113–114).

This messy, struggler image needs to be visible within linking narratives. As Marino (1997) shares:

> I deeply believe that one of the ways we can learn, especially in a social way, is by sharing what didn't work, what didn't come together, where things fell apart, as well as our successes or things that kind of went well. We've had years of training in which we have rightly learned to be cautious, avoid mistakes. . . . It helps to decode things like where did we learn it wasn't okay to make mistakes publicly? Grade One, probably kindergarten. . . . To privatize mistakes is to cut back on learning (pp. 50–51).

Marino (1997) goes on to state, "In the West, in North America, this is an *equivalency* that many of us make, that to fall down [make mistakes] is an inefficient way to learn—an equivalency that serves people in power" (p. 52). Unfortunately, exposing such messy struggles can be perceived as a threat within circles of ecological and social activist discourse. Often, injustice or arrogance is depicted as "out there" (in them) as opposed to also "in here" (in us). In this way, activist narratives can mirror many current hegemonic narratives where personal ambiguities, contradictions, and vulnerabilities are kept from view. Can the hero image be reconfigured enough to include this level of "imperfect" humanity? And if so, is this a useful project? Moreover, what possible traps may be encountered in this "new hero" package? These are some of the questions we are left to ponder.

SUMMARY REFLECTIONS

The Challenge of Narrating One's Linking Story

Single-issue, site-specific case study, and hero-based narratives can create problems in the articulation of linking activism generally, and in particular, for the group of Ontario activists I interviewed. Given these prevalent story frames it is not surprising many activists interviewed felt challenged when asked to narrate their linking story. In collecting and voicing their linking stories, activists can experience unfamiliar and awkward terrain. Western cultural discourses implicitly guide our messy life experiences into orderly, simplified, idealized, dualistic accounts before we even realize this has occurred. Being asked to speak to their activism through the perspective of the linkages they made was challenging for numerous activists. They needed time to gather stories and tally intersecting threads which many had not woven for themselves before. They needed to find the words to express the messiness of what they were being asked to relay about their experience. Most activists, I suspect, were more familiar with linking questions being a tangential or side-theme as opposed to being a central plot or organizing principle for an interview. Activists were also more likely familiar with being asked about one specific social justice-ecological connection as opposed to multiple ones. Another challenge was that activists' linking practice could also be implicit or nestled within existing discourses. Carol stated how surprising it was to look at her activism from the central point of the linkages she made, not realizing how much linking work she actually did. She states:

> This has been a very interesting process for me. Being asked to speak about the ways I link social justice and the environment in my activism has allowed me to see how much linking work I have done. I never realized I had done so much. I've never had the chance to put it all together. It makes me see my activism in a new way.

Kathleen emphasized the challenge of making linkages explicit. She indicated the interconnections were so deep and central to her activism it was challenging to know where to start in terms of outlining these connections. She states, "It's hard to know what to talk about first. I see the connection between social justice and environmental protection everywhere in my work. It almost makes it hard to talk about because of this pervasiveness." As such, looking through the lens of linking work can be a complex and awkward experience for activists.

Finally, narrating linking stories involves breaking out of the dominant cultural norms of specialization and simplification. This is not easily done. Chase (1995) points out that "the very thing that makes any group of people's life experience interesting may also produce narrative difficulties" (p. 13). Her insight could be aptly applied to the narration of linking work. To talk about one's linking activism involves, using Chase's words, "integrating two kinds of talk—two discursive realms—that do not usually belong together in American culture." (p. 14)—ecology *and* social justice; fighting oppression *and* being an oppressor; psychology *and* sociology as discursive realms brought together in activists' experience. Taboos in breaking these socially constructed boundaries may have produced narrative "silences, gaps, disruptions, or contradictions" (Chase, 1995, p. 14) in activists' narration of their linking work. For some activists, the experience of linking work may feel more akin to private as opposed to public discourse—a discourse written about in journals, spoken about to close friends or discussed during coffee or washroom breaks at environmental conferences.

A Greater Diversity of Narrative Forms

Much of the linking activist narrative has yet to be explored within Canadian academia. How activists are addressing social justice issues within their environmental change efforts is an inquiry that needs increasing attention. Within such projects, utilization of diverse narrative frameworks is important. The following questions could be used as a guide in creating such diverse narrative frames: Is the narrative relayed using a multi-layered or multi-voiced text? Are the intersections between social justice and ecological made explicit? Are activists portrayed in a manner which gives view to their multi or complexly-aligned identities? Are holistic conceptual frameworks being utilized to analyze the issues being presented? Is attention given to the interplay between personal and social change? Are small linking acts and gestures mentioned? Is the reader given view to the different kinds of linking efforts engaged by activists over time? Does the narrative show the connections across geographical locations (e.g, between the local and global)?

Narratives that coalesce these varied but intertwined dimensions will open the path to a more comprehensive and complex view of the realities and challenges facing linking activists in the context of hegemonic forces, which thrive on a reductionist, hierarchical model. Moreover, this broadened narrative format will facilitate the empowerment, expanded awareness, and understanding of both linking activists, and those participating in or observing their involvements.

Chapter Four

The Linking Activist as Linking Messenger: Challenges to the Communication of Social Justice-Ecological Connections

Journal note: "Powerlessness and silence go together," asserts Margaret Atwood. In her view, "a voice is a gift [which] should be cherished and used." While not indicated in a thesaurus, I have always experienced the words "agency" and "voice" as synonyms. Activism, in particular, brings this inter-relationship to the forefront. To be agents of social change, activists are called to use their voice—to articulate realities and visions in ways which can foster societal shifts and transformations. This "gift" of voice, I have realized, is not something to take for granted. As we take to heart the profound interconnectivity and complexity of our social-ecological world, we realize our need to be powerful spokespersons of these realities. In communicating these connections images of the linking activist as "linking messenger" or "verbal tapestry-maker" came to mind. That is to say, linking activists are challenged to weave different discourses and terrains into patterns of meaningful relationship. They are called to converse in the languages of circles, webs, spirals, and metaphors so as not to be tied down by forms of linear, reductionist discourse. As verbal tapestry makers, they need to be gatherers and weavers so that social justice-ecological linkages can be heard in ways which can effect social-structural change.

While the range and scope of linkages communicated were vast across the interviews, a central struggle of linking activism involves learning ways to communicate connections effectively. This chapter explores the communication of social-ecological connections and complexities. Specifically, five societal barriers which inhibit activists from speaking in more integrative ways are examined. These barriers include: 1) cultural simplification and the communication sound bite; 2) information overload; 3) specialization; 4) power of the hegemonic message and messenger; and 5) the limitations and challenges imposed by existing discourse and language.

LINKING MESSENGERS: COMMUNICATING CONNECTIONS AND COMPLEXITIES

Communicating linkages offers up the challenge to verbalize holistic narratives. Mann (1993) discusses the difference between common environmental messages or slogans and an attempt to "convey the total message." He explains, "It may not be as catchy as "auto-free" but what we're trying to say is that we want to reduce the use of autos, we want to improve your public health and we want to find jobs for you and the people in your community. If you can convey that total message, I think that people will listen" (p. 18). Many of the activists I interviewed were striving to convey more holistic narratives by connecting within and across issues. During the Gulf War, for instance, Dorothy strove to build a message that connected the ecological and social oppressions of war within a scathing critique of patriarchy and its institutions. This kind of integrative analysis was not being done in her environmental studies department, so she created forums to enable this discussion to occur. She recounts:

> [During the Gulf War in 1991] we tried to help people to think about how they could integrate the larger global violence against women, violence against the earth, the violence of militarism, the violence of structural adjustment, and the debt crisis. The whole oil issue was very much related to the Middle East and the questions of who runs the world and in whose interest, in terms of militarism being a way of living and thinking for so many countries in the world. Particularly, the big arms sellers who are on the Security Council of the United Nations. And of course you have to have these wars all the time to keep the motors running and to test the new stuff and to justify pouring billions of tax dollars into military equipment. And it's big business for everybody . . . a macho, patriarchal, violent, sexist environmental war.

Similar to Dorothy, Kathleen positions her environmental message within a larger socioeconomic and political frame which links environmental harm, social injustice, and democratic assault. Conveying the breadth of her message she shares:

> In my outreach to the community I work to show the big environmental picture so people see the link between what they do and say, so for instance, they can see their role in climate change. But more importantly, I strive to show the links between the underlying causes of anti-environmental behavior, anti-democratic process, social justice, and the nature of globalization and corporate control. This means coming up with analyses and perspectives on the issues I work with that enable me to talk about the complexity in a way that is understandable and in a way that draws the links between it all.

As these citations illustrate, Dorothy and Kathleen sought to be conduits of bigger pictures, weaving tapestries of social-ecological injustices which gave view to common root causes shared across these intersecting inequities.

Activists were not just messengers linking social and ecological problems; they were also spokespersons advocating integrative social and ecological solutions. Focusing on integrative solutions, Tonya's linking voice portrays the need to create forms of recreation that are ecological, intergenerational, and are able to welcome women to parks currently dominated by men's sports activities. Voicing the integration of ecological and social benefits in the creation of a community garden, Tonya states:

> I just finished building a community garden in my city with the environmental group I am a member of. For me this was an alternative initiative. Our current park system is full of recreational activities that are focused on men—sports clubs, baseball, hockey. In a park system there are very few recreational activities that are focused on women or on older people. When we decided to build the community garden, there were a lot of reasons why we did it. One reason was we were trying to build an organic garden. We wanted something that was going to be a heritage seed garden, something to maintain the bio-diversity of rare and old seeds. We were also looking for an activity that could be intergenerational. Something to bring together older people and younger people, experienced and inexperienced. We knew that the dominant gender in that garden was going to be women.

In advocating integrative solutions there is not only a drawing together of multiple domains and locations within our outer contexts, but also a coming together of our inner domains of identity, alliance, and experience. Serren portrays the need for multi-aligned identities as she reflects on the kind of person needed to convey connections around sustainable forestry and economy issues. She articulates the applicant qualities her environmental organization sought to fill a job posting in a community outreach project intended to foster dialogue on issues of forest sustainability and community economic health. Her description demonstrates her awareness of the connections between expanded notions of identity and integrative social change. Serren states:

> We were looking for someone who'd be good at dialogue and was a good listener. Someone who was not just saying, "I only care about the trees" but had roots in the community and cared about the life of the community. We weren't looking for someone who was strictly an environmentalist and we weren't looking for somebody who was strictly a community economic development person, nor were we looking for someone who was looking only for social justice for native people. We wanted to find someone who was able to integrate all those things together. We were also looking for someone with a strong activist commitment, someone who does the work out of the love of it and has enough vision that they knew where they wanted to go. Someone who could passionately defend what we were doing when reactionary backlash was encountered. In choosing those people you need somebody who's willing to stand up for and possess the courage of their convictions. This whole combination of characteristics is hard to find.

Not trading off one oppression or concern for another is another way to describe the challenge of linking work, and this challenge is more likely to be creatively confronted if we are in touch with our complexly-aligned selves—with our multiple concerns, alliances, experiences, and identifications. Clearly, taking a multi-positioned voice (i.e., for the forest, residents, the economy and First Nations people) within a context of community fractions around these very issues takes fortitude.

While she did not use the term, Serren was looking to hire someone who was a cross pollinator. This is how Si referred to herself. As communicators of connections, activists are cross pollinators—infusing knowledge, ideas, information, and analyses across organizational, sector, cultural, geographical, and discourse borders. Si discusses the importance of cross pollinator work, stating:

> I synthesize stories spanning social justice and ecological landscapes and try to be a cross pollinator of these stories. So when I go to the multicultural gala I try to tell the immigrant people there about the First Nations women's stories. When I am on a strike or on a picket line I talk about women's issues. When I am with some women's groups I talk about environmental issues. I try to open people's eyes in each sector. When I went, for example, to the LEAF breakfast this year, I was interviewed for television. It is a fundraiser for a legal education and action fund. It has become a middle class event. When I was interviewed during the event I deliberately said, trying to be a strategic

pollinator, of the 50 things I could have said, "I am really proud of LEAF for all the work they have done for immigrant women." It is really important that this group of primarily white middle class women reaches out to immigrant women and tries to enhance their well-being and that this is one of the reasons I came to this breakfast this morning. I could have said I came for the muffins, or to enhance women's issues, but I saw that as an opportunity to intersect—to highlight the intersectionality.

As these examples illustrate, the task of communicating social-ecological connections is challenging in and of itself. In examining activists' stories, however, I found their efforts as linking communicators were further complicated by five societal barriers—cultural simplification and the communication sound-bite, information overload, specialization, power of the hegemonic message and messenger, and the limitations and challenges imposed by existing discourse and language.

BARRIERS TO COMMUNICATING SOCIAL JUSTICE-ECOLOGICAL CONNECTIONS: A CULTURE OF THE COMMUNICATION SOUND BITE

The underlying tendency in our Western mainstream culture to value a communication style that oversimplifies our lives is clearly reflected in the media gimmick of the sound bite or concision. As Cogswell (1996) states:

> "Concision" is the name news media professionals give to the principle of cutting everything to a bare minimum in order to make it fit within the format of "news." The idea that all news has to fit into this kind of format is an unquestioned assumption. . . . It is impossible for anyone in our mass media to go into any issue at length. . . . Through the principle of concision, it is assured that only conventional ideas will pass through the media filter, because ideas that everyone knows by heart require no support (pp. 97–98).

This communication device which imposes the need to keep political messages short and simple poses a key impediment to the linking messenger. Kathleen expresses the lack of fit between the sound bite and her linking message(s). She vocalizes how the media sound bite serves to affirm mainstream culture's promotion of oversimplification which supports corporate interests. She states:

> In my work it is a challenge to communicate complex issues in sound bites, especially when I am trying to link across issues where the complexities and sensitivities become even greater. This style of communication is

reinforced in our mainstream culture which idealizes oversimplification, even to the point of idealizing ignorance. Like it is hip to be stupid. We have these popular media icons, especially depicting men as
idiots, like Homer Simpson and Al Bundy. When people are proud to
be ignorant it also serves the corporate interests who do not want an
educated public but a compliant public who will go along with their
agenda. The media sound bite affirms and fits this pride of simplification as well as affirms corporate interests.

Doug picks up on this theme of over-simplification, tying it to the power of
Western cultural dualism. He notes the challenge this simplistic aperture
poses for the person seeking to stay attuned to the complexity of life, indicating, "This is a culture of black and white, left and right, right and
wrong. It forces everyone to be too simplistic, and analysis suffers badly in
this kind of an environment. I have struggled to learn to live with ambiguity. This is really key. It forces me to realize both the complexities and the
subtleties more." Doug notes the tendency of even progressive political
movements to portray simplistic political messages, stating:

> It is also the political left that oversimplifies. Sometimes activists will
> oversimplify in order to make the argument seem more compelling. I
> am not sure if it is because they are being too simplistic and they don't
> understand, or they lack the analysis. Or, whether they are being a little
> manipulative and they're making it a more cut and dry, black and white
> issue because it is more winnable that way.

Environmental groups, for example, get caught in utilizing the sound bite
and its oversimplification of issues. Environmental campaign slogans such
as "Zero Discharge" (of a toxic substance), "Save the Old Growth Forest,"
"Save the Seals," and "Auto-Free Society" have been criticized as simplistic
messages which hide from public view the social, cultural, and economic
realities of communities and workers. Interviewed by Surman (1993), Eric
Mann speaks to the use of the slogan "Auto-Free City," stating:

> [T]he term "auto-free" has both positive and negative aspects to it. The
> positive is that it's trying to make a bold statement. . . . It's trying to say
> that the auto is a real threat to the public health. . . . But I'm a former
> auto worker—and not just an auto worker, but somebody who cares
> about working people, unions and thinks about the average people's
> attachment to the automobile. And the perception is that the people
> who want to get rid of automobiles are people who will also get jobs
> elsewhere—that is to say, the white collar or upper-middle class person
> who doesn't care about the working class. So working-class and com-
> munities of colour don't perceive it as an environmental issue—they

hear it as a class issue, and frequently as a race issue, if they hear about auto-free cities. Because they don't really believe that we're going to get rid of autos, instead, what they believe is that we may get rid of auto workers (p. 20).

The connection between the sound bite and ensuring one's message is bold is also one worth exploring. For instance, Marge stated that her environmental organization would not explicitly frame an environmental issue as a "social-environmental issue" because "it would not be sexy enough." While "Save the Seals" is a "sexy" sound bite, Marge states:

Social environmentalism is not as sexy an issue as environmentalism with a caption of a seal . . . , if we used a social environmentalism message someone in an upper middle class neighborhood might think, "Well, they are just lazy, why don't they just move [if they can't keep their jobs because of the need to protect the forest]"or "They are just welfare moms [we don't need to take their environmental health concerns seriously]." Social issues just are not sexy. Environmental issues are, and if you mix the two together you get a sort of lukewarm issue.

The racism, sexism, and classism that are implicitly attached to what is deemed a sexy environmental message within Marge's organization disturbed her. Seeing themselves as reliant on the financial contributions of many middle or upper class donors, as Marge implies, such environmental organizations can feel justified or impelled to keep their environmental message deceptively and uncritically simple. Staying keenly aware of who is included in the sound bite and who is excluded is a key task of linking activist work.

Helen gives us a flavor of the pressures she faced in getting across an interwoven message within the constraints of a "keep it short and simple" communication paradigm. She recounts her experience of trying to make a number of social-ecological connections in a radio commentary she did following the devastating ice storm in eastern Canada in 1998. She sought to get below the surface of this issue to expose root challenges and causes. For her, the ice storm was a "wake-up call" to issues of global warming and our dependence on over consumption of nonrenewable energy. Helen attempted to frame these issues within the context of a feminist analysis which looks at issues of power and the beliefs which foster social problems. It was a difficult task. She recounts:

I wanted to get people thinking about the environment, both cause and effect, how this is connected to global warming and how we are far too

dependent on electricity and consumerism and how this all ties
together. I wanted to highlight that we need to think about these things
and see the storm as a wake up call. I linked this to our illusions of
being in control of everything and therefore [thinking] nothing like this
can happen to us, that human beings—"man"—are in control.

Helen goes on to state:

I tried to make the point, without using the jargon of patriarchy, that
this is a patriarchal phenomenon, but each effort I made didn't work
very well. In the last minute discussion in the studio, we canned it. I say
now that a really good writer would be able to find a way to do it that
could be heard, and would fit into the three-minute time slot I was
under. The male producer and technician were saying it was a distrac-
tion—that I needed to stick to the main point in a three-minute blurb,
and that bringing in these connections would get people's backs up. I
said isn't that the point of a lot of the commentaries, you want to stim-
ulate people thinking. But they said, "What we are trying to do is get
them thinking about the ice storm, and stating this is a signal about the
environment. You might be sacrificing people's ability to hear that
point if you try to include this other thing because they are going to
hear it as anti-male." And they were right as far as that went in that
particular context. But then what I ended up doing was coming up with
this bland commentary. It is pretty namby-pamby in terms of what I
would normally say.

Clearly, restricted time and space for the presentation of information and
attenuated analyses greatly inhibits the possibility of integrated synthesis of
several related social and ecological issues. These examples also stress the
point that environmentalists and social activists are also influenced by our
educational system and cultural communication patterns, which encourage
such oversimplification. Not surprisingly, activists can and do opt for this
style of message. This concise but dumbed-down version of issues can be
seen to be more appealing and convincing as it conforms to a style that
audiences are familiar with. Dealing with the pressures to keep environmental messages simple, short, and narrow is challenging for activists
wanting to voice more integrative social-ecological messages.

INFORMATION OVERLOAD

In contrast to restrictions on activists' ability to share their message, there is
the countervailing explosion of the volume and sources of information.
This heightens a number of challenges for the linking messenger. Four of
these are: 1) having to work harder for audiences' attention; 2) facing an

already over-saturated, overwhelmed audience; 3) encountering the belief that to act or speak responsibly one needs to know all the information; and 4) confronting an atmosphere where information has become the message (i.e., synonymous with imparting a message).

In our age of information, massive amounts of data vie for our attention. Listeners must sift and sort this glut of information choosing which data-snippets to attend to, and which to ignore. Thus, linking messengers face a particularly competitive communication environment within which to get their message across. Linking messengers can thereby confront people who feel overwhelmed and weighted down by this information highway encircling them. Michelle described it this way:

> There is so much information one can access. People have to be able to pick and choose. It is easy to get overwhelmed. I can see sometimes in some of those I speak to, that they are already overwhelmed and overloaded before I even open my mouth and present the social justice and ecological connections I make around our whole food system and industry.

Information overload can make individuals less open or receptive to new incoming information generally, and specifically, to linking messages which are layered, complex, and require a concerted discernment on the part of the listener. In this sense, information overload may reinforce the attractiveness of the short and simple message for some audiences. Others hopefully will welcome linking messages which can connect and integrate some of the snippets of information "flying" around them.

Connecting information with responsibility poses a third challenge for the linking messenger. Some audiences and activists hold the belief that *all* the "facts" are needed in order to speak or act responsibly on an issue. This is an unrealistic expectation. Nevertheless, linking messages may only increase an individual's frustration at not being able to put this notion into practice. This is because many linking messages highlight complex social problems which lack simple solutions. Si makes this connection between information and responsibility. She feels people can resent her linking messages because they feel unprepared for or overwhelmed by the sense of responsibility that gets triggered inside themselves. Si states:

> When someone gives you information you can feel impelled to do something. Now that you have the knowledge, what are you going to do about it? But you may also feel resentful that someone gave you the information because you think, gee, now I need to do something about it. So as I go around doing my pollinator work of connecting issues I

think sometimes, while they may be enriched by the knowledge they may also not know what to do with it. They may not have the energy to do something and feel resentful because I have given them a burden.

Similarly, activists may feel a need to be fully versed in each aspect of a complex message before speaking. While very knowledgeable about pesticides for instance, an activist may possess only basic levels of understanding of labor unions or First Nations issues which are intersecting pesticide issues. Or, as Brennain succinctly states, "We have too much information and not enough education. I think many people are intimidated by the possibility of making the links. If they think about environmental issues and Native land rights, they wonder, do they have to learn about both of those things? This is pretty daunting and intimidating to people." Activists articulating linkages without demonstrating solid knowledge of the intersecting issues may appear neglectful or lazy. This is not a designation hard-working activists want applied to their efforts. Linking activists must creatively navigate the tension of being informed while not having to "know it all."

PERVASIVENESS OF SPECIALIZATION

A third force which challenges the linking messenger is the pervasiveness of specialization within Western culture. Specialization, like single-issue narratives discussed in a previous chapter, serves to impede integrative messages through the isolation and separation of issues. Three difficulties can be encountered within this terrain. One challenge is that through specialization the flow of information across issues and borders becomes restricted. This segmentation makes it difficult for linking messengers to integrate issues which overlap these constructed divisions. Activists referred to the problem of specialization in environmental movements. Many plainly confessed that environmental groups, in general, are still not very good at articulating the links to social justice even though these issues are inherently connected. Others spoke of social justice links as issues that are dealt with reactively and "in passing" within environmental groups. One activist states, for instance, that while feminism is respected it is not "up front and center." She comments:

> One of the environmental organizations I am part of is full of feminists, in terms of its staff and board members. Feminism is not usually an issue in our meetings unless something specific comes up. It is accepted if it is mentioned. If a passing remark is made noticing that a group is made up of all men and a very male way of doing things is being utilized, there is sympathy for criticism and it does not have to be

whispered about, but it is not right up front and center. It is not hidden but it is not what we talk about, only occasionally and often then only pretty much in passing.

Another activist articulates the problem of specialization by voicing the need for the environmental movement to broaden its scope, awareness, and interaction, stating:

> That connection between social, economic and political issues; we, the environmental movement, need to be much more involved in those issues. We need to be up-to-date on what the current social economic problems are—income, poverty, childcare, all those things. The environmental movement has to broaden its scope. . . . In a lot of cases you will find, generally . . . there are environmental groups and there are social justice groups, and there is still not a real meshing of the issues. It's very difficult.

Stretching environmental discourse was a key form of linking practice engaged by activists. For instance, in pushing her organization to develop a policy statement on First Nations issues and to build links with the labor sector, one activist states:

> I really pushed that we work closely with other groups and that we develop joint positions and actions where we can. Before I was involved in this organization we weren't part of networks. We weren't really working too closely with other groups. . . . This is how you can start bringing in social justice issues. If you don't even know what other groups are thinking or whether they're exploring that common ground, we are missing out. . . . My organization had never really taken any position period on Native land claims . . . and we ended up with a fairly positive working policy now in support of Native land claims.

While specialization serves to keep particular information in and other information out, this frustration is accentuated by these boundaries that are often subtle and unnamed. Negotiating these boundary crossings with "gatekeepers" (i.e., those with the authority or influence to direct what information comes into or out of an organization) can be challenging for activists. Speaking on this issue, one activist states:

> Often I've tried to fit this circle or this square in the opposite hole. There have been certain environmental organizations that haven't been doing particularly what I wanted. But rather than finding one or two other people who have my focus and just working with them, I've tried to swim upstream [and bring these linkages into these organizations].

> People resent you for doing that. Gatekeepers are so busy and pulled in
> so many directions that they work most of the time at keeping new
> ideas out and certain people out. They are quite exclusionary and want
> to keep their organization so focused that they don't allow sub-com-
> mittees or new people in. There is already a template you have to fit
> within.

Linking messengers themselves can get caught in details and not see the bigger
picture. In a cultural environment that has the tendency "not to see the forest
for the trees," a specialized focus distracts us from the broader messages. We
lose sight of the accompanying actions needed to make the underlying paradigm shifts which support and cultivate socially just and ecologically sound
communities. For the linking messenger, it can be hard to combat the pervasiveness of this way of seeing and bring audiences to hear broader, integrative
narrative pictures. Moreover, several activists indicated their organizations
were so busy working to understand and communicate a specific environmental problem that, in fact, they had little time or energy to address or speak
about environmental solutions or intersecting social equity or justice issues.

   Specialization also imposes a conceptualization of who is the valued
or legitimate messenger. The creation and validation of messenger as
"expert" denotes the expertise of the "specialist." For the linking messenger this characterization poses yet another challenge. The concept of the
linking messenger as expert or specialist excludes or devalues the insights of
more integrative communicators. Some activists saw themselves as general-
ist or big picture messengers, encountering opposition as a result. Other
activists were more specialized but saw an important role in speaking
across borders to the issues which connected to their issues of concern.

   Verbally stepping across perceived boundaries of an environmental
issue did concern some colleagues and audiences. Media pressure and
pigeonholing was often part of such expressed concerns. As gatekeepers of
how environmental organizations are perceived publicly, some activists
mentioned that the media does not like organizational identities to change
or be messy (i.e., more integrative). As Peter states, "I think the problem is
that the media does not expect our organization to comment on social justice issues." Fear of negative press and public opinion can stop activists
from voicing complex alliances. This resultant climate of discomfort is
expressed by Peter. He states:

> I often did not feel comfortable. I thought that the minute I started to
> branch out and talk about equity issues and social justice issues, I knew
> that I was potentially going to raise concerns on the part of people who
> saw the organization as a good environmental advocacy organization,

but the minute I ventured into social policy the organization would be perceived as outside its realm and told it was not appropriate for us to comment on social policy.

Desires within the public and media for clean and simple organizational/ activist identities are additional guises of specialization. Moreover, the pervasiveness of the hegemonic lens within the mainstream media encourages such identity simplifications.

THE CHALLENGE OF CONFRONTING HEGEMONIC MESSAGES

The ownership of most conventional communications and media industry by powerful and wealthy corporate interests is a fourth impediment for the linking messenger. These hegemonic political and economic messengers bend and shape our cultural narratives to reflect their interests and goals (Cogswell, 1996; McQuaig, 1998). Hegemony, as Bell (1997) states, "describes how a dominant group can project its particular way of seeing social reality so successfully that its view is accepted as common sense, as part of the natural order, even by those who are in fact disempowered by it" (p. 11). Corporate capitalistic ideological structures are invested in restricting the ways in which we can promote the communication (as well as conceptualization and actualization) of integrative or linking activisms by not wanting to give priority to perspectives which threaten their power or control. The management of news and public relations through these interests often serves to silence and put socially critical messages to sleep. Foster (1998) for example, states "in those cases where forest ecosystem defenders and forest product workers have gotten together the mass media has provided very little coverage" (p. 203). The restriction and sidelining of linking efforts and the avoidance of class, gender, and race critical analyses within societal messages are illustrations of hegemonic control over mainstream media institutions.

With few exceptions, activists possessed a critical view of hegemonic values, particularly those embedded in our current economic system. Activists saw hegemonic values, rules, structures, and processes as restrictive and at the root source of social and ecological injustices. Many activists shared stories of confronting forms of hegemonic oppression growing up. They spoke of experiences of sexism, racism, classism, ableism, and ecological and human threat—experiences which led many to activist work. In being agents and messengers for systemic social change, activists confronted numerous challenges. Serren's narrative, for example, articulates the power of the corporate forestry industry message which pits environmentalists against workers and their communities. Communicating an alternative message that illustrates common ground between environmentalists, workers, and forestry communities is challenging, especially within an atmosphere of advertised and promoted divisiveness.

Linking messengers face the gap that exists between mainstream power holder messages and alternative standpoints which priorize issues of environmental protection and social justice. Sue, for instance, spoke about the difficulty of trying to voice social-economic alternatives when government officials proclaim economic globalization as the only option. Sue states:

> There is a lot of educational work needed to encourage people to think differently. My concern is that we are being constantly bombarded with globalization, with change in the economic order. Our federal and provincial governments are telling us that is the only system that works. We've got one hell of a job to try and encourage people to think in a different way and see that there are other alternatives.

Messages promoting the status quo can make individuals feel unable to effect change, restricting individuals' confidence to explore alternative options and engage in critical thinking of dominant views, two essential components to getting linking messages heard. Speaking to the lack of class analysis, Karen indicates:

> There is a lack of good class analysis in our communities. Partly because relative to some other countries we are not doing that badly. . . . The contradictions are growing here but it is not at a point where you really see people talking about class and class analysis. This is a real barrier. Certainly, right now politically we are going through a swing in conservative ideology that is far away from any type of class or justice issue analysis. What we're seeing is so superficial in terms of how it is dealing with these issues in the province and that superficiality is at a municipal level as well.

Environmental organizations and movements have also participated in assumptions of hegemonic culture. Shirley, for instance, reflects back on the environmental movement, remembering its focus on recycling and all the unexamined classist assumptions that were wrapped up within it. She recounts:

> The focus about 15 years ago was on recycling. It's strange to go back and see that as the "cause" of the environmental movement, whereas

before it had been all about wildlife. This was a more urban version of the earlier environmental groups. When they were doing pilot projects where I lived, it was the upper class neighborhoods. There were a lot of assumptions there about who is in power, who actually will recycle, who cares about the environment in the first place. Also development was not looked at in the broad sense of where is industry placed, who lives by those industries, who benefits from those industries and who loses. The connection with workers and occupational health and the cause in terms of health . . . in terms of the smells of a working class neighborhood where your laundry is black and it is dusty and it smells when you step out your door. The broader economic connections with environmental justice in terms of who gets control and who is listened to when they have a complaint and why there are no incinerators in Rosedale were never asked. It was white middle class people. Maybe at that time the mining industry or certain industries were attacked for cutting down old-growth forests. They were not looked at as communities where people lived—that part of their life could be affected by this or not just part of their life, their whole life when it comes to trapping and wildlife.

Cecilia sees this lack of class and cultural sensitivity among some southern environmental groups today. Speaking to the realities faced by northern Ontario communities, she states:

> I think southern groups and people need to learn more about northern groups. They almost need to live in the north to understand the issues as opposed to just blanketly saying to us, "Why don't you just get rid of industry there? Why don't we lobby to get rid of those jobs up there?" That is not the problem. The problem is that the industry is putting pressure on people to do these types of jobs. But they need those jobs and mining and forestry industries are not going to go away. And, we don't necessarily want them to go away but we want them to operate in a sustainable way and we don't want them to hurt the health of our families and communities.

Brennain makes the point that we learn to put our critical thinking and awareness skills to sleep. Reflecting on the teaching of Canadian history in schools, she states:

> We are not well educated in Ontario in the sense that we do not know the history of the land or how Confederation really took place. We do not know the role of the Hudson's Bay Company or Louis Riel or the pressures of the American expansion on Confederation. If we learned these things we would know something about imperialism and corporate control and political dissent. But what we learn about Confederation is that John A. MacDonald founded the country in 1867 and there

was a railway. It is useless information in the sense that it does not give us the ability to think critically of what is going on around us. We are given a very pacifying education. People do not have a basic awareness or sense of how to broaden their awareness.

Marino (1997) raises this issue, arguing, "the patterns of interpretation and practices of cultural production, especially—becomes an impediment to education for social transformation" (p. 104).

It is not just the power and content of hegemonic messages that are problematic. The style and modeling of message delivery is also dangerous. From hegemony we learn to identify a powerful or "real" messenger as someone presenting a strong sense of ego, authority, rationality, status, and material success within society. It is a manner characterized by "I know and have the answers." The hegemonic messenger image and style is also strongly identified with being male. Several women recounted experiencing sexism, such as one activist stating that, "Being taken seriously is a constant barrier for female activists because credibility is accepted more in men and, in particular, more in men who are wearing suits." This issue of sexism adds additional challenges to women in their capacity as linking messengers.

Articulating social-ecological connections in competitive, ego-driven, controlling, and authority-based tenors is problematic. Activists highlighted the importance of speaking to environmental issues in ways that are not arrogant, condescending, or preachy. One activist boldly put it this way:

> We are talking about deep heavy stuff and advocating for change that will affect huge numbers or society at large. So if we are wanting the world to change we had better have our shit together. Our own personal shit. If we are ego driven rather than embedded in the issues themselves, we can cause a lot of damage. It is about treating people with curiosity and respect and having open lines of communication to figure out how to work out problems and share work in ways that are productive for the work as opposed to massaging our egos.

Boswell (1992) argues environmentalists can forget about being sensitive to the cultural diversity within North America when they speak. Referring to this lack of sensitivity, he states:

> It's a strange irony that environmentalists have learned how heavy-handed preaching about issues like deforestation, population and development directed at cultures in the South is an offensive, paternalistic and counterproductive activity, yet fail to recognize that North Americans, too, have a mix of cultures which demands sensitive treatment,

very careful reading and very, very careful "correcting" (Boswell, 1992, p. 16).

The bulk of tasks and processes characteristic of activists' linking activism, such as building links across cultural communities, dissuades them from embracing an arrogant and know-all preachy communication approach. Common cause work, consulting, and relationship building, for instance, require communication styles that are co-operative, respectful, and humble. Macy (1992) reflects and advocates such an approach of respect. She states:

> Hold yourself and those whom you meet in utmost respect and com-passion for simply being alive and conscious at this crucial turning of our collective journey. Don't scold, don't moralize, don't expect people to embrace easily the magnitude of what needs to be done. We have no experience for this, we don't have language for it, we don't have rituals for it. Pause reflectively, bow in reverence to the recognition that what is happening for us is really very new. And when your brothers and sis-ters want to stick their heads in the sand, just remember how much you'd like to do that too. Nourish compassion, knowing that they're not going to do that forever. And respect yourself for suffering with our world. It's a measure of your aliveness and your humanity. Listen when you feel that pain, listen for the accompanying message (p. 3).

Being humble and respectful in one's activist work requires fortitude. Activists work on issues they care about deeply. Their passion and concern, and the challenges they face in trying to effect change, can make it difficult to maintain a messenger style that is not preachy. While activists did not aspire to emulate hegemonic messenger styles, some caught themselves falling into an ego-driven communication approach at times. With blunt candor one activist admits:

> In doing linking work it is so important to be able to communicate well. Many of us are raised with this whole concept of ego, pride, and will. We are so oriented through our socialization to this whole concept of maximizing our external power that our whole vocabulary and our whole way of speaking is controlling and dominating. I speak as some-one who knows this intimately because I was raised in this way. It still pains me how poorly I speak at times without wanting to or without noticing that this is what I am doing. I can have a dominating voice and a controlling style and use of words which are counterposed to my fundamental philosophy and values which are of co-operation, sharing, tolerance, negotiation, appreciation, and mutual respect. We have to relearn our way of discourse within our culture to facilitate co-opera-tion and mutual respect. This is a big task. Within such familial and

cultural milieu activists are faced not only with outer systemic barriers
but the internalization of these aspects within themselves.

In voicing connections between social justice and environmental issues,
linking activists must repeatedly confront dominant discourses which minimize these issues and their interconnectivity. As activists relayed, given the
political, economic, and socio-cultural strength of dominant ideologies, this
is no easy feat. Activists must work creatively and with the confidence that
hegemony within any context (i.e., institutional) is never complete. As Ray-
mond Williams (as quoted in Marino, 1997) states, "A lived hegemony is
always a process. It is not, except analytically, a system or a structure. . . . It
does not just passively exist as a form of dominance. It has continually to
be renewed, recreated, defended and modified. It is also continually resis-
ted, limited, altered, challenged by pressures not all its own" (p. 105). One
of the ways activists challenged hegemony was through their critique of
language and their use and/or construction of alternative terms capable of
incorporating greater complexity and recognition of social justice-ecological connections.

THE LIMITS OF LANGUAGE

Communication simplification, specialization, and hegemonic messages
create language barriers to articulating linking messages. Viewing issues
and contexts in largely linear, reductionist terms, these three communication modes restrict forms of integrative and holistic communication needed
to best portray social-ecological connections.

Activists contested terms within social and ecological landscapes and
advocated for new terminologies. Terms such as "health," "risk assessment," "environment," "activism," "expert," "voluntary/host community," "epidemiological," "grassroots," "justice," and "equity" were
challenged. Activists at times implicitly, in other instances explicitly, named
underlying assumptions embedded in these terms, making apparent who
and/or what is included or excluded in a specific term. They wanted terms
stretched, reconfigured, or turned upside down, similar to the way these
terms are being debated and contested in various literatures (eco-feminist,
environmental justice, environmental health, environmental).[1] In this
respect activists' messages helped propel a fundamental rethinking of such
concepts, and the approaches they represented. Jack spoke about questioning the continued usefulness of well-used and well-worn concepts such as
"pollution" and "environment" because they do not best articulate the
reality of linked issues that need to be dealt with. He states:

> Some people think words like environment and pollution are old concepts. That these terms do not really say a lot or say what is important. I think there is a new lexicon developing to better reflect all the linkages we talked about. For instance, I feel a lot more comfortable talking to labor groups about clean production than pollution. Clean production assumes you are trying to find solutions. It means that society will still produce things because we have to live and eat but can we do it in a clean way. We still have to produce clothes but can we do it in a local way, and in a milieu where people are paid appropriately—local production and consumption but still production. So there are language issues which I think are fundamentally important which we have not really thought through.

Affirming (new) constructs that better express social-ecological relationships such as "clean production" and bringing these terms into the community were important messenger tasks. Terms such as "burden of proof," "weight of evidence," "(pollution) prevention," and "environmental racism" were used by many activists. These terms highlighted issues of social justice (e.g., environmental racism), challenged the level and degree of evidence needed to act to protect people against an environmental contaminant (e.g., burden of proof, weight of evidence), and emphasized preventative values as opposed to reactionary approaches (e.g., pollution prevention as opposed to regulation of contaminants).

The array of languages, discourses, and styles of communication across social and ecological communities also creates challenges. Rick states, for instance:

> There are tremendous communication problems. How problems are perceived through the day-to-day understanding of issues through media and what is really going on are not in synch. This is why I spend so much of my time on communications. There are people out there trying to understand what we want to do, but there's a semantic problem, a language barrier. We don't talk the same language.

Existing language and semantic problems manifest in many forms. Craig, Yuga, and Brennain spoke of the language barrier encountered in their linking work. Being a spokesperson on behalf of the Inuit while not speaking their language is challenging. Craig states:

> The language barrier is a huge struggle. The Inuit language is the most widely spoken aboriginal language left in North America. It's a very different way of thinking, in terms of the way people think in that language. It's a big barrier when you don't speak it and you have to communicate with the people you are trying to represent.

Brennain, who is not fluent in French, spoke of wanting to communicate and offer support to French-speaking environmental groups in her region. This language barrier hindered her ability to make linking connections.

Using the same terms across constituencies, like the word "sustainability," but carrying different meanings of these terms is another language challenge. Rick and Craig spoke of the different connotations of the concept of sustainability across environmental, business, labor, First Nations, and community sectors. "Environmental justice" is another term that held different meanings. Some activists saw the term representing the broad intersection of quality of life issues and rights of nature issues, while others used the term specifically to refer to racially and economically oppressed groups facing disproportionate environmental contamination (often from an existing or proposed development, such as a toxic waste dump). These differences of meaning were frustrating because of the miscommunication they bred.

At the same time, such differences in meaning across sectors can also be catalysts which challenge and expand an activist's view, lending greater integration of different worlds/ terrains/ discourses. Craig's work with a Chilean environmental group altered and expanded his understanding of terms like "sustainability" and "nature preserve." He states:

> Following my experience in Chile, my environmental values were challenged. We went on this tour of a nature preserve. There were some foreign exotic species planted in this supposed pristine nature preserve. A few people actually lived in it and I thought this isn't a park in the classic sense that I think of as a park. I said, why are they going to such lengths to protect this? Then I realized my definition of park doesn't have to be the same as theirs. A colleague and I talked about it a lot as it was all happening. I was having my own values tested constantly throughout the experience.

Tensions arising from different modes of communication were mentioned by some activists. Story-telling and flexible time allotment are different from a factual, scientific, and time-conscious manner of communicating in dominant white society. One activist spoke of the tension that developed between First Nations and white presenters at an environmental conference, stating:

> There was a lot of tension in the room. White activists kept their presentation short and concise and stuck to their time allotment. When a First Nations speaker did his presentation he did not follow this process. The First Nations speaker used stories and spoke over time. Many white activists felt frustrated by this but no one was sure how to address these tensions that arose. It was uncomfortable.

Activists are often concerned about how issues are framed and discussed. As symbols, terms can express and make visible vital aspects of our experiences, values, and identities. The use of certain terms can depict our resistance to hegemonic concepts that we experience as restrictive, demeaning or oppressive. This use of language as a means of naming and claiming is an important aspect of individuals' resistance and empowerment. However, the common use of terms across anti-oppressive movements can cause friction. Terms of discourse such as "Left," "racism," "grassroots," "patriarchy," "feminism," even "environmental issue" have become loaded, invoking strong emotional reactions. Doug strongly expresses his frustration over this situation, stating:

> Part of the problem is that the language has been so fucked over. Language has become a problem. Finding terms that are not loaded is increasingly difficult. Speaking common language that speaks to people that isn't dogma. It is an ongoing frustration for me that we aren't sophisticated enough, generally speaking, and as a movement there is not enough care taken to thinking in terms of the linkages and complexity.

One activist recounts the tensions she has encountered in initiating a feminist dialogue within her environmental work. She states:

> I feel very close to feminist issues but I get tied up in all these other things and then there is something yelling inside me, "But what about women?," "Why isn't there a feminist analysis here?" and, "Why are people so able to ignore it? " And when I try to insert it, it often either backfires on me in the form of "Oh, you are just being anti-male." or "Well that is a tangent." or "We don't want to get men's backs up, or some women's too." Women are often as defensive as men about it because, after all, we depend on their good will for our survival. There is definitely some tension in integrating feminism in my environmental work.

The frame of "environmental issue" can also be loaded and problematic because it "sometimes scares people away" as Cecilia states:

> Most people [in my northern community] do not see the problem as environmental issues. They see it as a health issue and human quality of life issue. The pollution from the steel plant is not categorized as an environmental issue because that sometimes scares people away. People see it in terms of their neighbor getting sick and you feel for them because they are your neighbor and you get involved in that capacity.

Moreover, Cecilia states many of the terms used in southern Ontario are not familiar to northerners. She states:

In the north we are not really familiar with some of these terms, like environmental racism, sustainability, consensus decision-making. These are not terms that tend to be used even though the thinking and process can be the same in the north. It is just thought in terms of "[t]his is the way we live and work in the community." I think they are fairly educated terms because they are not the terms we use.

Another activist experienced how having a certain critical discourse can work to exclude the very persons you want to support and include in your activist work. She shares a hiring process experience which unfairly disadvantaged a candidate being interviewed. Because this minoritized man did not use a white discourse of critique, she, and the others on the interview committee, unwittingly perceived him as a weaker candidate. She explains:

We just interviewed people, two were white women of Anglo descent and another man who is of Indian descent. One of the criticisms was that he was not critical enough in the interview of the partnership between the community and the university. So then it occurred to me after we were saying all this, that when you are not in a power position how could you possibly critique a relationship between the community and the university? Why would you be critical? Where would you receive the strength to be critical when you are trying to look for work? It only occurred to me afterwards that I can't believe I did not give that person leeway. I did not give the room for that critique to come. I did not make room for him to be comfortable to talk about that. I was expecting that analysis to come out of his mouth because the previous interviewees addressed the issue. The women had power. They are in the system. They feel strong. They have had jobs. They know they will always have jobs. They know they belong. So they have the power to critique. Why would someone who is a new immigrant and who is struggling, even dare or have the ability or strength to critique? I was entrenched in the paradigm that the good interviewee would talk about critique instead of helping that person in a way that would help us understand how analytical that person was.

She goes on to reflect:

I struggle with do we just hire people who are like us? Can we not get out of our frameworks? Is it that we don't want to take the time to train people? We don't want to take the time to understand where people are coming from who are from different social locations. We are constantly pushed to adopt a white paradigm. Our [organizational] lingo is privileged to people who are educated and who are in circles of privilege which are white. There is a lot of lingo and jargon we use and expect the person interviewed to use. If I believe strongly in hiring people who are

underemployed so they have avenues of employment. These barriers
get in the way of doing that.

This activist's experience expresses the challenges of staying in touch with
our multi-identified selves within organizational contexts and social change
cultures that are not aware of how their language and discourse can work
to include some, and exclude others. As these citations have illustrated,
finding terms that engage and open communication channels rather than
close or confuse them can be challenging. This stems from the fact that
social change concepts can become so loaded in ideological and political
meanings that their use triggers disparate responses.

Linking messengers confront numerous communication barriers in
order to communicate the common ground that resides across different
constituencies. For linking messengers the issue of translation is pivotal.
This section introduces the theme of translation, a theme which also arises
in the following chapters and that is discussed in more detail in Chapter
Ten. Yuga, for instance, spoke to the numerous ways environmental
groups' messages are not literally or figuratively spoken in a language that
is heard or understood by new immigrants. He points out multiple areas
where translation is needed in order to rectify these communication
impasses, including: a) an over-emphasis on written material and lack of
materials translated into other languages; b) lack of connection to culture
or health within environmental messages; c) speaking environmental messages in venues new immigrants do not tend to frequent or feel comfortable
in; d) holding environmental events at inconvenient times; and e) not utilizing environmental messengers new immigrants can relate to or feel comfortable with. In his own words, Yuga succinctly states:

> From our experience it is not enough just to have written material. We
> have found that printed material is not the best medium to educate new
> immigrants around environmental issues. Utilizing songs, stories or
> posters which make the link to culture, health, and their everyday expe-
> rience is what is needed. Environmental messages to save the seals or
> owls are not very popular to new immigrants who often cannot relate
> to these campaigns. . . . In addition, the information has to be in their
> community centers, apartments, churches, Mosque, and Synagogues,
> places where new immigrants feel comfortable. Then there is the issue
> of who delivers the message. Is it somebody they are comfortable with?
> Somebody they can relate to? Somebody who understands both worlds
> (their initial home culture and Canadian culture)? The other aspect is
> timing and being able to present your message outside of nine to five
> working hours when people are able to attend.

Rick also raises the theme of translation. He states the language used by environmental theorists and writers is often not understood by others. While very active in environmental issues, Rick himself has struggled to understand the works of social ecologist Murray Bookchin and the writings of "ecological footprint" theorist Bill Reese, stating that he has called on his son's assistance (a student studying these issues) to interpret these works. While indicating that their material is good, Rick states, "We can't communicate with people on the street with this." In another instance of bringing environmental literature and videos on sustainability to a labor union meeting, he recalls, "I took it to the Congress and we all scratched our heads going, 'What the hell is that?' I still have problems with a lot of what this activist says, but I understand where he is trying to go, what he is trying to do. The language is the problem." It is not just academic or theoretical environmental terminology that is problematic for many listeners. Boswell (1992) argues that Canadian citizens often do not resonant with social change terms such as "struggle, conflict, resistance, democracy, and power" (p. 16). He argues, in Canada, softer words are more radical. Leaving us with something to think about, Boswell (1992) states:

> [T]he words I'd hoist to the top of the social change lexicon are *reconciliation, community, wisdom, nuance, caressing, convincing,* and *embracing*. Yes, these words have a soft exterior; on the surface, they seem opposite to words like *resistance, power, struggle*. But their strength lies in the bonds they create between people, and in the deep change in values and ideas and actions that they portend. Ideas and movements that are rooted in people's lives . . . are ultimately more radical (p. 16).

Being an effective translator across constituencies is an ambitious undertaking. Brennain leaves a hopeful tone in being able to accomplish this task. While she speaks to social groups not necessarily using the same language, she also demonstrates her flexibility as a communicator across these different contexts and constituencies. She states:

> Other social groups would not necessarily use the same language. First Nations would probably not describe the problem as corporate control. They would probably describe it as one of colonial control. There is a fine line, an invisible line between corporate control and colonial power. It is all basically colonial power exercised for the benefit of expanding corporate control over a larger land base. In the final analysis it would pretty much come out the same thing. It varies issue by issue, case by case and person by person. With First Nations groups, some of them I would and some of them I would not. There are a couple of people I work with who

> I talk about the political philosophical analysis between us. With others, it is much more concrete and pragmatic, like how can we make a government ministry have a meeting with us before they take this action and what are the arguments that we can put forward to try to alter their action. With labor and other community groups it really depends on a person-by-person basis, and on time constraints.

Jack underscores Brennain's outlook. He contends that there is no agreement on what terms or language are "correct" because activists come from different locations. He states:

> I do not think there is an accepted term to denote social justice-ecological linkages. It depends on the situation. A lot of people come from the social justice movement and work in the environmental field so they bring in their own language. Many environmentalists who do not work in the social justice field use different language. So I do not think there is agreement on what language is right. Environmental justice can sound fairly esoteric to most people. I think when I deal with communities I just deal with it in words and not labels. If we are trying to deal with a polluting facility we say we have to accommodate the community. We want it to be healthy. So we are trying to reconcile environmental protection and economic development. And if we are discussing with our labor friends it's jobs and the environment and clean production.

Jack's emphasis on the importance of dealing in words not labels based on the specifics of each individual situation is an important skill for linking activists to utilize given the diverse socio-cultural landscapes of linking work. Awareness of who and what is being included or excluded, in the use of terms, is equally essential, as is forging a lexicon capable of offering critique while simultaneously elucidating connection and integration such as terms like "clean production." As activists strive to relay social justice-ecological connections, one can argue they become like maverick linguists who dare to use existing terms in novel ways and have the creative confidence to construct new terms. They shift our thinking beyond linear, reductionist, imperialist constructions that predominate our discourse.

SUMMARY REFLECTIONS

This chapter illustrates that it is not only the complexity of linking issues and the sensitivity of boundary issues which come into play, but also numerous societal forces which inhibit integrative verbal expression. Even when activists broadly analyze situations, when they not only have great intentions but are practicing linking work and maintaining a holistic approach, there remains substantial pressure to reduce things verbally. Activists can feel pressure to relate social-ecological issues in ways that are short, simplistic, and quick so that listeners do not become confused, over- whelmed, or restless. It can be hard for them to step outside this pressure and be more complexly-aligned communicators. Activists need to be aware of the forces discussed in this chapter so that they are better able to work consciously and creatively among these constraints. Moreover, greater attention needs to be given to examining the skills of complex communica- tion and the ways these messages can support socially just and ecologically viable social change.

Part Two

Exploring Forms of Linking Activist Practice

Chapter Five

Living Democracy through Linking Activism: Fighting for the Rights of Information and Participation in Government Environmental Decisions

Journal Note: The newspaper headlines on January 19, 2002 read, "Judge blames Tories: Inquiry concludes cuts doomed water victims." "The Report of the Walkerton Inquiry" has been released. The newspaper headlines have sat staring me in the face for days but I haven't had the heart to read the coverage of the report.

Justice Dennis O'Connor's investigation into the death of seven people, as well as into the thousands of Walkerton, Ontario residents who became sick from contaminated drinking water, brought up lots of emotion, more in fact, than I thought it would, almost two years after the tragedy occurred.

I felt grief for the residents of Walkerton who were confronted with such a community disaster. I felt anger for what this occurrence tells us about government cutbacks, lack of government accountability, insufficient public knowledge and involvement, and the predominance of the global economic paradigm. I felt upset that the warnings, sounded by citizens/activists (about the impact of these government cuts) were not heeded by government officials.

One, among the many lessons from the Walkerton tragedy is the lesson that tragic consequences occur when the government does not inform or involve the public in environmental matters.

Several years prior I confronted my own naiveté about the impor-
tance of our democratic rights to information and participation. I wanted
to believe our democratic frameworks are flawed but tolerable. Or else, I
liked to think that I would succeed in maneuvering these flaws when I
encountered them. This attitude displayed forms of my own denial, privi-
lege, and individualism.

I realized it can be difficult to fully understand the complex configu-
ration of subtle and not so subtle systemic barriers until you crash into
them. Working as a citizen activist on the proposed Environmental Bill of
Rights legislation, now law in Ontario, I was given a firsthand opportunity
to experience the synergistic effect of multiple citizen participation barriers.
This experience of encountering not just one barrier but numerous inter-
connecting impediments was when I realized the real significance of
activists' efforts to address barriers to democracy. The Walkerton tragedy,
which occurred several years later, is a chilling reminder of how far we have
yet to go in safeguarding and expanding these democratic rights.

Without access to environmental information or the ability to participate
in decisions which affect the environment, citizens are excluded from
matters which deeply influence their lives—matters of the quality and
treatment of the air we breathe, the water we drink, and the soil that
grows our food. In a democratic society, effective environmental citizenship calls on two process-based justice issues: the public right to know
and the public right to participate. While all activists interviewed were
engaged in the activities of public awareness and participation at some
level, involvement with these issues at governmental levels varied among
activists. Yet, whether they were actively involved in government lobbying and policy mechanisms or not, when asked to relay their linking stories, the themes of the public right to know and participate were relayed
by activists as social justice issues.

The activists I interviewed saw rights of access to environmental
information and participation as issues of power and empowerment. Experiencing a lack of access in these areas gave many activists firsthand knowledge that these barriers are not merely coincidental but are embedded in
forms of inequity within existing government legal, bureaucratic, and political mechanisms (laws, policies, and regulations). This chapter narrates the
varied dimensions of struggle engaged in by activists to safeguard,
strengthen, and/or expand citizen knowledge of and participation in governmental environmental decision-making. Specific attention is given to the
following nine themes:

1) the complexity and political nature of environmental issues
2) the mistrust of government to uphold its environmental responsibilities
3) the legacy of government decision-making behind closed doors
4) the lack of level playing fields within government forums
5) the struggle to secure more meaningful levels of citizen participation
6) the lack of resources to enable effective citizen participation
7) the attack on information and participation rights by the Conservative provincial government
8) the reductions in environmental protections impacting human and ecological health
9) the connection between provincial regressive actions and global economic forces

THE RIGHT TO KNOW AND PARTICIPATE AS SOCIAL JUSTICE STRUGGLES

Environmental issues are complex. This complexity makes public awareness and involvement in these issues all that more vital. Activists relayed accounts of the often contested scientific details of ecosystems. They, moreover, recognized that environmental decisions are embedded within the relations of ruling in societal, socioeconomic, and cultural spheres; thereby they viewed these decision-making processes as value-laden and political. Advocating for citizens to have meaningful venues of participation so that their interests are represented in environmental decision-making processes was a central linking practice among activists. Kathleen speaks of these variables, stating:

> There is a crucial need for public knowledge and involvement in environmental decisions because those decisions are value judgments directly affecting people's lives. They are not decisions based on pure science, which is why people who are directly affected and those who are disproportionately affected need to be involved. They are value judgments that need to be made as a community and should not be imposed from above.

Expanding on the significance of these justice issues, Kathleen asserts the potential for the manipulation of power without strong citizen rights of information and participation by arguing:

> Not only is knowledge power but the manipulation of knowledge is power. This manipulation is especially true for environmental issues

since information is almost always incomplete and highly complex. When decisions need to be made in the face of incomplete information, value judgments and political decisions are made and the effects of those decisions are felt by others, often by the disenfranchised or non-participating members of the public who are not in a position to influence those value judgments or political decisions.

As Kathleen alludes, part of the complexity of environmental issues is the lack of available knowledge which leads to environmental decisions being, in part, the result of "informed" guesswork. The risk assessment process underlying regulatory decision-making is one example where a lot of estimations are made in the deliberation of decisions. This ambiguity factor makes the rights of information access and participation crucial social justice issues because the impact of such "guess-work" can disproportionately affect some people.

Mistrust of the government's ability to carry out its environmental responsibilities also places the rights to information access and participation within the domain of social justices issues. Activists recognized the government's key role in demonstrating and upholding environmental values and standards to ensure safe and healthy environments, and felt strongly that government officials should be held accountable for these responsibilities. Repeatedly, activists witnessed governments not taking seriously their role as public guardians of our commons (our forests, water, air, soil). This created a climate of activist mistrust in the ability of government to do its job. Activists spoke of government inaction and mis-action. Identifying proof of this, Carol states:

> At a provincial level, you just have to look at the "Report of the Environmental Commissioner of Ontario." This is the body which monitors the environmental behavior of provincial ministries. It documents many, many ways our government is not living up to its environmental responsibilities and calls for needed change if we are to take our environment seriously as a province.

Central to this inaction and resultant distrust of government was the sentiment that hegemonic interests dominate the resolution of government environmental decisions. Activists expressed that government decisions continually favor economic and corporate interests over the public's need for safe, clean, and sustainable physical environments. Brecher, Costello, and Smith (2000) concur with such views, stating, "In reality . . . states are largely and increasingly subject to corruption and coercion by global corporations, so that they represent the latter far more than their own people.

At present, few if any states could be proven not to be illegitimate outlaw states" (p. 45). Government enmeshment with corporate/industrial interests is voiced by Rick. He states bluntly that governments are fearful and unable to deal with the corporate agenda. Indicating that this agenda maintains the dichotomies between jobs and the environment, he asserts:

> Corporations, industry, and government are working together now. That is the problem. For instance, looking at the federal gasoline regulations makes me shake my head with what the federal government has done to accommodate industry, something they call "economic flexibility." There are no politicians working for the common public interest anymore. . . . It is not just the Harris government, it is all these governments not being able to deal with the corporate agenda. Politicians are being held ransom locally now because of the fear of trade and the fear that industries will by-pass them. They won't bring jobs into the community. . . . There is still that trade-off that either you are going to have a job or you are going to have an environment, you can't have both. We have executives at Ford, Chrysler, and some of the biggest corporations in the world still saying that to us.

Irene is equally candid in her cynicism concerning government "doing the right thing." Speaking of the short-sighted approaches to hazardous waste problems she reports:

> Local government and regulatory agencies cannot be trusted to do the right thing in solving hazardous waste problems. They have to be pushed into it. Their interests are making a fast buck off the taxes or grants they receive from industry in taking their waste. Local governments will bring in a booming population even if it is a boom and bust outcome. As long as the economy is booming when they are in office so they can collect the taxes and build new arenas and roads they proceed. It is a very selfish and irresponsible approach to leadership.

Many activists voiced the negative ecological and human health impacts resulting from the government's over-enmeshment with the business sector's "progress" and "profit-driven" ideologies. Speaking of the need to raise public awareness of this imbalance and its implications, Michelle states:

> Making citizens aware of what is going on between corporations and governments is a social justice issue. My choice to learn more about and inform others of the wide ranging corporate control of food production, such as apples, where small farmers have been dictated to by corporate giants, such as Weston, regarding species of production, pesticide use, and distribution channels is one example. This has led to significant reduction in the numbers of available species of apple and

quality of apple, along with soil and land degradation. Clearly, it has not been in the interests of Weston, or Liberal and Conservative governments who are financed in large measure by corporate donations, such as Weston, to promote this awareness of control over food production and its negative environmental and health impact, and the underlying restriction of democratic choice by citizens. There is much work to do letting people know what is going on here.

The legacy of government decision-making behind closed doors, with citizens outside and powerful interests within, is a third reason rights of information and participation are social justice issues. Clearly articulating this imbalance Maynes (1989) states, "Consultation is nothing new. Governments have always consulted before making major decisions—behind closed doors, with powerful interests like corporations, professional bodies, and other governments" (p. 1). Consonant with activists, Maynes (1989) sees access to information and participation as crucial citizen rights. Affirming the movement by activists and citizens to lobby for such entitlements, he goes on to state:

> What's new is the demand by citizens and grassroots organizations to share in the opportunity to shape important decisions before they are made—during the planning or policy-making process—through open, systematic public consultation. . . . Public consultation is our right. We have the right in a democratic society to participate in planning the projects, laws, and policies that affect our lives and our environment (p. 1).

Rights to environmental information and participation have been lobbied for and won by citizen and activist groups, as Maynes (1989) alludes. Numerous activists interviewed were participants in these struggles and successes for legal and policy tools and reforms throughout the mid-1970s to the early 1990s. The creation of the Canadian/Ontario *Environmental Assessment Act,* the *Environmental Protection Act,* the *Planning Act,* the *Pesticide Notification Regulation and Spills Bill,* the *Intervenor Funding Project Act,* the *Environmental Bill of Rights* each conferred rights of public notice and participation to citizens (Estrin & Swaigen, 1993; Muldoon & Winfield, 1999). For example, before the creation of the *Pesticide Notification Regulation,* lawn spray companies were not obligated to post signs indicating they had sprayed pesticides. While gaps in rights of public notice and participation still existed (Muldoon & Winfield, 1999), these legal and policy tools were important successes leading the way for another layer of inequity to be confronted.

Once inside the consultation/decision-making room, power imbalances loomed between citizens/environmental activists, on the one hand, and government and industry stakeholders, on the other hand. This lack of a level playing field is vividly described by one female activist. She states:

> My experiences working at provincial and national levels in various forms of environmental consultations have brought home the link to social justice for me. I know how it feels to be in a room full of bank presidents and CEOs of big corporations and senior bureaucrats with only maybe one or two other people from the environmental sector and the feeling of having to hold your own in such a forum. It is an experience of feeling incredibly outnumbered and of having no financial and political clout in comparison to these other interests at the table. The experience of hearing very wealthy and privileged members of society dismiss concerns for environmental protection that serve the larger public interest. The experience of watching government officials, elected to represent the public interest, failing to do so.

These *power imbalances within the process of consultation* comprise a fourth rationale for conceptualizing the rights of participation and information as areas of social justice struggle. As Arnstein (1969) and Maynes (1989) reveal there are varied levels of citizen involvement. Arnstein (1969), for instance, configured an eight-rung ladder depicting different levels of citizen involvement in political/government institutions, ranging from the pseudo or token involvement of manipulation and therapy at the first rung, to delegating power to citizens and citizen control at the top of the ladder. Within the many different venues and levels of participation (e.g., hearings, open houses, committees) that comprise notions of public involvement in governmental decision-making, often participation rights allotted are those that allow less rather than more public influence in decision-making. Getting decision-making processes closer to the top of the participation ladder was another important terrain of struggle mentioned by several activists. For instance, Carol states:

> Another part of my linking story, as you call it, is just the struggle to advocate for more powerful degrees of participation. Often what the concerned environmental citizen gets is the chance to write a letter to the Environment Minister. They call this participation when in fact it is input, not true involvement. It's really a joke. Even open houses can seem pointless. Sometimes it's like government officials are just going through the motions of public involvement, it's not really meaningful. If citizen values are going to make a difference in the decisions government makes they need to have more voice and more power, more

weight. I try to voice the need for greater levels of participation. I talk
to government officials. I talk to other activists.

The *lack of resources to permit and enable meaningful participation
within existing forums* comprises a sixth area of social justice struggle.
Referring to participation within government environmental decision-making, M. Gardner (1993) has stated, "There is increased recognition that
effective public participation in decision-making processes is closely linked
to access to the necessary resources" (p. 3). While there are different configurations of resource support needed for citizens and groups depending on
the situation, Maynes (1989) outlines three general categories of needed
funding support: 1) "independent research, independent experts, and writers to prepare briefs"; 2) "networking activities such as workshops, conferences, and newsletters, and caucus meetings so we can develop and
co-ordinate our input"; and 3) "travel expenses, childcare, translations,
and other miscellaneous costs appropriate to the circumstances" (p. 16).
Like Maynes (1989), activists interviewed were aware of resource barriers
and needs. They spoke of financial barriers, time constraints, distance barriers, discourse/language hurdles, childcare challenges, and lack of information and contacts as obstacles to participation. As Carol asserts:

> The lack of resources to participate come up all the time in my environ-
> mental work and also for others I know. It may be easy for those living
> in downtown Toronto, who can take time off work or don't need to
> work, or don't have kids to take care of, or who are in paid activist jobs
> to go to government forums, but I don't possess any of these advan-
> tages. This is a big equity issue and it makes me mad that the govern-
> ment does not provide funding so I can use my democratic right to
> participate. In theory I have a right to participate, but not in practice.

Groups within the environmental movement facing the greatest resource
challenges were also mentioned by numerous activists—these included
small groups, volunteer groups, rural, and northern groups. Acknowledging her privilege in relation to other activists and organizations working for
environmental change, Kathleen states:

> I work in a large environmental organization in a large urban center
> and am a paid staff member of this organization. I have access to
> information, resources, and networks because of where I am. Many
> others in the environmental movement do not have these privileges.
> They are volunteers, have limited time, and are far from the decision-
> makers.

Keeping government officials aware of these resource needs, and pressuring them to address these disparities to make public participation in government forums more effective and inclusive, was work engaged by numerous activists interviewed. Kathleen speaks of her awareness and efforts:

> You have to remind government officials of the barriers many face to participation every time. We are always dealing with new people in government and their frame of reference is Monday to Friday, 9 to 5 and often in Toronto. The notion of making hours and locations accessible to volunteers or people living at a long distance from where the information may be located or provided, is often just not considered. The internet both helps and in some ways hinders. It is a good way of providing information to anyone in any location but it of course requires access to a computer, but is now being used as the only means of issuing a one-way push of information. If you aren't looking for it you won't hear about it. Also, by now being able to provide information so easily on-line, the face-to-face meetings are still during weekday work hours, if they happen at all.

Information and participation rights as social justice issues, took on a new level of significance for activists with the election of the Conservative government in Ontario in June of 1995. Progress made by activists in these areas was significantly weakened and in some cases lost. *This political shift was a seventh reason why rights of information and participation were seen as social justice issues by* activists. Changes were made to the public participation provisions within numerous environmental protection and environmentally related statutes. Several activists, for instance, spoke of changes made to the *Freedom of Information and Protection of Privacy Act*. These changes meant they would have to pay several hundred or thousands of dollars in photocopy service fees to access the information they needed, costs beyond their means. The *Intervenor Funding Project Act* was not renewed, which meant there was no longer any funding for citizens and citizen groups to prepare their cases when participating in complex and lengthy environmental hearings (Muldoon & Winfield, 1999). Lindgren (1999) speaks to more of these changes, indicating:

> Ontario had set up several expert advisory committees which served as important vehicles for soliciting public input into environmental decisions and standard-setting. For example, the Advisory Committee on Environmental Standards (ACES) was a forum to bring various stakeholders (government, public, industry) together to develop new or more stringent environmental standards. Similarly, the Environmental Assessment Advisory Committee (EAAC) solicited public input and

provided advice to the Minister of Environment on specific projects and on improving Ontario's environmental assessment process. The MISA (Municipal-Industrial Strategy for Abatement) Advisory Committee received public and stakeholder input and provided advice to the Minister on the water pollution standards for specific industrial sectors. These advisory committees were extremely efficient: they were inexpensive to operate, thorough in their reports, and balanced in their recommendations. Unfortunately, the government abolished the advisory committees in 1995 without warning or public consultation (p. 5).

Kathleen summarizes five ways rights of information and participation have been attacked by Ontario's Conservative government since 1995. I have quoted her publication rather than her transcript because it is succinct and consistent with what she shared during our interview. She states:

> Changed laws, budget, and program cuts also mean that hard-won citizen rights are being lost in five significant ways. First, as noted, environmental laws are being changed in ways that serve to cut off or greatly constrain public access to information and to environmental decision-making. Second, the public consultation on these legal changes frequently has been a farce. For example, in the summer months of 1996 the government held brief consultations on environmentally significant changes to four laws and over 80 regulations. Third, the move to "voluntarism" or "self-regulation" of polluters and resource extraction industries has little or no room for public involvement. Fourth, elimination of modest funding to environment organizations, particularly the Ontario Environment Network and its caucuses, cripples a democratic and cost-effective consultative relationship between the Ontario government and concerned citizens across the province. Fifth, the elimination of key environmental advisory committees has removed important avenues for public input to government decision-making (Cooper, 1998, pp. 79–80).

In the Conservative reign, aspects of access to information and public participation rights were not the only setback in democratic rights; measures protecting ecological and human health also suffered. Environmental laws and reforms were deregulated and natural resources privatized. This strategic double strike on the part of government was a real source of pain and anger for many activists. *In knowing that the public's access to information and participation are essential tools of resistance against the weakening of environmental laws and regulations, these rights, again, became more deeply framed by activists as part of the social justice struggle: this contextual evidence is an eighth reason to situate rights of information access and participation within a social justice framework.*

Let's get a clear look at this picture. What laws and reforms were deregulated? What specifically do these changes mean in our lives? While such questions were addressed in bits and pieces by a number of activists, I am going to quote from Kathleen's article, "Trashing Environmental Protection: Ontario's Four Part Strategy" at length. Again, she offers a clear and succinct overview of the situation and demonstrates a tone of concern, congruent with other activists who spoke to this issue. Naming the thirteen laws affected, Kathleen states:

> In Ontario, environmental de-regulation is in full swing. In less than two years, the government has implemented major rollbacks in environmental rules and citizens' rights in 13 laws: Aggregate Resources Act; Conservation Authorities Act; Environmental Assessment Act; Environmental Protection Act; Freedom of Information and Protection of Privacy Act; Game and Fish Act; Intervenor Funding Act; Lakes and Rivers Improvement Act; Municipal Act; Mining Act; Ontario Water Resources Act; Planning Act; and Public Lands Act (Cooper, 1998, p. 77).

What are the general ramifications of these legal changes? Kathleen answers this question stating:

> In general, the many changes to these statutes have served to greatly reduce the government's role in monitoring pollution or resource use; issuing permits for polluting activities or resource extraction activities; enforcing environmental laws; and ensuring democratic access to decision-making. . . . The names of these laws may not immediately suggest how the environment will be affected by legal rollbacks. However, taken together with numerous additional changes to regulations and policies, every aspect of environmental protection is at risk. Controls have been weakened to air pollution, water pollution, pesticides, waste disposal and recycling, urban sprawl, energy use and climate change, pit and quarry operations, natural heritage and biodiversity protection, mining and forestry (Cooper, 1998, p. 77).

Kathleen continues to give us a sadly detailed picture of the increased air, water, and soil pollution that will result. Moreover, these impacts will hit vulnerable groups the hardest. She states:

> [W]ith weaker rules, Ontario will experience more air and water pollution including increased releases of toxic chemicals. Pulp mills will no longer be required to phase out highly toxic organochlorines. A decision to eliminate the Ontario Waste Management Corporation was not accompanied by any new powers to regulate the reduction, reuse, and recycling of hazardous wastes. Mining companies will no longer have

to obtain government approval for mine closure plans, a move that will worsen the already serious problem of toxic run-off from abandoned mine sites. The lifting of the ban on municipal waste incinerators opens the door to new incinerators that generate toxic air emissions and large amounts of toxic residual ash that must be landfilled. Proposals to weaken landfill standards and changes to the environmental assessment planning process may well contribute to a legacy of toxic groundwater from landfills for decades into the future. Groundwater and surface water are further threatened by the loss of sound land use planning tools to protect wetlands, rivers and streams, and groundwater recharge areas from inappropriate developments. . . . Everyone will be at greater risk to exposure to pesticide residues because testing for these residues has been eliminated (Cooper, 1998, pp. 77–78).

Hand-in-hand with environmental deregulation was the move towards the privatization of public resources by the Conservative government. It is crucial to note that the privatization of the control of public resources cuts into the public's right to participation in the use of those resources. Moreover, with the privatization of publicly owned resources, the information regarding those resources also becomes privatized, which means citizens lose access to information on those resources. This loss of the right to know, through privatization, occurs because private corporations are exempt from the "Access to Information" laws, which apply only to public sector corporations (Muldoon & Winfield, 1999).

Activists interviewed linked provincial environmental rollbacks to global economic forces. They saw funding cuts, deregulation, and privatization as part of a larger distressing picture. This comprises a ninth and final reason information access and public participation work resides within the context of social justice struggle. The global economic trends behind provincial environmental rollbacks are well summarized by Swenarchuk & Muldoon (1996). They state:

We live in an era when the very concept of the "public interest" is under attack by neo-conservative voices and the corporate world. One of the important aspects of this attack is the strategy of de-regulation, or elimination of public interest laws, including in the field of environmental protection. . . . The de-regulatory initiatives are international, through the current round of trade agreements (FTA, NAFTA, GATT), national and provincial. . . . De-regulation and self-regulation remove . . . hard-won current rights of public involvement in legal processes, so fundamental to our democratic legal system (pp. 1–2).

Describing the broad workings of globalization, Henderson (1999) states:

> Globalization today involves the increasing interdependence of national economies, financial markets, trade, corporation, production, distribution, and consumer marketing. This globalization process is driven by two mainsprings. The first is technology which has accelerated innovation in telematics, computers, . . . and other communications. . . . The second is the fifteen-year wave of deregulation, privatization, liberalization of capital flows, opening of national economies, extension of global trade, and the export-led growth policies that followed the collapse of the Bretton Woods fixed currency-exchange regime in the early 1970s (p. 1).

Caught within these larger political-economic forces, the politics of information and participation rights in environmental decision-making, and environmental protection itself, becomes further intensified, complex, and challenging. As authors have stated, globalization trends can serve to reduce access to information and decision-making through greater levels of corporate concentration which by-pass or erode state legislative processes, processes which have served to safeguard the social and ecological interests of communities (Athanasiou, 1996; Brecher et al., 2000; Henderson, 1999; McQuaig, 1998). With few exceptions, activist interviews spoke of these corporate global economic forces and the challenge they present. Rick passionately asserts, for instance:

> Our big struggle is the corporations. If we are going to get serious about environmental change and social economic changes, we have to look at the root cause of the problem. It's the corporate sector, the NAFTA, the general agreement on tariffs and trade and the GATT, the World Trade Organization, MAI. Those are the things that people have to be much more aware of and we in the environmental movement have to be able to take those issues and put some environmental languages to them too. There has been an attempt to do that. These larger, global, international forces are having a direct impact on a very local grassroots level . . . in terms of democracy, in terms of who defines how, what, when and where.

Offering the same message but framed differently, Brennain speaks of the struggle between the values and visions of the corporate world in contrast to those of the community, in the "Lands for Life" land-use planning process. This government exercise comprised a provincial review of forestry, mining, and protected areas on thirty-nine million hectares of northern Crown land, which involved 45 percent of the province (Canadian Environmental Law Association, 1999). Referring to this review process as a struggle between community versus commodity, she states:

In the Lands for Life project the issue is corporate control over the land
and all the consequences of that. The land is the home of all living
beings and if you have corporate control over all living beings and the
corporate worldview is that the land is a commodity then there is a
struggle between the values of commodity versus community. [As citizens and communities], we are tugging at the fabric saying it is community and they [corporations, government] are tugging at the fabric
saying it is commodity.

Like Rick, Kathleen, and Brennain, the majority of activists interviewed
linked rights of information, participation, and environmental protection
itself, to a social justice struggle against these larger hegemonic economic
forces.

EFFECTING CHANGE

Naming and voicing the barriers to meaningful and effective public awareness and participation in government environmental decision-making comprises an important sphere of social justice effort within the realm of
environmental advocacy. Recognizing and bringing together these varied
and inter-meshing challenges helps us to see their collectively combined
power to keep citizens at arms-length from the very issues upon which their
wellness and health depend. In their various capacities, many activists were
engaged in informing others of environmental rollbacks and their potential
threat to human and ecological health and democracy. Activists also spent
time struggling for increased access to information and greater levels of citizen involvement within government environmental forums. Before the
election of the Conservative government, several activists, for instance,
were involved in lobbying for the creation of what is now *Ontario's Environmental Bill of Rights*. This law gives the public access to government
and industry/business proposals that have a potentially significant environmental impact and provides venues for public response. Numerous
activists, moreover, supported citizens so that they could participate more
meaningfully in government forums, providing information, contacts,
analysis/strategy, translation of legal and technical issues, and so forth. The
generosity of many activists, with respect to these issues, cannot be over-
valued. They used their privilege to foster citizens' ability to effectively act
on environmental concerns citizens had. Kathleen, for instance, states, "I
have spent so many years trying to get the information out to the grassroots
and democratize the process and ensure that there is a place for the grassroots around the consultation table. I try to 'work for the little guy' using
the privileges I have to serve those with 'less.'" Some activists also spoke of

using their access to government forums to voice views and concerns that had been relayed to them by citizens—citizens who could not attend themselves or did not have access. Irene and Brennain bring to life some of the issues that have been discussed in this chapter.

IRENE'S STORY: HOLDING POWER HOLDERS ACCOUNTABLE TO INFORM THE PUBLIC AND HONOR RIGHTS OF PARTICIPATION

Irene's story powerfully illustrates the significance of the public right to know and participate within the sphere of environmental concern. When asked about the origins of her nuclear awareness activism, she recounts a childhood experience. Awakening to the connection between industrial pollutants and issues of human health and safety, Irene saw the centrality of the public right to know. Reflecting on her father's work at a chemical plant, she remembers:

> My desire to work on environmental and pollution issues comes from my experience within my family. My father worked at a large chemical company and shared his daily horror stories at the dinner table about what had gone wrong or who had screwed up at the plant that day. He shared some of them, and some were confidential incidents he didn't share. As a ten year old, I certainly got the sense that there was a lot of bad stuff going on down at this industrial plant. My mother would always get up in the morning no matter what shift my dad was on. She would pack his lunch and see him off at the door. When my sister and I used to bug her about that every once in a while, my mother would remind us that this could be, if there was a bad accident at the plant, the last time she saw my father. So she told us she was not about to lay in bed when she had the opportunity to see him out the door. Her words and actions instilled in me the notion that industrial processes are hazardous, and in some cases, workers are at great risk.

In realizing the real risks her father faced at work, she also witnessed her father's courage to "blow the whistle"—to take the stance that communities have the right to know what is taking place inside the workplace that affects them. Irene recalls:

> My dad became a whistle-blower at his plant and his job was threatened. He had a lot of personal decisions to make about how much he valued his job versus would he be able to expose the wrong doing in terms of toxic substances from the plant being illegally dumped in the river. Mercury was being routinely dumped into the river along with carbon tetrachloride chemicals and the other components which became known as the blob.

These childhood experiences rooted themselves deeply inside Irene, leading her to over two decades of nuclear energy activism—an activism grounded in the need for the public right to know and participate. She realized the public has the right to know: What goes on inside a nuclear plant? What ecological and human health risks and impacts result from these energy production processes? Are communities with nuclear energy plants informed on such issues? And, if so, by whom? She explains:

> Living through that process with my family and having my dad share this information with us made me realize as soon as I knew there were nuclear reactors that the same kinds of risks were probably going on there too. This made my hair stand on end and still makes my hair stand on end. The research I have done reveals that, yes, these things are being done at nuclear plants. The potential loss of control of the reactor and uncontrolled release of radiation means that not only are workers at great risk, but so are the surrounding human and ecological communities, and the economic base for the entire province which could be permanently damaged. These are issues the public needs to know about and have a say in.

Irene embarked on the work of public awareness and participation in a serious way. Holding information brokers accountable, doing investigative research, getting the information into the public sphere, and successfully getting government bodies to give the public greater access to information are all practices in which Irene was intimately engaged. Having worked to increase public knowledge of what goes on in nuclear facilities and governmental decisions related to nuclear energy, Irene recounts successfully accessing Ontario Hydro's documentation of their nuclear facilities:

> Funnily enough most of our information and research comes out of Ontario Hydro's own documents and the regulator, the Atomic Energy Control Board. I did research in their [Ontario Hydro's] corporate library. I was doing a lot of research for a few years. I read almost every document that board members of the Atomic Energy Board read. Through that we have put our finger on almost every problem that they are facing. One of the things that I do is track the accident reports [at the nuclear facilities] which have to be filed at the Head Office Library for each nuclear plant. Most people would not know where to look for them if they went to Hydro's library, but I know my way around so I can put my finger on almost anything. The accident reports are called Significant Event Reports. I log and read these reports. The challenge is whether I can get an actual copy of something before they object. These reports range from someone slipping on a sidewalk in the parking lot to an operator making a major mistake to the reactor core. Sometimes I

will be trying not to fall asleep, at which time I will find a real incident and be wide awake and shocked to read what has happened.

Breaking the silence by placing this information in the public eye, Irene recounts its impact on Ontario Hydro practices. She states:

In recent years we made a habit of releasing information [via media release] about accidents in the plant that people would have no other way to know about. So generally now Ontario Hydro will do a news release the minute they have a major problem just so that the news comes from them and not from us. Our work has forced them to operate in different ways.

Successful in pushing Ontario Hydro to make nuclear plant incidents public, Irene and her nonprofit group also experienced the backlash against their public right to access such information. She reports:

[When] we hit them really hard on particular issues and they realized that all the evidence came from their own documents, they decided to clamp down in their library. As a result, we no longer had unrestricted access at the library. Ontario Hydro has clamped down now. We are having difficultly getting anything out of them. We have to use the Access to Information Act more and more and we are getting turned down more and more, or sent huge bills where they say to vet and copy information it will cost 18,000 dollars. Needless to say, we do not have that kind of money.

Increased barriers in getting access to Ontario Hydro documents, were, however, dealt with creatively by Irene and her group. They shifted focus to the Atomic Energy Control Board where they could push for change. They were successful in increasing access, quality, and notice of information and board acceptance of public input. Irene recalls:

We no longer had unrestricted access at the library. In the meantime we have gotten much better at tracking the Atomic Energy Control Board. We have also pushed them to operate differently too. We have been intervening at their board meetings since 1992 in a very active way. We have fought with them over access to documents, better advance notice of meetings and better provision of background materials prior to deadlines for filing basic kinds of public consultation process. They have come to accept our presence, and we have encouraged other groups across the country to intervene on the licensing of the nuclear facilities in their areas. So there has been a general increase in the level of interventions. The Control Board members have become less hostile

to public interventions. They realize it is a step they have to undergo
and they can't get away with treating us like dirt.

Subsequent to this interview, Irene's voice could yet again be heard in a
press release indicating the further removal of public rights to information
stemming from the privatization of Ontario Hydro into two corporations,
under Bill 35. With this privatization, as noted earlier, the public loses
information access, as private corporations are not subject to the Freedom
of Information legislation. The press release states:

> The break up of Ontario Hydro may lead to increased environmental and
> health risks. The Canadian Environmental Law Association, Nuclear
> Awareness Project and other environmental and energy watchdog groups
> reacted with alarm at news last week disclosing that Ontario Hydro will
> be exempt from Ontario's Freedom of Information legislation as of April
> 1, 1999. . . . There have been many occasions when Ontario Hydro has in
> the past refused to provide environmental, emergency preparedness,
> health and safety information to Ontarians, and that information has
> only become available because of the provisions of the Freedom of Infor-
> mation legislation. . . . The Canadian Environmental Law Association,
> Nuclear Awareness Project and other environmental groups are calling on
> the government and the opposition parties to commit to ensuring that the
> Ontario Electricity Generation Corporation and the Ontario Electric Ser-
> vices Corporations are designated under the *Freedom of Information and
> Protection of Privacy Act* by April 1, 1999.[1]

In the telling of her story, Irene's account traces the attrition discussed in this
chapter. We saw Irene's journey from freely accessing information in Ontario
Hydro's library until her access was restricted after she publicly released information about Hydro incidents. Barred access, Irene and her group began
using Freedom of Information law. Changes to this law, when the Conservative government came into power, limited her ability to use this legislation due
to charges now levied to citizens for the copying of public documents. Following this barrier, the privatization of Ontario Hydro dealt another blow to public rights of access and participation, as these new private corporations were
exempt from the *Freedom of Information Act*. In striving to expand rights of
information and participation within her advocacy on nuclear energy, this
account reveals the layers and angles of Irene's linking efforts.

BRENNAIN'S STORY: PARTICIPATING CREATIVELY
WHILE BEING OUTNUMBERED

Experiencing the lack of a level playing field when participating in government forums is something Brennain knows well, as a seasoned activist

representing environmental and social justice concerns. Here she recounts an experience of being isolated and outnumbered as the only environmental community representative on a government environment committee. She also relays the fact that she was the only woman appointed to the committee, creating an interesting mélange of unwelcome reactions by existing committee members. What is so appealing about Brennain's account is the effectiveness and clarity of response she brought to a challenging situation. Brennain recalls:

> Sometimes there is some mean spiritedness in the room which is really hard to take. And sometimes, it is really hard to deal with people thinking the worst of you or people making a lot of negative assumptions before you have even said hello [because you are an environmental representative]. There is one government [environmental] committee I am on that was running for a couple of years before I was appointed to it. The group was very hostile to me being appointed to the committee. They did not want me there. And this is the committee where I am the only woman, except for the secretary. It is sometimes really difficult going into the room knowing that they do not want you there. Just the sheer psychic weight of that can be a barrier.

Acting to make the situation work for her as much as possible, Brennain describes her success in forging an acceptance of her presence. She recounts:

> To deal with that situation I just decided to be helpful. So, for the first couple of meetings I acted only in an information capacity. It was a fluke that three or four items came up during the first meeting that staff members were unable to answer for committee members. Items I knew about and was able to answer. I was helpful and non-intimidating and just explained information in a way they could understand. I identified where I thought the concerns were from a northern perspective and I left it at that. They came right around. I go to the meetings now and no one flinches when I arrive. It is quite relaxed.

Importantly, Brennain illuminates her strength in using her participation strategically, stating:

> I don't think I will ever win an issue that is on the table at that committee. But I don't go to win. I go because it is a great place to get information. The other members are finally relaxed enough around me that after a couple of years they will talk about all the screw-ups happening in the industry. And, every now and then I am able to move them on something.

As the token environmental representative in a committee full of government and industry players, Brennain knew she faced an uneven playing field, a power differential additionally expressed through the initial sexism and mean spiritedness in the room. She dealt with this unwelcoming situation not as a victim but with her competence and community-building approach—listening, offering support, acting respectfully towards others (even when her views were very divergent from the views of other members at the table), and seeing and focusing on the opportunities the experience offered her amidst the challenges (i.e., to gain information within a political-economic climate that is making such access increasingly difficult). Moreover, Brennain's account illustrates the importance of keeping a sense of humor within the challenges of advocacy work, seeing the successes in the small steps and opportunities to increase public knowledge and participation on environmental matters—all important skills of linking work.

SUMMARY REFLECTIONS

Disparities in Ability to Know and Participate: A Closer Examination

What if meaningful access to government information and participation is secured, but minoritized and disenfranchised groups are not accessing these participatory tools? This chapter has stated that resources affect the ability and effectiveness of participation in government environmental forums. Resource differences among citizens/groups were also cited by activists. This concluding section explores some of these issues and their connection to the challenges of linking activism. Speaking within a Canadian context Schrecker (1995) moves us in the direction of this inquiry. He asks the questions, "Can institutions for public participation be designed that would be conducive to a genuinely inclusive politics? . . . Perhaps more importantly, will people who promote expanded opportunities for public participation even be concerned about selective or biased inclusiveness?" (pp. 212–213). Schrecker (1995) goes on to state, "[I]f environmentalists hold distorted beliefs about class and the universality of affluence, they are likely to be relatively unconcerned about the ways in which time, money, vocabulary, and networks of political contacts serve as prerequisites for effective political participation" (p. 213). Moreover, he argues that the use of categories by activists like "citizen" and "community" hide or "decontextualize" social inequalities stemming from class, race, and gender, asserting, "Superficial solicitude is shown for the concerns of citizens, the public, the community, the grass roots or some similarly decontextualized category. All these terms obscure the relevance of such issues as class and gender, and thereby ignore the manifold practical barriers to participation that confront many individuals" (p. 231). Articulating another concern, if, in fact, activists are aware of these differences, Schrecker (1995) states, "An alternative view is that environmentalists may be cognizant of such barriers, yet are willing to live with pseudo-inclusions (in March's words) at the institutional level, on the basis that it is (a) better than nothing at all, and/or (b) the best that can be hoped for" (p. 213). During our interviews, activists were not specifically asked to speak to the issues raised by Schrecker (1995). However, ignorance of barriers to effective participation was not found among those activists interviewed as Schrecker posits. Keen awareness of the challenges of participation and the ways these challenges increased with layers of marginalization were recognized by activists. It is also true, however, that activists interviewed saw themselves as sensitized to social justice issues and therefore they may not be a representative sample of activists engaged in environmental change.

While activist accounts reveal that they used concepts such as "citizen" and "community" in their advocacy work, activists also employed more contextualized terms such as north-south, small-large, and volunteer-paid differences to acknowledge disparities (of time, resources, access, contact, power) between different citizen and environmental groups in Ontario. Moreover, activists were sensitive to the fact that while Caucasian, English-speaking, economically stable members of a northern rural group encounter real barriers to their environmental participation, the obstacles for disabled, unemployed, or working poor citizens, and/or minoritized and/or non-English speaking community members would be, more likely than not, that much greater. Activists recognized that forms of societal racism, classism, and ableism permeate all social arenas, including environmental forums.

Sexism, classism, and racism encountered in government environmental forums, and policy-making processes and agencies were articulated in a number of activists' accounts. Some shared personal experiences of social discrimination, while others shared experiences encountered by others they were striving to support. Sharing her personal experience, one activist stated, for instance:

> I have experienced being dismissed because I am a woman in a room full of suits. Here I felt my femaleness keenly. Moments which brought home the importance of the feminist movement and the sexism it is trying to change. All these experiences have shown me the ways in which environmental decision-making processes and the decision themselves are social justice issues. White men and Western capitalist values still tend to dominate these kinds of decision-making processes.

Did activists, however, use the language of sexism, classism, and racism when they voiced barriers to government environmental participation and information access? In some cases they did. In others cases they did not. On this point Schrecker (1995) is correct. At times activists choose to live with "pseudo-inclusions . . . at the institutional level, on the basis that it is . . . better than nothing at all" (p. 213). However, did activists also believe, as Schrecker posits, that this is "the best that can be hoped for" (p. 213). To this assertion, I believe the majority of activists would articulate a resounding, "No!"

One feminist activist interviewed gives us an inside view of some of these dynamics raised by Schrecker (1995). In this account she speaks frankly about raising gender issues in government forums. Illustrating some of the messiness and challenge of being an effective linking messenger, she recounts:

> Gender issues we generally do not raise, not on the record, not at the table, occasionally we will. I remember a Ministry of Natural Resources (MNR) meeting last April, I can't remember what I said around gender but the room just went dead. I was a bit sharp and maybe a bit sarcastic in the way I said it. The man at the front of the room went beet red and the whole room just froze. Then someone else said something else and the meeting just continued. Raising gender issues usually does not go over that well. Usually I raise the gender inequity with a helpful sense of humor. I will say, "Hey, good gender parity here, guys." . . . But I will usually do that over lunch to the meeting organizers.

While attempting to raise gender parity with a sense of humor, in fact, the situation is far from being a lighthearted one. She confesses she sees gender parity backsliding, reporting:

> We are going backwards on the gender issue. I feel that things were better a few years ago. If you compare MNR policy tables in the early 1990s, the Old Growth community was 5 women, 4 men. Now you look at the Round Tables for Lands for Life and it is about 12 men to 3 women. It is a concern to me but it is not a concern that I will go on at length about to them. I will name it and make sure any list of suggested names I put in are equal women to men.

While voicing her concern over the lack of gender parity, this activist also gives her reasoning as to why she did not make gender parity a central issue and articulates her ambivalence about this choice. She continues:

> I will not go on at length about gender parity because in this case I do not think they will remedy the situation. For me to go on at length about gender when they are not going to remedy it, did not make sense.

I am using up my bingo chip. Maybe I need to use my airtime for something they can remedy. So my compromise is that I name it and leave it. That is what I have to do in that instance. I am not completely confident that is it the right thing to do. Most things I decide to do when I approach things in a certain way is a judgment call. I assume that sometimes I am going to make the right one and sometimes I am going to make the wrong one. But in this case that is the decision I made in terms of effectiveness.

You have to think about the people you are raising it to. In the Lands for Life process the target audience, the people we are most wanting to move are the Round Table members. So, are the Round Table members going to benefit from my going on at length about the fact that they do not have gender parity? Well, no. They are not, because they are not able to change the gender balance. They are appointed by the minister. The Round Table members who are the target audience that we need to move and affect, they are not able to do anything. And in fact, we run the risk of making them feel personally criticized and inadequate on the basis of gender parity when it is not their fault. They were set up in a twelve to three ratio.

In a context where she experiences the realities and pressures of little time and voice, so too, does she experience the pressure to be pointed and specialized. At the same time, knowing who calls the shots on which issues, this activist will not waste offering aspects of herself to those who don't have the means to recognize or empower issues of gender parity in environmental decision-making. Importantly, she does not devote herself to a fatalistic attitude with respect to gender parity in environmental forums. About this, she states, "Proactively, the next time we are making nominations for something like this. Or the next time we hear the minister is going to appoint a committee, the point needs to be made quite strongly before the appointments occur that there was a problem with the lack of gender parity on the Round Tables." Struggling with how to get the message of gender parity across in a manner that will be heard, whether doing so explicitly or covertly, her reflections raise a number of questions such as: To what extent are social issues raised within an environmental forum contingent on what the government is willing to recognize? How can one articulate social inequities (such sexism, racism, classism) in a manner that will be heard by government representatives or officials? This activist, for instance, goes on to ponder:

There is also the issue of how do you convey your concern in a manner that is culturally acceptable to them? The Round Table members are made up of a mix of people. I do not think that the 70-year-old member is going to be moved by my launching a formal complaint to the Round Table about gender parity. But he might accept it, understand it, and remember it better if I say to him in a personal conversation, "Gee, X you really don't have very many women in your group do you. What do you think about that?" Then he will tell me what he thinks about that and I will tell them what I think about that. Given that they do not have the power to change the gender composition the more effective way of changing him is probably using a one-on-one approach.

As this account reveals, the problem with Schrecker's (1995) analysis is that it is overly simplistic and falsely situates activists with fixed views on issues of inclusive participation. In setting up categories of "better than nothing at all" and/or "the best that can be hoped for" to portray his fear that environmental activists do not advocate for genuinely inclusive participation in governmental forums, Schrecker neatly objectifies activists, cutting himself off from deeper insight into the issue at hand. In sharing her inner/outer struggle over whether to voice sexism, the account portrayed demonstrates how one activist's approach is shaped on a case-by-case basis by the varying and complex array of factors at play. While Schrecker's analysis raises crucial questions highly relevant to linking activist practice, his approach to these questions eliminates linking practice from view. He misses, for instance, activists' struggle to weigh issues strategically, and to find and create open spaces to raise social inequities *and* relay their environmental message effectively. In this discussion, the activist used humor and the strategy of confronting power-holders informally to make sexism visible. She knew *who* had the power to effect change, avoiding confrontation with officials who lacked the ability to shift gender imbalances. She conceptualized her experiences in environmental forums as learning opportunities to act more effectively (on gender parity issues) in future involvements. Moreover, she acknowledged her ambivalence towards her own actions or inaction at times. She alludes to wanting to push harder on issues of gender parity but struggles with how to get her message heard by power-holders who are asleep, intentionally or unintentionally, to sexism within governmental environmental politics. These are all key issues to explore in understanding linking practice and its messenger work.

Asking Questions and Going Beyond Liberal Policy Arenas and Solutions

The rights of information and participation comprise two areas of social justice struggle for activists engaged in environment advocacy. Depicting these layers of power inequity between citizens and government/corporate sectors within environmental politics has been the focus of this chapter. Clearly, attempts to safeguard, enhance, and meaningfully utilize the public right to know and participate within the governmental sphere is a complex one. It is a terrain imbued with questions, deliberations, and gray zones for activists to maneuver. Is lobbying for greater access to information and participatory mechanisms a constructive use of time and resources? Will created mechanisms embrace inclusive participation? Can citizen and advocacy group participation be used to further legitimize existing hegemonic interests? Should one participate without the accompanying resources needed? Are accessing rights of information and participation at governmental levels effective strategies for protecting the environment and human health?

Additional questions may include: What are the negative consequences of government consultation for socially disadvantaged groups (outcomes such as the ways advocating for tighter waste disposals laws may result in companies illegally dumping waste in low-income residential areas)? How should inequities in ability to participate be framed, in terms of group characteristics, such as small, volunteer or rural and/or in terms of class, race and/or gender or both? Is participation in a government consultation going to strengthen or weaken connections among social justice allies (labor sector, First Nations, women's movement)?

Given these questions and the challenges outlined in this chapter, is lobbying for public access to information and participation within government realms worth the effort? I suspect activists may answer, in some cases yes, and in some cases no. This ambivalence is important to maintaining a healthy sense of cynicism within government forums and to staying cognizant of the multiple layers of power inequity that exist therein. Overall, I surmise, however, that the majority of activists interviewed would say that having and utilizing the rights of information access and participation at government levels is vital. Procedural mechanisms for public information and participation push forward a paradigm whereby citizens are included and recognized as consistent stakeholders in government environmental matters. This creates the potential to: 1) increase the voice of citizens; 2) contest government and industry dominance in state environmental decision-making; and 3) facilitate a greater balance between values of resource utilization (prevalent in corporate globalization) and community values of participatory democracy, ecological, and human health in government decision-making. Richardson, Sherman, and Gismondi (1993) argue that public voice can make a difference in government decisions. Reflecting on the public hearings of an Alberta-Pacific bleached kraft pulp mill in northern Alberta, they explain how activists won against huge odds:

> If you are wondering whether participation is worth the effort, consider the inequality of power among the groups facing each other at the Alpac hearing. Relatively uninformed, unorganized individuals in rural

northern communities found themselves up against the money and influence of transnational corporations, the authority of specialists and experts, and a provincial government that had already approved the mill in principle. Yet public intervention was so effective that Alpac could not persuade the Review Board to approve the mill. The provincial government could not even buy Alpac a reversal of the decision with the Jaakko Poyry review. In order to push through the mill, the Alberta government had to create a kangaroo court which was not allowed to consider the effects of the "mitigative" process on the environment. Thus, the government's political decision could no longer be masked by the hearing process and dressed up in such phrases as "environmental integrity," "sustainable development," or "ecologically sound." The public denied Alpac and the Alberta government claim to these words. . . . It is clear that public participation in the Alpac public hearings did make a difference. However, participation in public hearings is not enough. Sustained political activity is required beyond the hearing process (pp. 175–176).

A second far-reaching example of citizen influence over government policy is the case of the pesticide bylaw in Hudson, Quebec. Citizen pressure to ban the cosmetic use of pesticides within their community, including private property, led the municipality to create a pesticide ban bylaw. When this happened, two spray companies took the municipality to court arguing that the town did not have the legal authority to create the bylaw. In court, the town won against the spray companies twice. Taking their case to the Supreme Court of Canada, the spray companies again lost their case. The Supreme Court decision stated that the municipality has the power to respond to local concerns by instituting a pesticide ban bylaw, a bylaw that incorporated the "precautionary principle." On the basis of citizens' lobbying, the town took precautionary action because of public pressure and concerns.[2] Citizen concerns empowered and legitimated a municipal government's response that could not then be derailed by business/corporate interests. This example illustrates the potential power of citizens to spearhead and create policy at the municipal level, in order to meet their needs, even when corporate interests are not supportive.

Both examples situate the public right to know and participate (within environmental decisions) in the larger discourse on participatory democracy and the politicizing and radicalizing of the constructs of "citizen" and "community." In this latter discourse, the roles of the citizen and community are expanded and deepened beyond a liberal democratic framework which is invested in attempting to "level" rather than change the "playing field" itself. Citizens and communities are envisioned as playing a much more central and influential role in the direction of their lives and society at large. This vision includes, but also goes beyond, equitable access and influence within existing government forums. Brecher, Costello, and Smith (2000) depict the tone I felt from many activists regarding expanded notions of citizen involvement within societal life. They refer to the concept of "transborder participatory democracy," stating:

> Conventionally, basic values are the province of priests; policy the province of officials; and strategy the province of the top brass. But in a social movement, people must act on their own initiative and on the basis of their own convictions. So values, policy and strategy cannot be handed down on a transmission belt from high, but must be something that people make day by day in the process of determining their own actions (p. xi).

They further state:

> Sovereignty is being redefined not as the absolute right of states, but rather as a right of peoples at multiple levels. . . . This broader concept of the human right to participate in decision making has been described as a "transborder participatory democracy" that declares "a universal right which recognizes no borders": "the right of the people to intervene in, to modify, to regulate, and ultimately to control any decisions that affect them" (p. 44).

Many activists were conscious of the need for more radical discourse and fundamental social change spearheaded by citizen movements and held views consistent with Brecher et al.'s depiction of transborder participatory democracy. Other activists did not have these issues clearly formalized in their stories, yet a number of their efforts and views fit within this broader framework.

Chapter Six
Linking Activism as a Catalyst for Organizational Change: The Challenge and Promise of Environmental Organizations

Journal note: In my early years of environmental group involvement I remember meetings where we talked about our promotion of "No Flyers Please" signs on household doors and mailboxes. Our reasons were three-fold: to protest the number of trees cut for the publication of consumer ads, to express concern about the amount of waste this activity created, and to exercise our democratic right to choose whether or not we wanted to have these flyers delivered to our door. During this time I remember an occasion where I paid concerted attention to a woman delivering flyers in my neighborhood. She walked up my front steps about to place a handful of ads into my mailbox until she saw the no flyers sign posted on my door. I recall the pleasantness of her face and the way it was shaded with tiredness on this hot summer day. At that moment I realized that the more our environmental group was successful in encouraging our local citizens to post no flyer signs on their doors, the more this woman would have to work and walk to be able to deliver her stack of flyers; or even yet, the more likely this woman could face unemployment.

In our discussions as an environmental group, we had never considered the potential implications of our actions on those who deliver flyers for their employment. We hadn't thought about the fact that employees are paid on a per flyer basis and not on an hourly rate. We forgot to remember and gather together our observations that many of those who deliver flyers are among the working poor and/or are minoritized citizens in our community. We didn't think to critically examine our social, cultural, and economic locations when we discussed the use of these signs as an act of environmental change-making that we wanted to promote.

Now in the twenty-first century, I still recall this experience almost two decades earlier and continue to see the need for environmental organizations to address social justice issues in an increasingly proactive and significant manner.

Environmental organizations are not homogeneous. Among environmental groups, the philosophies, political stance, size, level of involvement (local, regional, national, international), financial means, strategy, and decision-making process, to name a few, can vary widely. A number of authors such as Milbrath (1984), Eckersley (1992), J. E. Gardner (1993), Naess (1989), and Paehlke (1989) outline various categories to depict these diversities of philosophy and characteristic within the environmental community and its organizational contexts. While organizations may be placed within a particular category, they may also possess characteristics that cross different classifications, such as displaying characteristics of both big group (e.g., taking a policy perspective) and small group (e.g., having a strong grassroots, local base) perspectives.

Within such diverse landscapes, attention to social justice issues will vary as organizations demonstrate different stages of awareness, growth, and commitment to social justice-ecological linkages. This variation will leave linking activists clearly more supported in some organizational contexts and more frustrated in others. As discussed in Chapter One, Athanasiou (1996) provides hopeful council as he argues social justice realities are becoming unavoidable.

While my research question centered on the activist and not the organizational context, most activists engaged linking practices from organizational settings.[1] The connections, separations, and tensions between the individual and organization can be messy and difficult to discern. For instance, in numerous accounts, activists' linking practices and their organization work were narrated as being one and the same. In other accounts they were not. What is clear, however, is that activists' linking practice is shaped and informed by the organizations in which they work. Three things can be said, in particular, about environmental organizations: 1) they have ignored or minimized intersecting social oppression and inequity issues in varied ways; 2) real and perceived obstacles can impede them from engaging in forms of linking practice; 3) they are also contexts where linking efforts can be made possible. Within these gaps, barriers, and possibilities, activists strove to bring their complexly-aligned identities of who they are to environmental organizations, working to assess and strengthen a social justice mandate and practice within these contexts.

This chapter addresses these three themes. First, a summary of some of the ways activists saw environmental groups failing to address social justice issues are outlined. Second, constraints impeding the embodiment of a more integrative organizational practice, which were noted by activists, are listed. Third, some of the ways activists worked to strengthen a social justice lens and practice within environmental organizations are described.

IGNORING, DENYING, OR MINIMIZING SOCIAL JUSTICE CONNECTIONS

There are many overt and inadvertent ways environmental organizations can and do ignore, deny, or minimize social justice aspects of environmental degradation and change. Naming ways social justice realities and implications get left out of environmental organizational mandates and practices is one aspect of activists' accounts. Some activists referred to social justice gaps they confronted in their own environmental organizations. Numerous activists expressed these gaps with a tone of irritation and frustration. Others spoke pragmatically about making social justice links visible when organizational discussions or plans left them out. Underlying these differences in expression were differences in the extent to which activists felt their organizations were supportive of their desire to express their complexly-aligned identities within their practice.

In their organizational critiques, activists often wavered between talking at an organization level and movement level, portraying their perceptions that these gaps are realities within the environmental movement at large. Many activists articulated their connectedness to the Ontario/Canadian environmental movement and felt linked to its successes and failures. In contrast, other activists, in either tone or words, specifically set themselves apart from non-linking environmental organizations and from the environmental movement in general. These activists located their environmental work in the context of the social justice movement, women's movement, or First Nations political action, for instance.

With respect to organizational gaps, Rick shares an account of the limits of his environmental organization to address the sober realities of socially disenfranchised groups, stating:

> Through the years we've had big problems bringing environmental issues to activists in the city of Detroit because of their economic problems. Eighty percent of the city is Afro-American, low income.

Forty-five percent are unemployed between the ages of 15 and 24. It was very difficult to get the black population concerned about issues such as cleaning up the Detroit River and air pollution. It was perceived as a white issue, a suburban white issue. We did all kinds of leafleting in the streets of Detroit when we fought the Detroit incinerator. I can still recall some poor guy digging in the garbage, probably looking for something to eat, and one of our guys ran up and gave him a leaflet about the incinerator. So here is some guy trying to stay alive and somebody saying, "You've got to get active and fight the incinerator." And some of the black workers at the incinerator saying to us, "We don't disagree, but we need a job."

In a similar vein, another activist describes her realization of the need for greater sensitivity in engaging environmental campaigns in socially disempowered communities, stating:

One thing that really disturbed me was an experience I had when I went to the United States with my environmental organization. We did an action there and I got arrested. We were in a body of polluted water. It was 100 degrees out. We had these full dry suits on. I was ready to faint because it was hot and the fumes from the water were just awful. I was in the water trying to plug the spout where all the effluent was coming from when I saw a woman who was up on the bridge. She had her baby and was balancing her infant on the bridge above us looking down. I thought, "She shouldn't be here and she shouldn't bring her baby!" That night we were on a radio call-in show. All sorts of people were calling in and saying, "You're trying to take my job away!" and "Like, can't I work?! You environmentalists and bla, bla, bla." And then one woman called in and said, "You environmentalists jumped in here and as quickly as you came you are going to leave. And so what are we going to do with this mess in our community, with everyone in this town dying of cancer?" And we did. We left the next day and it was just like, "What do you do?" It made me wonder why did I do that action. Before I thought these actions were so cool and after that I didn't know anymore.

Both these accounts raise key issues of environmental change process. Providing brief visits or literally flying in and out of a community to "save the environment" is incongruent with the spirit of linking work. These practices lack connection to and investment in the affected local community and serve to harm community members who are most socially and economically vulnerable.

The issues of class and poverty underlying these former accounts are confronted directly by Doug. He shares that he has not seen an effective activist campaign that addresses class, stating:

I have not really seen a lot of fully integrated activist campaigns or projects. When I mean fully integrated, I mean that address class. I think that even in our community we have done some pretty inventive community projects, everything from public education campaigns around Environment Week that obviously go beyond trees, water, and air, to talk about underlying values of the culture, about economies and how economies are structured and all that. We have really tried to get at some more fundamental concepts including gender and patriarchy and all that, but not class. It is definitely one of the things that I feel personally has been one of the weakest parts of my work, and I have not seen it dealt with in a lot of people or other groups.

Kathleen looks at this sense of disconnection to issues of class and poverty and other forms of marginalization on an international scale. She describes how she became starkly cognizant of the "naiveté and narrowness of the mostly middle class, mostly white, North American environmental movement" while attending a conference in Brazil. Stunned by the enormity of what she saw Kathleen recounts:

During my trip to Brazil to attend a conference on globalization there are so many unforgettable images which have stayed in my mind. One that sticks out was a young girl I saw from the window of a taxi during the dangerous madness of the busy Belo Horizonte rush hour traffic. She was crossing the street. Her bare feet were the filthy black of the streets; the color that is only now rubbing off my running shoes six months after I spent so many hours of walking through that city to and from our many meetings. She was quite tall, desperately thin, wearing filthy rags of clothes. She looked about 14 years old, her eyes were blank and dull and she was sucking on a baby pacifier. She absently scratched her crotch as she walked across the street, dodging the cars. She was such a poignant example of the millions of people that are quite literally being treated as just as disposable as the rest of the trash of our throw-away society. She embodied the link to social justice and environmental justice. This was a key thing that I learned on this trip both by simply looking around me but also by learning about so many other examples of the social impacts of globalization. I learned about the many "export processing zones" where workers, mostly women and often children, endure unbelievably harsh working conditions (below a living wage, excessively long hours, child labor, harassment and abuse) to produce "First World" t-shirts or calculators or plastic toys or whatever. And, of course, the communities they live in are contaminated, often horrendously so. To see the link between social justice and environmental protection, we need only look at these people.

Questioning the "relevance" of the environmental movement, Kathleen goes on to state:

> My thoughts also dwelt a lot on the naiveté and narrowness of the mostly middle class, mostly white, North American environmental movement. Seeing the circumstances of so many millions of people, and not just their environmental circumstances but the lack of meeting basic needs like food, shelter, land, clothing, health care, employment. I recall thinking that our advocacy in the north on environmental issues can have little relevance or value unless it understands and integrates these broader issues of justice and equity both at home and around the world. Without this understanding and integration, our activism becomes almost as arrogant and ruthless as the global economic forces that cause the injustice in the first place.

Ontario environmental groups are not fully inclusive, anti-oppressive contexts for their members and the larger communities in which they serve, but are in varied places of resistance to and movement toward these goals. For instance, diversity of membership (in terms of ethnicity, race, class, gender, and geographical representation) continues to be limited in Ontario environmental groups according to activists interviewed. Moreover, in contrast to the efforts of many women's organizations (over the last 20 years) to become more diverse and inclusive (Desai, 1996; Johnson, 1996; Minors, 1996; Novogrodsky, 1996), the majority of Ontario environmental organizations are in the early processes of clear and consistent linking practice. Jack elucidates such a viewpoint:

> We don't have any magic formulas. But what I see is many activists and groups trying to become more cognizant and sensitive of the links. I see some people talking to other people, forming new networks, new relationships, not formal, but just talking. So, that even though we may not have a grand formula such that when we see a problem we know how to analyze it, or know how to account for social justice issues and all the other issues out there, we *are* suddenly looking at an issue and saying, "Oh boy!" Some lights are going off and we are wondering whether we should talk to this person and that person. So that is not a formula but we are trying to educate ourselves in these areas. And I do not know how far we have come. My guess is that we haven't come very far in Ontario. But in certain situations we have.

At local, national and international levels, activists recognized that (Canadian) environmental groups need to embrace (organizational) change if they want to meaningfully address the realities of socially marginalized groups in their environmental change efforts. Looking across these and other activists' accounts, at least six areas of environmental organizational critique can be delineated. They include:

Lack of organization membership diversity

- predominance of white, middle-class membership
- failure to recognize and solicit the skills and contributions of marginalized communities

Weak social critical analysis

- staying single-issue focused and ignoring the broader social context in which environmental issues reside
- displaying inadequate analytical understanding of and sensitivity to specific social oppressions, whether racism, sexism, classism, ableism, or other forms of discrimination
- working under the assumption that environmental protection is good for *all*
- possessing a broad understanding of social oppressions without knowing relevant details of these lived experiences
- possessing insensitive, arrogant, and preachy educational approaches
- supporting government environmental initiatives that disadvantage workers, the poor, and/or other marginalized groups. Examples include user pay schemes such as household garbage fees that do not address the impact on those who cannot afford these added costs; racist policies of population control which ignore the variables of culture and poverty on family size; closures of polluting industries that do not give fair compensation to workers; pollution control laws which lead to increased illegal dumping in poor communities by industries; and animal rights and conservation groups which fail to consider impacts on First Nations communities.

Too problem-focused

- concentrating on environmental problems while ignoring attention to transitions, solutions, and alternatives to address social-ecological challenges

Lack of contact and consultation with other communities/sectors

- being out of touch with local/grassroots, ethnic, and/or marginal-ized communities
- failing to consult those who will be disproportionately affected by environmental change proposals or campaigns
- working in ways which are insensitive to communities or groups. Examples include flying in and out of a community to do an envi-ronmental campaign without consulting community members or maintaining community contact after the campaign event; failure to support or join local activist/citizen environmental struggles; not giving local groups credit for their environmental work; and sabotaging local ecological groups' efforts to tackle their environ-mental problems themselves.
- failing to develop projects that specifically seek to ameliorate the environmental problems in vulnerable or marginalized communi-ties/constituencies
- lack of available or effective educational outreach to women's groups, low income neighborhoods, minoritized communities, poverty groups, and disabled groups

Lack of effort to work in collaborative partnerships with social justice sectors

- not giving attention or priority to networking, partnering, and collaborating with social justice sectors
- failing to support and join social justice sector struggles and cam-paigns
- lacking the interpersonal, group process, and cultural awareness skills to work effectively with social justice sectors
- not working with groups concerned about the same issue but from a different entry point. For instance, attempting to strengthen municipal public transit but ignoring work by women's organizations to make public transit safer for women.
- taking grant money for environmental projects without sharing these funds with local groups, communities, or marginalized groups who are directly affected by the issues

Over-reliance on liberal or neo-liberal approaches and solutions

- over-emphasis on environmental change through measures of reform, technological-fixes, incrementalist, or top-down strategies.

For instance, focusing on pollution control rather than pollution prevention.

- over-reliance on advocacy at governmental levels by working in the system to effect policy, legal, and regulatory changes
- promotion of an organizational culture characterized by professionalism, hierarchy, institutionalization (large, centralized), and compromise (with government and industry)
- lack of focus on social justice and environmental health issues

The areas of critique outlined above are supported by various literatures which outline similar criticisms of mainstream environmental organizational work in the United States.[2] Areas of organizational/movement critique have arisen on many fronts, including environmental justice movement actors, feminists, labor unions, First Nations communities, anti-poverty activists, environmental theorists and historians, and activists within environmental organizations.[3] What is clear from both activists' stories and this literature is that environmental organizations (and some more than others) have new paths to forge if social justice links are to be seriously addressed.

ORGANIZATIONAL BARRIERS TO LINKING WORK

Many activists, as environmental group/movement insiders, saw both sides of the challenge. While they acknowledged social justice gaps and the need for change, they also saw impediments inhibiting organizational shifts in mandate and practice. As a result, the overall portrayal of barriers by many activists was an interesting mélange of disappointment, frustration, and impatience with environmental organizations on the one hand, and an appreciation of organizational challenges to address these issues on the other. For instance, even when environmental organizations have explicit social justice mandates, many variables can impede these principles from being meaningfully addressed. Addressing this theme, one activist states:

> Even though our organization has a clear mandate to address environmental issues in low-income communities there are constantly obstacles which keep us from really digging into the full complexity of the issues. For instance, while we are effective on case-by-case situations with individuals or individual groups, we are less effective at infusing social justice issues into the broader social policy landscape of environmental reform. The lack of data, lack of public interest, differences in priorities among staff members and volunteers, lack of depth of analysis even though we have the mandate, lack of the funding and resources needed

to explore these links effectively—these are all barriers that challenge our work in implementing our mandate. For instance, we have had one funder who became miffed at the notion of a focus on poor people and environmental problems when they considered environmental issues to affect everybody and by implication to affect everybody equally.

Three terrains of organizational barriers articulated by activists include:

Lack of time and resources

- lack of financial resources to invest in linking initiatives
- linking work is too time and resource intensive
- organization is already working at its capacity

Lack of organizational mandate

- does not fit within organizational mandate
- lack of expertise in social justice areas (e.g., anti-racism)
- lack of organizational history and relationship with social justice sectors
- sense that it is better for environmental and social justice groups to work separately

Linking activism is too messy, complex, risky, and/or politically loaded

- not wanting to carry the added burden of social justice issues
- fearing loss of membership, public, and/or media support
- realizing that linking work often lacks immediate "pay-offs" which organizations need to survive
- lacking scientific proof to validate linking campaigns
- lacking sociopolitical economic fit
- too much mistrust, stereotyping and politics to address between sectors
- fearing of offending and making mistakes
- fearing "nature" will get lost or marginalized if social justice issues are brought in
- waiting for social justice sectors to approach our environmental organization

The barriers identified above are rooted in issues of organizational identity and history; sociopolitical economic dynamics; funding structure and resources, as well as organizational campaign structure and orientation.

Understanding the variables which impede environmental groups from incorporating social justice principles and practices is an important aspect of linking work. Without being aware of impediments which intersect and collide with activists' expressions of their complexly-aligned identities, activists are less likely to succeed in their linking efforts. And, in maintaining awareness of organizational barriers, activists can stay conscious of how their linking efforts are dynamic tapestries of agency and constraint.

Strong organizational identification is both a strength and weakness to linking practice. While activists may be more likely to collude with non-linking organizational practices when they are highly identified with their organization, in these situations activists may also feel organizationally safer to express themselves and may feel the ability to push their organization towards increasingly integrative actions. In either case, these experiences highlight the importance of activists staying in touch with their complexly-aligned identities, and in situating themselves in organizational contexts which provide space for activists' linking goals. While some activists expected more from environmental organizational contexts than others, the reality is that in their linking aspirations, activists experienced both being facilitated and supported as well as being criticized or minimized within organizational contexts.

Marge's story elucidates some of the organizational gaps and barriers to linking work. Groups discussed by Marge and others are primarily large mainstream environmental groups that are issue-driven, campaign-focused, rely predominately on private monies for their organizational survival and lack an explicit social justice organizational mandate.

MARGE'S STORY: EXPLORING GAPS AND BARRIERS

Working with local communities disproportionately afflicted by environmental degradation or negatively affected by environmental protection efforts challenge facets of mainstream environmental group culture. Environmental group culture can be centered on being savvy, fast paced, singularly focused, having clearly defined pay-offs, and on juggling multiple campaigns simultaneously. As Bob Ostertag states (as quoted in Seager, 1993b), "[Greenpeace] eco-warriors cut bold figures when getting in the way of whalers on the open seas. Making Greenpeace make a difference in places like [a] Brazilian slum requires a lower profile-and messier politics" (p. 183).

Marge depicts these disruptions beautifully. She captures multiple actual and perceived obstacles to linking work within her large mainstream environmental organization. As discussed in Chapter Four, Marge indicated that her organization would not explicitly frame an environmental issue as a "social-environmental issue" because "it would not be sexy enough." This kind of campaign angle, Marge indicates, would not secure the financial pay-off or rise in membership base needed to be viable for her nonprofit group. In relaying her account, Marge points to social discriminations among middle-class donors that would stop them from financially supporting a social justice linked environmental campaign.

Fear of the complexities and messiness of working with community groups was also depicted by Marge. Clearly, working effectively with community groups takes concerted effort. She explains that outreach work can be seen by some environmental groups as taking them off-track because of these complexities. Avoidance of community building can be particularly acute when organizations operate under panic to "save the planet." She states:

> When an environmental organization starts dealing with community groups it takes a long time to build this relationship. Dealing with the community and doing it in the right way takes a lot of work. Some groups do not want to deal with that. They want to circumvent this level and go another way they find easier.
>
> Some environmental groups have had bad experiences. They have gone into communities and then had the communities hate them and not allow them to come back. In such situations, maybe the activist got a lot of pressure from his boss to do the campaign and get out. We don't have much time. I know many environmental organizations say, "We have no budget to work with the community. We are doing a gazillion things at once," and so forth.
>
> If your organization is working on an environmental issue and is really focused, it is like feeling you are running and can't stop and turn around. You can't sit back and look at other variables. You just keep plowing ahead because you don't want to lose the momentum on the campaign that you already have. So, when it comes to looking at the social aspects of that issue you don't look at them because that would bring in another can of worms. These issues might get you off track and you can't do that.
>
> There can be this attitude in environmental groups that you have to act now because there is not much time left to save the earth. It is this notion that you cannot afford to stop and look at the social aspects of environmental problems. I think we have to look at these social dimensions. I think that it would only help but some groups do not see it that way.

Marge continues to explore how addressing social justice links within environmental issues would alter the way some environmental groups operate—

campaigns would span longer periods of time, expend more financial and staff resources, and not likely achieve immediate returns. Marge argues:

> A lot of groups do not want to do this work because it is long-term. They will have to pour more money into these campaigns than in their other campaigns. And then, in some ways it becomes a can of worms. You may help out a small union or a worker's association and once they become affiliated with a bigger union the union may remember your support and work and write you a fat cheque. And then they may not. In some cases your group may get added respect for this work but many organizations feel they do not have the time to wait for these kinds of positive results.

How one's environmental organization financially supports itself helps set the boundaries of how, and to what extent, social equity and justice issues get addressed. Further, if linkages take time to form and develop because they require relationship and trust building, but the organizational strategy is structured to demand quick change and financial pay-off to survive, groups wanting to make social justice links can find themselves in a dilemma. Moreover, public attitudes towards linkages also sway how environmental problems get framed by groups. Marge's account highlights the question, who are environmental group members and potential public supporters? Are public constituents who embrace social justice being effectively tapped by environmental groups? In many cases, activists working in environmental groups may possess a social justice lens not shared by colleagues or by their organizations' membership or target audience.

A few more points need to be included in this discussion. First, environmental organizations that receive government funding can also find themselves weighing their public linking messages carefully. Speaking of her publicly funded environmental organization, Kathleen indicates, "All the power we have lies in our name and credibility as an organization." While Kathleen's organization does have a mandate to support economically disenfranchised groups with their environmental problems, specific linkages her organization makes between environmental and social justice must be done with a clear sense of the facts and with integrity. This detailed work takes time and the financial means to initiate primary research to demonstrate these links empirically within the Canadian landscape. These variables can be real obstacles to deepening and expanding an environmental group's social justice mandate and practice. Without Canadian-based research that documents specific linkages, environmental organizations will be tentative in how much they will say about such connections. Unlike U.S environmental groups that have numerous studies to back specific race and class environmental linkages (see research discussed in Chapter Two), Canadian groups, by and large, lack this empirical foundation.

Second, there is also the reality of extensive funding cuts to Ontario nonprofit environmental groups carried out by the Conservative government in 1995. Rick speaks to the resulting disorientation among many environmental groups. He states, "The environmental community got overwhelmed by the Harris agenda and its cuts [to environmental group funding]. . . . In terms of volunteers and numbers we haven't quite recovered to where we were prior to Harris." In this disorientation, groups may put aside linking goals. Jane argued that these and other provincial government attacks on environmental reforms may result in some environmental groups spending less time on linking practices. Jane argues:

> To survive today as an environmental organization you have to be savvy. And being savvy means not so much about expanding linkages but going to court and suing polluters. This is the smartest thing you can do today. To get the best example you can find, get an out of court settlement and get environmental enforcing agencies to do their job of protecting the environment.

And third, there is the issue of environmental campaign structure. Morag is clear and articulate about the way campaigns are framed, at least within the organization she works for—a large international environmental organization with offices in Canada. She argues that environmental campaigns are framed in ways that reflect the dominant political economy they are in. Campaigns need to mobilize the constituency that environmental groups are targeting so environmental groups receive the support they need to effect change. Morag states her organization does not organize campaigns around environmental justice issues because, "there isn't that kind of history of separation and marginality here [in Canada as compared to the United States]. . . . By and large it is very difficult to make that kind of [environmental injustice] analysis for the whole of Ontario or for the Canadian situation." Morag goes on to say that, in contrast, her sister organization in the United States *does* take on environmental justice campaigns because there is a historical and political economic fit. Morag argues that the U.S. history of black slavery and its civil rights movement enables environmental justice campaigns to resonate within the United States. The perception that Canada does not have a national environmental justice issue which would rally concerted public support is an interesting one that can be explored from many angles.

A number of questions requiring further research and exploration can be raised. For instance, what other factors may explain Morag's assertion? Is Morag using a U.S. based understanding of environmental discrimination (which concentrates on pollution and waste siting) to determine whether Canada has a central linking issue? Are there environmental discriminations regarding the use and control of public natural resources issues that unite Canadians? Are the negative social and ecological impacts of economic globalization unifying Canadian political action?

Additional questions can be asked: Is oppression more subtle in Canadian communities? Does Canada's stronger welfare state mean we have less environmental discrimination? As compared to the United States, are Canadian communities too socially blended to show specific identity groups disproportionately affected by environmental degradation? And, in what ways does our approach to delineating environmental discrimination inhibit social-ecological injustices from being recognized?

Interestingly, while Morag argues that her organization does not organize or frame campaigns as environmental justice issues, she has no difficulty identifying environmental justice issues in her urban community and across Canada generally. Injustices against First Nations people, northern communities, and poor urban neighborhoods are three examples. In fact, through her organization, Morag did work with different disempowered groups facing environmental injustices but in a "behind the scenes" manner that her organization did not publicize. This kind of potentially creative shape-shifting in the expression of organizational linking priorities and practices across different contexts is interesting to note. It would appear that different environmental groups may be linking *practitioners* without extending this work to being linking *messengers*.

STRENGTHENING THE SOCIAL JUSTICE LENS AND PRACTICE WITHIN ENVIRONMENTAL GROUPS

Activists were not just engaged in naming organizational gaps and constraints. They also found and created opportunities to strengthen the social justice lens and practice within environmental groups. Nine of the initiatives taken by activists to support and strengthen a social justice perspective within organizational contexts include:

Revisiting issues of organizational identity and membership

- raising dialogue about the lack of diversity within environmental groups
- reviewing organizational identity and membership criteria
- organizing outreach to new audiences

Creating new policies to address justice and equity issues

- developing positions on First Nations rights and labor union issues

Initiating and developing research on linkages

- investigating links between children's health and pollution
- assessing connections made between forest protection and forestry worker job loss

Expanding the complexity of environmental organization messages

- voicing positions that make social equity/justice aspects visible
- incorporating a critical global economic analysis
- expanding one's organizational ecological story to incorporate social aspects of ecological environments

Developing ecological initiatives which have a strong social justice/equity focus

- creating a community garden which promotes participation of less powerful members in the community
- working to translate public education materials in languages other than English
- initiating and participating in transition planning forums

Becoming more informed and supportive of other social constituencies and groups

- becoming a watchdog of social constituencies, such as First Nations, to make sure these interests are not being left out at environmental decision-making tables
- subscribing to newsletters of social justice groups
- sharing organizational resources (time, information, contacts, expertise, funding)

Networking, collaborating, and building relationships with other social constituencies

- listening to criticisms that challenge and expand one's awareness of social connections
- building coalitions and relationships of common cause
- inviting other sectors to organizational events
- creating joint conferences, protests, initiatives
- networking with other sectors and being a messenger between sectors

Consulting affected groups

- consulting affected groups on ecological initiatives
- speaking out against environmental groups that fail to consult affected sectors

Shifting organizational process and/or campaign procedures to link more effectively

- changing organizational timing and procedures in order to address social implications of environmental problems
- initiating and/or expanding local community work

Across these and other examples, activists contributed to extending and reorienting organizational boundaries. They were voices and agents of organizational evaluation and questioning, disrupting organizational identities, agendas, knowledge, priorities, discourse, strategies, and actions. As agents of organizational change, it was not just the exertion of angry resistance activists brought, but an energy of curiosity, openness, and insight. Activists were motivators, innovators, facilitators, and enablers within their organizational contexts. Activists creatively made use of organizational information, resources, ideas, contacts, influence, credibility/legitimacy, strengths, and other supports to make integrative organizational work more viable. They also used organizational contexts as spaces to awaken and act from their complexly-aligned identities as they learned about linking realities related to their work.

BEING MORE CONSULTATIVE: CASE EXAMPLES OF ACTIVISTS' ORGANIZATIONAL EFFORTS

This chapter ends by exploring five illustrations of activists' organizational efforts to be more consultative with affected constituencies facing ecological and social challenges. In the first example, Helen describes how she and a forest ecological group had to backtrack. In developing an ecological initiative, they forgot to consult with the First Nations community in the area. In the second example, Irene tells her story of bringing two sets of citizens together—one group wanting to send their toxic waste to a northern community, the other group comprised of citizens who would be on the receiving end of these radioactive nuclear tailings.

In the third account, Serren tells the story of how, in listening to the perspectives of local residents, her organizational project was able to reach community members more effectively. In the last two examples, Jack relates moving himself and his organization to start exploring the concept of transition planning in shifting from "dirty to clean industry." Kathleen, in turn, outlines the shifts in her organization's consultations with the labor sector over time.

HELEN'S STORY: TAKING THE TIME TO CONSULT FIRST NATIONS CONSTITUENTS

Helen describes forgetting to consult regional Native people on a rural forest and economic sustainability project which was spearheaded by an urban-based environmental group. She states:

> I worked on an environmental project aimed at addressing ecological and economic aspects of the forest area where I live. Just as the project group heard that the project had received funding and was getting off the ground I suddenly realized "Oh my god, we haven't talked to any Native people in the region." I felt very responsible for this mistake because I had been consulted on the project several weeks before and it hadn't occurred to me to talk to the Native community. Yet, I go around talking about how important it is to make sure Native people are taken into account, that it is their land, that all Canada is Native land, and most notably *this* land, which has never been subject to a treaty.

While there was organizational pressure to start the project quickly because of funding arrangements, a decision was made to delay the commencement until the Native community was consulted. Helen recalls:

> So we quickly rallied and said we must talk first to some of the Native people. Then, they became involved. This meant a delay in getting the project off the ground. We had pressure on one side in that the funding covered a certain period of time. And, on the other side, [for the Native community the] processes [of] thinking through "Do we or do we not want to be involved?" [would] take time in a geographically spread-out

Native community. We did take the time and wait and allow the process to happen, which took a couple of months.

Following this process of consultation, Helen shares the nuances of engagement with the Native community during the project. Specifically, she reflects how they can welcome Native input and involvement in ways that do not repeat oppressive, colonialistic relations. Helen reflects:

> We received the consent of the Native community and to some extent got their involvement. We kept looking for them to be more involved, but we wanted at the same time to respect that they had other priorities. They were not that clear about the importance of this project to them. They certainly did not want it going on without their input, involvement, and information flow. But, they weren't necessarily concerned about devoting that much time to it.
>
> So, on the one hand, we kept saying (and meaning) that Native involvement was very important. On the other hand, we didn't want to say "Hey, come to all our meetings!" which could almost turn into another form of cultural imperialism saying, "These are our meetings. This is our project. We got funding for this. You do it our way!" And "I thought you said you wanted to be involved" kind of response.

While upfront about the different organizational implications of striving to practice a non-oppressive, consultative relationship with the Native community, Helen also suggests that in acting from more complexly-aligned identities (in caring for the forest, Native community, and town residents) positive seeds were sown. She explains:

> Throughout the two-year life of the project, we were working on that stuff pretty constantly. It took an immense amount of time and energy to practice what we preach. I think we did fairly well on that. I think we came out with good feelings for the most part on the Native and non-Native side. Getting Native input got the backs up of some non-Native people in the area who felt we were giving special treatment to the Native people. They had fears and beliefs that the Native community wanted to take away all the land from non-native people because they have a land claim in process.

IRENE'S STORY: SEEING THE IMPLICATIONS OF ONE'S PROPOSED ECO-SOLUTIONS

Irene also supported her organization to tread new ground by facilitating the principle of consultation. Like herself, her anti-nuclear organization felt strongly that "we need to look for local solutions for radioactive waste, so that communities are not just opposing this waste and dangling money in front of desperate communities in northern Ontario to take the waste—communities which are economically deprived and don't feel they have any other alternative but to take it." What had not been undertaken before, however, was to bring these different communities face-to-face. Communities wanting to send their waste elsewhere do not see the face-to-face implications of their proposed "solutions." The host community of the waste remains the "other" who resides "out there." Working in conjunction with her environmental group, Irene brought these two groups together. Sharing her powerful story Irene states:

> A couple of areas emerged in northern Ontario where I actually knew people, environmental groups in those areas where they were saying, "Holy Shit! Look at what we have to fight! We don't want this radioactive waste sent to our community." So one of the things I did, was introduce the activists fighting to have their toxic waste taken out of their community and housed elsewhere, those who were saying, "Move this shit out of here. We don't want it anymore!" to activists in the north who were saying, "Holy shit, look what they are trying to do to us!"

Being faced with the implications of one's proposed environmental solution can be painfully eye-opening and disturbing. During this wrenching encounter, Irene recalls:

> The activists advocating that their waste be sent elsewhere were shocked and scared by the experience. They were so shocked to find out that what they believed in was a total problem for another group of friendly, warm people. Northern Ontario is not an empty void with a bunch of rocks. People live there and people in these communities care. They had no idea that what they were asking was so unworkable for these northern communities. Some activists felt the waste could be put in a safe place somewhere outside the community where it would not affect people, and that they were doing the right thing by opposing the siting of the waste within their community. For these activists, the lesson that it wasn't the best plan to ship it somewhere else was very hard and has impacted them to this day. Some felt very guilty for having advocated that it be moved to northern Ontario. It took some of them back quite a bit.

Irene was gutsy to do what she did. Through her facilitation, community members gained firsthand experience of the social inequities of their proposal, an encounter which had a profound emotional impact on many of these members. Irene provided a forum for these citizens to realize that while they needed a solution to their communities' radioactive waste, this did not mean they were willing to find solutions that would be at the expense of another community. The encounter led to a dramatic shift. Irene informs us that this experience led the community group to seek local solutions to their environmental problem. This, in turn, led to their energy being spent on preventive solutions such as promoting a closed system and zero-discharge approach for industry—solutions which do not move an environmental problem from one (usually more privileged) location to another (more vulnerable) location.

SERREN'S STORY: LISTENING TO RESIDENTS' NEEDS AND IDEAS

Serren tells the story of working with her environmental organization to reorient its initial linking message from one that was dry and abstract to one that was able to creatively engage the community members her organization was trying to reach. Here linking issues were expressed via a community newsletter, which blended community voices with research statistics and facts. It is an account which illustrates the value of an organization's flexibility to be open to doing things differently. Recounting her fascinating story, she shares:

> We've gained an understanding of the way that you make links with different elements of the community. Sectors of the community that are very important. We learned what strikes chords with people and what doesn't. One of the most effective things we did was start a small community paper which talked about sustainable forestry. We did a series of tests. We interviewed local people and came up with a paper, which presented their own voices and what they thought about the issues. It was really critical for us to know and to recognize the fact that it's one thing to write up the best information in the world, but if it doesn't have that community focus and voice you're not going to get very far.
>
> It was an interesting process because from the very beginning there was this realization that to do this community outreach, we had to be really flexible and pay attention to what people in the area wanted. Our original proposal for working in the community and where we ended up were quite different. We were taken in a different direction than we had expected.
>
> We started out with a conventional idea that we'd have a series of little fact sheets talking about what was going on in the region . . . well, people weren't as interested in the information sheets as they were in reading about what their neighbor thinks and seeing a lot of pictures and little bite size pieces that people could take with them. They wanted information that was very regionally oriented which had lots of references to places and names they knew.

So that was what we did and it went over really well. It got people talking about the issues, even some of the things that people found really difficult. One of the things that somebody said in the area was that they'd never seen something so good on biological diversity that explained it in really simple terms that people could understand.

We managed to get a number of tabloids out. The first one was on land use. The second one was on biological diversity. It was really interesting because by the end of the second one, people were saying "Oh this is just a rag that talked about forests, we've seen it all before." The third one was on the forest industry. We had gone around and talked to many people involved in the forest industry and through their perspective said that these are some difficult issues in relation to forestry and here's one viewpoint and here's another. This third paper was timely because it came out a few days before a community public meeting. It was a meeting organized as a public roast by this very well organized group of reactionaries in the community. The paper diffused the oppositional stance of this group. It was now difficult for them to say that our organization was only representing and talking about forests when it was clear that we weren't. We were really trying to pull in these other elements.

The original idea for these little papers was that they would just present facts. What they ended up being was a key tool for the whole project. The tabloids were a way to bring people together and talk about these issues.

JACK'S STORY: INCLUDING TRANSITION PLANNING WITHIN ONE'S ORGANIZATIONAL WORK

Connecting and consulting across sectors, Jack depicts an experience of working to stretch himself and his organization towards a more integrative change-making approach. Seeing the need for transition planning, he speaks to some of the challenges and possibilities that are raised in designing the transition "from dirty to clean industry." Here you can see the expansion of discourse and effort within environmental organizational culture. Reflecting on moments of naive and simplistic thinking, and naming what gets left out, Jack states:

> I look at my sort of knuckle brain thinking that says ban chemicals. And when I say this, all of a sudden communities are in the way, labor is in the way, everything is in the way. . . . There are huge job implications, huge community and economic implications that have to be addressed. There are all these kinds of implications. Moreover, society wants certain things and to make those certain things we need the use of chemicals, without them they would be debunked. So we either redo the process, we redo the product, or find alternatives. . . . So all of a

sudden we realized that in the process of doing that there was a transition phase needed—the transition from dirty to clean technology. So we talked to labor and they talked to us. We talked to all kinds of people. What we heard made a lot of sense. So, then we said, how do we label all this and we used the term transition planning.

Revisiting the concept of transition planning from the Cold War to look at equitable environmental solutions, Jack relates:

> There is this whole thinking now of what we call transition planning from dirty to clean industry. Transition planning is not a new concept. In the United States, after the Cold War, there was a demilitarization conversion from military institutions and all kinds of communities were affected. So there was a whole network of people dealing with transition planning. We are trying to use some of their expertise and apply it to the environmental realm. So that is a concrete example of how we are thinking through it.

Awakening to a multi-aligned expression of self in their work to eliminate toxic chemicals, Jack and his organization found themselves treading on new terrains of reflection spanning economic restructuring, gender quality, job sharing, and more. Here, environmental concerns became one among many additional social issues to address. Jack shares:

> What we also found was that in our dialogue and consultation, people wanted to put more things on the agenda, such as the recognition that there aren't a lot of jobs out there. Therefore, can we put on the agenda a four-day workweek or job sharing? . . . These signify major change. They are talking about restructuring jobs, restructuring the economy through different industrial sectors. This became an opportunity to talk about new innovative ideas. Everything from gender equality, to how you accommodate families, to daycare subsidies, to how do we ensure quality of life of workers and make sure they have jobs but also ensure that families are taken care of. All these issues were being considered which is fascinating. How do you relate a four-day workweek, job sharing, gender equality, and toxics? Well, it is called transition planning. What is this economy going to be like? Is it going to be a service economy? What does it mean for the worker? What does it mean for the environment? Is it part of transition planning? And then other people said, wait a second, if we get involved in these issues we should look at what new technologies and materials we want to use. If you don't want to use chlorine then what are you going to use? If you are not going to make mercury, then what are you going to use? What are options for workers? All of a sudden these issues mushroomed.

KATHLEEN'S STORY: REVIEWING ORGANIZATIONAL SHIFTS IN HOW AFFECTED GROUPS ARE CONSULTED

Kathleen's account shows different kinds of organizational consultations that can occur with affected groups. As her environmental organization established regular lines of consultation with a sector, such as labor, mutual familiarity, comfort, and respect developed. These consultation successes allowed the consultation process to be less intensive and more streamlined. Furthermore, Kathleen relates how technology provides the vehicle to support such a streamlined approach. She states:

> There is a whole progression we can talk about in terms of consulting impacted sectors. I have seen my own linking work and that of my organization move from not consulting labor on our proposals, to realizing the importance of doing so, which has resulted in setting up meetings to address the labor implications of our environmental ideas and proposals. Then, as time progressed and a whole lot of good work was done on just transition we developed strong working relationships with labor representatives and we got to the point where we could put our proposals forward and automatically incorporate the principles of just or fair transition that had been worked out between us. At this point we often only need to double check minor points with labor rather than consult closely together on the entire proposal. And even more recently with the internet and the availability of good sectoral information on-line, we can now find their positions on issues on-line and take these views into account when developing our own positions, so that our positions are complementary. The internet has been an incredibly valuable tool for NGOs, in particular to those who have limited resources but who can use the internet to economically publish their information.

SUMMARY REFLECTIONS

This chapter has outlined an array of organizational gaps and barriers that keep environmental groups from addressing the social justice dimensions of environmental problems and solutions. Greater depth and exploration needs to be given to each of these findings, a pursuit which was beyond the scope of this book. Many of the organizational challenges articulated across activist accounts have been noted in U.S. literature, such as the environmental justice, environmental movement, and labor literatures.

Clearly, environmental organizational contexts play a significant role in shaping activists' expressions of linking work. Activist accounts suggest that many organizations are in the early processes of understanding and moving towards a more integrative environmental practice. The main goal of this chapter has been to show how activists were able to look critically at their organizational contexts without denying the organizational impediments on the one hand, and the possibilities to strengthen a social justice-ecological practice, on the other. These efforts on the part of activists were, moreover, conceptualized as another form of linking practice.

Chapter Seven

Constituency-Oriented Linking Activism: Voicing Environmental Concerns from the Realities of Socially Marginalized Constituencies

Journal Note: How do the social locations, values, and experiences of activists shape their environmental change efforts? Activist Eric Mann argues that environmental activists who come from previous social justice movements engage environmental challenges differently. He states, "I think if you've come out of the women's movement, if you've come out of the civil rights movement, or if you've come out of the workers movement, you would come to environmentalism in a different way. You'd come to it in a more holistic way and you wouldn't talk about auto-free cities, banning this, we don't want that, no price is too great. But you'd talk more like an organizer and say, 'Look, there's a multiplicity of problems your family faces. Let's see—as a society—how we can solve these problems'" (Eric Mann cited in Surman, 1993, p. 19).

More than simply physical systems under stress, environmental problems are embedded in social power relations which give influence and control to some constituents more than others. As a result, when you have experienced forms of social oppression, it is hard to imagine viewing environmental problems in isolation from these inequitable power relations. Mann brings attention to this issue. He also raises the notion that many activists work more holistically because they are not only bringing their environmentally concerned identities but their experiences and identities as, for instance, women, minoritized persons or labor unionists.

Examining the interplay between our multi-aligned identities and integrative social change are issues at the heart of linking activism. Linking

151

work raises the questions: How do we use the breadth of who we are to justly navigate our complex social-ecological landscapes? What are the varied meanings of giving visibility to one's multi-aligned identity within one's environmental efforts? What would it feel like to speak within the arena of environmental change from the voice of one's complexly-aligned identity?

In reflecting on these questions, I am cognizant that activists can feel the desire, need, and/or pressure to keep their multi-aligned identities out of environmental politics. Often in donning varied suits of (activist) professionalism, activists blunt or hide the contours of their complex selves. I've wondered which is done at greater cost (to self and social change)—hiding our complexities of self within the political arena or revealing these complexities of locationality. Creed and Scully (2000) relay some of the challenges and benefits of bringing our multi-aligned selves into our work, an excerpt, I contend is equally relevant to activist work. They state:

> *Inclusivity is a challenge when visible social identities trigger potentially judgmental and divisive reactions (e.g., Wharton, 1992). A distinct set of challenges arises when employees bring invisible, marginalized, or even stigmatized aspects of their identities into the workplace. Making a social identity visible or not only sets the stage for other reactions, whether positive, negative or mixed, it also lays the groundwork for social changes that may reduce the stigma and costs of the social identity (Creed & Scully, 2000, p. 391).*

Our social locations can feel like unwelcome weights as we feel the challenges, hardships, and injustices of our individual and collective stories. And yet, our identities are also narrative containers which carry the power and empowerment of our histories, experiences, and values. Moreover, our identities are intimately connected to our ways of knowing and forms of expressed agency in the world. In relaying stories of honored relationships to one another and to the land, many activists attributed this sense of connection to their experience as women or First Nation people, for instance. Similarly, numerous activists linked their environmental analyses, approaches, and priorities to their experiences as an African-Canadian, northerner, trade unionist or other form of social locationality.

In striving to address social justice within the context of one's environmental advocacy, I imagine activists donning varied expressions of identity in relation to the dynamics or variables of each context. This would mean, that at times, linking activists would wear their complexly-aligned identity as undershirts, other times as well-worn jackets, and other times still, as evening gowns or as valuable protective armor.

The needs and perspectives of marginalized constituencies motivated many activists' environmental work. Many of the activists I interviewed were members of such constituencies and engaged environmental issues through the lens of important aspects of their social locationality. For instance, with a deep history of connection and membership to the labor movement, Rick's environmental efforts were strongly positioned from the labor sector. Dorothy, Linda, Shirley, and Si's environmental work was rooted in feminism and in the women's movement and its organizations. The ecological efforts of both Gail and Dwayne were rooted in their cultural traditions, and from First Nations organizations seeking empowerment for their people, which is intimately connected to honoring Native people's relationship to Mother Earth. As an African-Canadian who immigrated to Canada, Yuga was a co-founder of a grassroots environmental organization for new Canadians which was created to empower the voices, needs, and contributions of new immigrants within the landscape of environmental issues. As northerners, Brennain and Cecilia's environmental passion and activism were strongly tied to the challenges and complexities facing northern communities—a geographical area of Ontario faced with numerous environmental challenges and injustices. As activists, they fought against these injustices and vocalized the northern-southern geopolitical disparities that perpetuated these injustices. In "deploying" aspects of their identity (to use Berstein's [1997] term) in their efforts for socially just environmental change, these activists often illuminated a sense of strength and authenticity in their linking work which was personal and profound.

Other activists worked as allies within a constituent community (as they were not members of these communities). For instance, while not a member of the Inuit community, Craig worked for a large Innuit organization as their environmental policy advisor supporting the protection of Innuit environmental needs and rights. Similarly, Nita's linking efforts were based in an urban community health center and the movement for community health. Working as an environmental health promoter, she was engaged in supporting vulnerable minoritized and economically disadvantaged community residents facing exposure to environmental health threats. In their work, both Craig and Nita were provided opportunities to see environmental issues through the eyes of another community and support the empowerment of a constituency's blended social and ecological needs—ally work affirming their complexly-aligned identities.

This chapter examines seven main themes depicting activists' constituency-oriented linking efforts. Specific attention is given to ways activists worked to foster ecological and social empowerment within these contexts. These seven themes are:

1) naming forms of environmental discrimination;
2) creating innovative organizations and projects;
3) voicing constituency needs and perspectives to environmental groups;
4) designing environmental strategies to effectively reach constituency members;
5) situating environmental efforts within the larger fabric of constituent's social, cultural, and economic needs;
6) voicing constituency strengths within the terrain of environmental change; and
7) challenging constituent members to move forward on issues of sustainability.

NAMING FORMS OF ENVIRONMENTAL DISCRIMINATION

Social marginalization and oppression have resulted not only in different constituencies' social, economic, cultural, and/or political disempowerment, but have resulted also in their ecological disenfranchisement. As outlined in Chapter Two, less socially advantaged constituencies can be disproportionately affected by environmental degradation. Moreover, such constituencies can be unwittingly left unprotected by environmental reforms and strategies, or even face added ecological and/or socioeconomic burden from environmental change efforts. Understanding and voicing these realities is central to constituency-oriented linking work. In the naming of environmental discriminations, activists pointed to a lack of political clout, regional isolation, economic instability and social discrimination (stemming from structural and attitudinal prejudices/oppressions, such as racism, sexism, classism) as factors which enabled constituent-based environmental injustices to occur. Further, these constituencies often encounter difficulty in environmental reforms and initiatives. Stigmatization and language barriers as well as lack of time, resources and/or contacts dissuade their effective involvement. This section looks at environmental discriminations facing three marginalized communities.

Brennain and Cecilia both engaged in northern Ontario constituency-oriented work. They vocalized power disparities between Ontario's northern and southern regions. With a predominance of political and economic clout in southern Ontario, they asserted that northerners have experienced a loss of control over their communities' ecological and economic landscapes. Northerners have felt their ecological and social resources literally and figuratively being unsustainably "mined," "developed" and "clear-cut" by powerful outside interests. Reflecting back, Cecilia describes starting to make these northern social justice-ecological links in high school:

> I think the connection between environmental and social justice came for me when I was in high school. We were still in the Cold War and under this nuclear threat. They used to fly these big test bombers above our community. You would hear the jets go by our community. It really made me think about why up here. Probably because they won't hear a peep out of us because we are mainly poor people, mainly non-educated people. They thought we just wouldn't pay attention to something like that, and I thought they were wrong. But they weren't wrong because not many people did pay attention. It was bringing some sort of income into northern communities. For me this was a peace issue and a social justice issue. Then when I got involved with a local group which looked at the toxins in the Great Lakes, the connection between the environment and social justice was made evident for me. I asked myself, "Why does industry want to dump up by our beautiful lakes?" Because it is easier to sometimes, and nobody is going to raise a fuss or notice because that is how our industry is.

In the Adams Mine landfill case, involving a proposal to dump Toronto's garbage into a northern mine, Brennain commented that the northern community was targeted because of its economic and political vulnerability, and then was further disenfranchised by the barriers to citizen participation encountered in the decision-making process. Brennain also asked why over 4,000 abandoned mines sites across northern Ontario have been left unremediated. She estimated that over half of these sites would be deemed toxic and yet this environmental injustice is being ignored by the provincial government.

Nita identifies environmental discriminations facing a low-income, ethnically diverse urban community where she works as an environmental health promoter. Making the link between poverty and indoor-outdoor environment health exposures and risks, she describes:

> I work in a community within the city where people are exposed on a daily basis to poor housing and poor air quality. This is a community where people go to places like Bi-Way to buy cheap plastic products that are off-gassing every day and have high solvent content. They often live in housing with poor storage possibilities and poor ventilation.

She goes on to state:

> I work with tenants in a subsidized housing complex. Many are single mothers. It is an ethnically diverse community. They live on low

incomes. . . . Sewage was leaking up into tenant basements. . . . In the winter, there are a lot of problems with bleeding noses and inability to breath because of electric heat in their homes making their noses really dry. Tenants do not have control over their own heat. Sometimes it is extremely hot and they are boiling to death and sometimes it is extremely cold and they are freezing to death. There is a lack of ventilation which creates poor air in the units. Some of the bathrooms are extremely moldy. The problems are in part due to poor maintenance and part to poor design. . . . There is also chronic spraying of pesticides. Tenants began to realize they were feeling sick because they were coming in and spraying all the time. Long-term solutions at the root of the problem were not being addressed, the structural issues, such as leaky taps, holes in pipes and caulking. Nutrition may be poor because they have low incomes. Moreover, the air quality is quite bad because of historical land use. People live beside major traffic arteries. The whole set of risk factors are there to create a high-risk situation, both environmentally and socially.

Nita's description reveals how poverty, sexism, and racism make residents vulnerable to multiple environmental health risks because they face poor housing, polluted neighborhoods, and lack funds to purchase many quality foods and household items.

A third account of environmental injustice explores the layers of environmental discriminations surrounding the tragic PVC fire which occurred at a recycling company in an Ontario urban community neighborhood (an incident which was introduced in Chapter Two). As a member of the community affected, Ann became an activist overnight, identifying and challenging the environmental injustices she saw her neighborhood facing.

Looking back, the company storing the PVC plastic materials where the fire took place was able to locate adjacent to housing because of land-use planning bylaws. This lack of foresight in locating housing next to industrial activity was intertwined with classist land use values which grant the economically disadvantaged access to parcels of land or housing that are less valuable (such as in industrial areas). Ann voiced that the company would never have been located in wealthier sections of the community even if bylaws allowed this possibility. These factors comprise *one layer of environmental discrimination*.

The company responded to the desire across society to reduce waste and recycle auto parts by stock piling recyclable PVC plastics. Over the years, however, the company practices became increasingly sloppy, dirty, and unsafe. Owners began stacking PVC-based materials in their plant beyond safe limits. The owners were able to get away with these practices, numerous activists stated, because the plant was located in a less socially empowered community. So while social policy began encouraging recycling as a societal environmental solution, poor company practices meant these policies have inadvertent negative consequences for less socially advantaged communities. Such negative implications of environmental protection policies reveal *a second layer of environmental discrimination* faced by this community. These kinds of occurrences have been noted in the U.S. environmental justice literature.[1]

While residents complained about unsafe incidents at the company (like small fires in the plant), government officials failed to effectively monitor or put a stop to these practices, resulting in a major toxic fire of PVC plastic. This lack of effective government monitoring and enforcement of environmental laws and regulations was enabled, in part, because of the social stigmatization of the residential community by more powerful governmental interests. This less politically, socially, and economically powerful neighborhood community was not given the protections of responsible monitoring and enforcement. As noted in Chapter Two, when less privileged communities receive less enforcement of environmental regulations and wait longer to get a response to complaints (than do more privileged communities), they are not being equitably protected by environmental laws. These variables illustrate *a third layer of environmental discrimination* facing the community surrounding the plant.

During the fire this social vulnerability led, in part, to *a fourth layer of environmental discrimination*. Government and local public officials were insensitive and ineffectual in their immediate response to this neighborhood in crisis. Ann, a mother of two, living across the street from the fire recalls the horror of the situation. Her story is frightening and powerful. She recalls:

> There was a fire on July 9, a Wednesday night. I was working that night downtown. My husband phoned me before the fire trucks arrived to say there was this huge fire. Right away I said, "Are they going to evacuate you?" I talked to him every hour until I left work at eleven. He talked to the Emergency Services people at the side and they assured him that everything was fine. We have two young kids. The only thing they said was close your doors and stay inside. It was July and stinking hot. We had an air conditioner which you couldn't really use. That night there wasn't a lot of smoke in our area, but there were fumes. . . . We live literally right behind the fire. . . . Technically there are no buildings between us and them. My daughter, who was four at the time, her room backs onto our backyard. She could see the flames and it was scary with all the noise going on. She was hysterical and refused to sleep in her room. That causes me to be very, very angry. They traumatized my child.

We evacuated on the Thursday afternoon. The smoke changed
and there was the inversion. We could not see through our yard the
smoke was so thick, and it was choking us. This was chemical smoke.
It didn't just take your breath away, it burned your throat. When that
happens to an adult it is very frightening, but when you think of your
kids breathing it, you go hysterical. I phoned my husband at work in
Toronto but he had already left for the day. When he pulled up an hour
and a half later, I was hysterical and I am not a panic sort of person. I
grabbed garbage bags and ran around the house throwing what I could
into them, because at that point I had no idea how long we would be
gone from the house. As soon as he arrived, we left and he was very
distressed. This is day two.

Further describing the trauma of the situation, Ann speaks of the ineffectual approach that was taken in dealing with the fire. She depicts the dehumanizing treatment they received from public officials—being told that
"everything is fine." Ann continues:

The Emergency Services people around us were all wearing gas masks.
How does that make you feel? We have a lot of elderly people in our
neighborhood and a lot of young families. We have a lot of people who
do not speak English as a first language. Basically, what you are saying
is you do not care about these people one lick, they aren't even people
to you. I am talking about the city officials, public health and the fire
dept, those who were involved in the decision-making. Not the firemen
working in the field. They do not make decisions. They are told what
to do by a fire fighting bureaucracy.

The way they chose to fight this fire, and this is what the firefighters have told us, this could have been over in 12 hours, and they
know that. Even I know putting water on something that is burning
that has chemicals in it is the stupidest thing you could do. As soon as
you pour water on it you are forming gases. We asked the officials why
they didn't use foam. They said they didn't have enough. When we
asked the firefighters they said that was a load of crap. They could get
foam trucks from every city in the area within two hours and certainly
the ones from the airport. They were telling us you would never use
water for plane crashes.

As well, the way that this stuff burns, especially the PVC plastics,
they are hard to get burning but once they start they burn at a very,
very high intensity. When they are burning at that intensity you have a
minimal amount of crap being released into the environment. It also
burns very quickly. The firefighters have told us the best thing they
could have done that night, because it wasn't windy and there were no
homes close enough to reach the fire, was stand back and let it burn.
The second option would have been to use foam. By putting water on
it, you reduce the burning temperature and you are releasing a variety

of chemicals and gases into the atmosphere. You are putting soot and ash up into the atmosphere which will come down somewhere and it is all contaminated. The information we kept getting was that everything was fine. Everything is fine Wednesday and Thursday and all of a sudden not fine Friday and now miraculously everything is fine on Saturday. When told this many community members would ask these officials, "Do you have kids?" Generally, they would say, "Yes," and they would then ask, "Would you bring your kids over to my house then to play to with my kids?" and the officials would say, "No."

Naming the political elitist and classist response by public officials, Ann angrily states:

The public health people had an opportunity to assist in making the decision to take out the risk, err on the side of caution, and get everybody the hell out of there that night. They chose not to. Knowing what I know now, of all the different people we have dealt with in the levels of government, if this had happened in the upscale section of the community, and of course it would never bloody happen there because there is nothing like that there, you can bet those people would have been chauffeured out of their homes within five minutes of that fire starting.

The arrogance, paternalism, and dehumanizing treatment they received by officials, "experts" and decision-makers continued throughout their struggle to get their concerns addressed. For instance, traumatized by the fire, community members faced the added assault of being met at a public meeting by a riot of armed police officers. Additionally, the impact on the residents was played down and dismissed by officials under traditional epistemological jargon. Ann describes this later experience:

Resulting from exposure to the fire my husband had an eye infection. We all had burning throats making it difficult to talk. There was a chemical taste in our mouths that didn't go away for weeks. You had no saliva, severe headaches, diarrhea, sore throat. We thought we would receive some help from the public health department. All they wanted to do was take down our symptoms. We asked what they could do for us, "Oh, nothing," they said, "The symptoms will just dissipate." Again, I'm not a stupid person. If we suffer symptoms for a week, that tells me there was a good chance there was permanent damage done. "Oh no, you would have to be exposed for 85 years," they said.

Whenever they talked about limits, this was a little game they played depending upon who you were talking to and what they are talking about and what the results are. They would say, "Yes that exceeded the half hour acceptable exposure limit for this, however, it was well within the industrial guidelines." From day one my husband

and I and others kept saying, if you are talking industrial guidelines, you are making assumptions: you are male, between the ages of 18 and 65, you are in good health, you are using safety materials, your average weight is at least 165 pounds. What about our "little workers" who are 40 pounds? I have since learned children take in significantly more air per body weight than adults do. Anything that they breathed would have a significantly higher impact, even in a limited exposure.

Ann's story reveals the layered social, political, and economic power inequities and prejudices which contribute to acts of environmental injustice being imposed on her neighborhood community. Naming the forms and nuances of environmental discrimination imposed on socially marginalized constituencies by dominant cultural institutions, policies, attitudes, and practices is a central task of constituency-oriented linking work.

INNOVATORS OF NEW SPACES AND PROJECTS

In addition to naming and voicing environmental discriminations, activists created new spaces and projects to tackle social-ecologically blended issues more effectively and proactively. Activists were often mavericks within their constituency on environmental issues. They formed new organizations, committees, working groups, and projects within their sector, such as Yuga's efforts to establish an environmental organization for new immigrants. Dorothy describes the formation of the Women's Network on Health and the Environment (WNH&E), a project of the feminist Women and Environments Education and Development (WEED) Foundation. Through WNH&E, campaigns were created to explore the links between environmental toxins (such as pesticides and chlorine) and women's breast and reproductive health. Dorothy states:

> Shortly after I was asked to go on the WEED board after moving to Toronto we were forming the Women's Network on Health and the Environment, a project of the WEED foundation. . . . It grew out of the Stop the Whitewash campaign and expanded and broadened in ways that reached out to wider communities. It's not only women who are affected by all these things. It's children, it's men, it's the whole ecosystem.

Beginning back in 1985 when he began connecting labor and the environment, Rick was involved in forming environmental committees within the labor sector. He described the need to stretch the labor movement's notion of the environment to include the local communities surrounding the workplace. Similarly, Rick worked to bring labor groups into existing environmental organizations, forming for instance, a labor-environmental caucus within the environmental sector. Creating new spaces in both sectors to recognize the labor-environment connection and thereby honor his multi-aligned identity, Rick shares:

> In those days we were saying that labor could no longer ignore environmental deterioration in the communities around them. Labor needed to work with the community to clean up the environment and the workplace, goals in the best interests of the labor sector. Labor's definition of the work place had been the environment with a fence around it. We were taking the exposures, the occupational health and safety issues [in the plant] into the community. . . . We set up environment committees with two or three CAW locals. Labor council set up an environmental committee of which I still chair. We brought the labor groups, particularly the CAW into [the environmental group] Great Lakes United. We set up [a] labor environment task force. We set up a labor-environment caucus. In that sense it was successful in making both the environmental and labor movements realize that there was a connection.

As innovators of organizations, committees, and projects which prioritize the intersection of environmentalism and social constituency concerns, linking activists supported organizational structures and processes in becoming more complexly aligned.

VOICING CONSTITUENCY NEEDS AND PERSPECTIVES TO ENVIRONMENTAL GROUPS

Activists focused on constituency-oriented work had varied levels of connection, liaison, and networking with mainstream environment groups. While some activists were heavily involved with environmental groups (as either a member or by having regular liaison on issues of joint concern), others engaged with environmental organizations on an ad hoc basis. Regardless of their level of contact, however, these activists brought perspectives of their constituency to environmental groups, enlarging mainstream environmental politics and discourse. Rick, for instance, describes bringing worker issues to his involvement with environmental groups. He states:

> What we tried to do with groups like Greenpeace, Pollution Probe, and Canadian Environmental Law Association and all the rest was to remind them that there was a labor position that needed to be taken into consideration—quality of work, jobs, livelihood. In fighting for policy changes and new rules and regulations, worker issues had to be taken into account. If they weren't, those very same workers would end up working with management against us. We didn't want to turn the

labor movement into a larger movement of enemies. We said, we either work with them or we lose them. I certainly came across as a strong advocate for the labor position. That was deliberate on my part, keeping in mind that I wanted to give labor a good head start and to give the environmental movement a good understanding of what labor's issues are. We did a lot of educating, particularly the grassroots movement and some of the bigger environmental organizations were very open to understanding to what was going on.

Craig's constituency-based efforts were focused on the linkages between culture and the environment, specifically through his work with the Inuit. He expresses his frustration with the lack of understanding of Inuit culture within some sectors of the environmental movement. In particular, Craig refers to the lack of understanding and analysis of the link between the protection of Inuit culture and the protection of the natural environment. Wanting this link to be understood, Craig talks to environmental groups who have failed to make this connection. He states:

> I immersed myself within the environmental movement and have found an extraordinary level of naiveté among many of the people I worked with in the movement. . . . One good example I can give you today, in terms of what I have to deal with on a regular basis, is animal rights groups and the seal hunt. I work for an Inuit organization as a non-aboriginal employee. Their whole way of life is dependent upon the earth around them. The fact that they use their resources doesn't compromise the earth in any way. At least if you look at their traditional uses for their resources. Yet, I see people who are very opposed, you could call them deep ecologists, to people seal hunting in the arctic who have no other options. They don't have a lot of money. They don't have a lot of choices in terms of the food they eat and even in some communities in the clothing they wear. The Inuit have been under assault from southern and other non-aboriginal peoples in terms of their own cultures and values. . . . The fact that they can still be among the strongest aboriginal cultures on the face of the planet, despite all those challenges, I have a lot of admiration for. A lot of people within the environmental movement never see that side of the environmental equation and in my conversations with these kinds of groups I talk to them about these Inuit realities.

Genge (1994) provides further weight to Craig's criticism of environmental groups who want to end the seal hunts without considering the social justice ramifications. Genge levies heavy criticism on Greenpeace for its approach to the seal hunt, which he argues, ignores marginalized groups. He states:

When Paul Watson, Greenpeace and the International Fund For Animal Welfare (IFAW) led the successful campaign to close down the seal hunt in the mid-80's, absolutely no regard was given to the people whose lives were dramatically affected by the closure . . . while [they] went on to become international eco-stars, the people of Newfoundland were left to deal with the consequences of being on the losing end of the largest and most successful eco-war ever waged. . . . He [Paul Watson] is definitely not speaking for the marginal societies that suffer the economic, social and cultural consequences of being the target of the eco-warriors' environmentally selectively actions (p. x).

In her linking across numerous movements, including the environmental movement, Dorothy brings her feminist analysis of the interconnectedness between social problems and oppression. From this perspective, she states that she continually poses the question to environmental groups, "How can we better integrate these issues?" Noting that environmental campaigns constantly isolate as opposed to integrate environmental concerns, she states:

It's really strange the way many environmental campaigns are run in environmental organizations. In one large environmental organization they have a excellent toxics campaign but they don't talk about nuclear issues because it is not one of their campaigns anymore. It used to be, but they don't have that anymore because of various political power reasons within the organization itself. Another smaller environmental group I know does wonderful work on pesticides and air quality but they don't touch nuclear issues. . . . Their campaigns are limited. It's a pesticide campaign or plastics campaign or dioxin campaign.

As a policy analyst for a First Nations organization, Dwayne spends time networking with environmental organizations as part of this work. In these linking involvements Dwayne indicates that he has encountered environmental groups that are "too anti-development," groups that don't "respect our autonomy as a separate nation," groups that want to tell you what to do, and groups that "swallow you up" or "treat you like a token Indian." Fortunately, states Dwayne, there have also been environmental groups that do "understand where we are coming from." Across these interactions Dwayne shares an ecological perspective that is culturally rooted and articulates the social and ecological problems faced by First Nations communities. He challenges "false assumptions" made about his people. Changing perceptions within environmental groups, he states:

A significant part of our cultural makeup is our relationship with the land and Mother Earth. In everything we do we are always reminded by the grassroots people who we work for not to jeopardize the values that we hold in relation to the land. . . . In my interactions with environmental groups we are still raising awareness about the problems we are facing. The number one benefit of my interactions with environmental groups is when you go there and you share your perspective on things, it may take awhile, but sooner or later you start changing some of the assumptions that people have made about you. We've dispelled a lot of those false assumptions in our part of Ontario. A lot of people see us as a bunch of freeloaders and bums who don't do any work and see our rights as privileges, like special tax exemptions.

From their different constituency locations (labor, feminist, First Nations) Rick, Craig, Dorothy, and Dwayne all worked to expand the politics and discourse within environmental groups so that connections between environmental issues and the needs and perspectives of their constituency would be recognized.

DESIGNING ENVIRONMENTAL STRATEGIES TO EFFECTIVELY REACH CONSTITUENCY MEMBERS

Addressing environmental issues in ways that are reflective of sector needs and perspectives is a central goal within constituency-oriented linking work. Several activists note that the educational messages and change strategies of many environmental groups often fail to speak effectively to their constituency members. In their constituency-oriented environmental work, activists sought to bridge these gaps. As constituency insiders, activists had knowledge, experience, and perspectives which enabled them to respond to constituency-relevant environmental problems in tailor-made ways. This section outlines some of the strategies used by Yuga, Nita, and Dorothy to reach constituency members in relevant and meaningful ways. As discussed in Chapter Four, Yuga has watched new immigrant communities fall through the cracks of mainstream environmental campaign efforts. Tackling these gaps through his organization, Yuga utilized and advocated for an array of immigrant directed environmental strategies, such as:

- linking environmental issues to issues of culture and health, enabling new Canadians to relate to environmental issues;
- advocating educational approaches that go beyond written materials to include songs and visual art;

- conducting outreach work to make new Canadians aware of environmental health hazards in their neighborhoods;
- providing a clearinghouse for environmental information;
- assisting new Canadians in understanding technical information presented in environmental documents; and
- translating materials into local languages such as Somali, Swahili, Arabic, and Spanish.

Similarly, Nita sought to facilitate effective environmental health strategies for minoritized and low-income tenants living in public housing. She offered tenants her time and presence to discuss their housing situation. She shared environmental health information with tenants and utilized community-based educational and advocacy approaches which helped tenants empower themselves. Here are two examples of her work with tenants.

Working collaboratively with tenants, Nita tackled the environmental discrimination of stopgap environmental "solutions" implemented in public housing. One such stopgap measure was the habitual spraying of pesticides in tenant homes while ignoring structural problems such as leaky pipes and taps, which encourage pest populations. Working with tenants to make the link between their right to housing and their right to healthy housing, she recounts:

> Tenants were saying my stove is not working. There are bugs everywhere. They are spraying all the time. It is irritating and stressful. But no one said this is impacting on my family's health nor were they providing examples of how it is impacting their health. When tenants heard my message about the toxicity of pesticides they started to connect their sense of feeling sick to the chronic exposure to pesticides and began to talk about the need for long-term solutions rather than about the need to spray all the time. Making the links between health and the physical built environment and maintenance led to writing letters, advocating with tenants, that presented the issues through a health slant or lens. Before, the message that got out focused on saying, "There is a general right to housing," "There is a general right to having stoves that work and living without bugs!" Here the link to health was not necessarily being made or understood.
>
> The tenants and I have been working a lot on maintenance issues. Three years ago we brought in an energy and water audit through Greensaver, part of the Green Communities Initiatives. We collected data. Ventilation and pest control were identified as key problems. And in fact, ventilation and heating issues were not identified on a mass scale until we did the audits. Nobody identified it as a key issue until they realized that everybody else had the same problem with heating and saw

that it was affecting everybody's else's health too. One of our goals is to use the results of the audit as ammunition to get property management to deal with these concerns.

Let's look more closely at the layers of Nita's work to effectively address tenant needs. The isolated aspects of tenants' lives needed to be connected by making environmental health linkages and their justice implications explicit. In this case, the relationship between housing maintenance and physical health needed to be explored. Additionally, tenant experiences needed to be gathered to understand whether these problems were isolated or common. Nita knew that the movement from the individual to the collective experience was, in itself, insufficient to get to the root of the challenges tenants were facing. There needed to be an examination of these connections through a socially critical lens in order for issues of power and control to be made visible. Asking tenants, for instance, Who decides who sprays pesticides? How often and where? What is the relationship history of the landlord (Housing Authority) to tenants? Is this relationship respectful, empowering, patronizing, or oppressive? Why do tenants live there? What are the choices available to them in terms of where and how they live? Through this movement of bearing witness, asking questions, and critical analysis, Nita was able to assist tenants in reframing their problems and in finding the solutions they needed. Making environmental health and power inequities explicit altered the narrative tenants had of their own lives and challenged the narrative power holders (housing officials) held of tenants' lives. Previous narratives had kept these social justice-environmental linkages from view.

In another example, Nita describes the creation of a popular education theater skit. Nita used this play as a vehicle to effectively reach marginalized groups facing indoor environmental health hazards. Using creative doses of humor to get across issues of household toxic exposure and its connection to social inequality and corporate control, she recounts:

> I brought our play "Indoor Exposure" to the tenants group at the housing project. . . . I have a group called "indoor equality workers" who are doing a lot of popular education work. We've been doing a interactive theater piece about indoor air issues. We approach the issues of indoor air quality from a power perspective. What we've been doing is trying to address the issues of exposure, understand its ingredients, understand notions of control such as who actually can tell you you're sick. In our play we created a scene with a doctor who tells you you're not sick enough because the tests don't show anything and yet you

know you are. We incorporate alternative health care practitioners and the whole gamut of power as it relates to exposure to chemicals in the indoor environment. Our play has been fabulous. It's innovative and different.

Describing the play in more detail, Nita continues:

The first scene is about going into a bathroom using mime and humor. Everyone pretends they are using all these products like hair spray, perfume, and air freshener because they are going to the bathroom. It is pretty humorous. The second scene is about furniture and the furniture talks. So the sofa and carpet talk about the carpet deodorizers, and the curtains, table, and window talk. The next scene is an assembly line of people making cleaning products who are wearing gloves and masks. They are saying benzene, chlorine, tellurian. Then, there is a scenario where this family says I nearly got a case of food poisoning. They say, "Luckily we had kitchen cleaner," being sarcastic. The next scene is about a place where people have to line up because they have to buy their oxygen. There is a woman who has a child and she can't get oxygen because she doesn't have a card and the child is dying. And then there is a portrayal of a black marketeer selling oxygen. The scene is a spoof on oxygen bars. The play talks about equity, access, technology, toxins, and pollution, corporate and government control. If you are not plugged into the system you do not have access.

Indicating that tenants laughed, got involved, and really made the connection to their own lives, Nita states:

The tenants group really got it. They loved it. They laughed their heads off. They got up and they replaced the characters acting the parts themselves from their experience. Later tenants came up to me and said "Oh yeah, I've stopped using hair spray after seeing the play" or "Yeah, I really got it, those cleaners really bug me too." It was effective! It was fun! I love doing popular theater.

Like Nita, Dorothy engaged creative and effective constituency-oriented outreach practices. She has worked on several groundbreaking films linking social and ecological issues from a feminist perspective. In her work on the film "Exposure: Environmental Links to Breast Cancer" Dorothy sought to engage women through film and workshops on the connections between health issues, such as breast cancer, and an array of environmental contaminants. Utilizing a feminist popular educational approach, Dorothy sought to make these connections in ways that are meaningful, accessible, and sensitive to women, and in ways that support women to understand the power dynamics underpinning these issues. Exploring connections between breast cancer and various environmental contaminants in the film, she describes:

> Our strategy is an educational one. One part of the [educational] strategy was the making of the film, "Exposure: Environmental Links to Breast Cancer." The film deals with nuclear issues, it deals with nuclear fallout, radiation, X-rays, contamination. Rosalie Bertell talks about the effects of radiation on our bodies. It examines pesticides, electromagnetic fields, types of plastic, and chemicals, like chlorine, and their potential role in breast cancer. In the film, Anna Soto talks about how everything impacts on everything else. You take different things and they synergistically act in our bodies. It explores the medicalization of breast cancer prevention with the drug tamoxifen, and the need to use new scientific standards such as the "precautionary principle" and "weight of evidence." The film also looks at issues of power, such as the power of the military and pharmaceutical industry and the need for women to be activists.

Recognizing the importance of educational strategies that are relevant to participant needs (the majority of whom are women), Dorothy states:

> In conjunction with the film we also do educational workshops. We need to look at big pictures and we need to look at small pictures. We need to work in both ways. We do the workshops so that people can start from where they are and then can go back and work with their groups in ways that are good for them. There is no one way. This is the beauty of working in a workshop where people can come and articulate their particular needs and the needs of their groups. In the workshop, we work to present information in a way that touches people in their hearts and their heads and then with their feet, so they are empowered to effect change.

In their constituency-oriented environmental efforts, Dorothy, Nita, and Yuga all supported the making of important social-economic-ecological linkages. Furthermore, they worked to bring awareness of these connections in ways that would reach their constituency. They each engaged in processes that gave constituents tools to understand the meaning of these links in their own lives and to foster their sense of agency. Such examples are illustrative of community building and popular education approaches as opposed to mainstream outreach strategies which emulate top-down, transmission-based educational approaches. Themes of participatory democratic process, empowerment, self-reliance, and community control underlying these activists' efforts illustrate their desire to support, not only constituents' environmental health and empowerment, but also their psychological and social-cultural empowerment.

SITUATING ENVIRONMENTAL EFFORTS WITHIN THE LARGER FABRIC OF CONSTITUENTS' SOCIAL, CULTURAL, AND ECONOMIC NEEDS

Numerous activists sought to address more than their constituencies' environmental needs. Here activists blended issues in a constant multi-tasking effort to complement social and ecological needs. Yuga, for instance, understood that ecological efforts needed to be linked to the larger issues of social (tackling racism) and economic (dealing with job barriers) empowerment of new Canadians. He asked not only questions such as: What kinds of environmental information do new immigrants need access to most? And, how can the voice of new Canadians be heard in environmental decision-making? But he posed questions such as: How can the empowerment of visible minority youth be supported within his organization? Do new Canadian families have smoke detectors in their homes and properly working electrical appliances? How can racist perceptions and attitudes of black males be challenged? Do new Canadians know their civic rights and duties? Supporting visible minority youth in gaining work experience and employment, Yuga explains:

> Through our organization, visible minority youth can come and learn how to use the computer. They can come to write resumes, write covering letters, use our fax, phone about jobs and look for jobs. We can give them tips. I encourage them to volunteer here because even if you worked in your country of origin and used that as a reference the employer will not make a long-distance call, for instance, to Africa. But if they volunteer here I can be their reference. Others on social assistance are under pressure to look for jobs and in order to do this they need to have some experience and access to a computer and so forth.

Yuga, like other activists such as Shirley, Dorothy, and Si, recognizes the complexity and variety of constituent social-ecological needs and sought creative ways to include rather than exclude these needs within the context of their activist practice. In maintaining a holistic view of constituents' lives, activists can work to catalyze change in their constituencies at multiple levels, supporting change that is integrative and transformative.

VOICING CONSTITUENCY STRENGTHS WITHIN THE TERRAIN OF ENVIRONMENTAL CHANGE

As environmental issues cut across all sectors of society, each sector is needed to further the movement towards ecological protection and health. And yet, the wealth that resides within this potential diversity of contribution is often overlooked. Activists engaged in constituency-oriented practices voiced the strengths and gifts embodied in constituency perspectives and experiences. They saw the strengths of their constituencies—values, priorities, processes, and experiences that will strengthen socially just environmental change. Engaging in this kind of constituent capacity-building and strengths-based focus is central to effective linking work. Constituencies facing forms of social-ecological inequity and oppression are repeatedly framed in deficit terms by powerholders/hegemonic interests. They are framed as causing their own social-ecological challenges stemming from inherent and/or learned character flaws, behavior problems, and/or poor cultural practices. Activists also used their own experiences of oppression/disempowerment/exclusion and of privilege/power/access/empowerment as both motivators of their linking work, and as strengths they applied to their linking efforts. For instance, many female activists saw their exclusion from power structures as providing them with a different perspective on and analysis of environmental problems, one that was sensitive to power imbalances, social inequity, and the need for just environmental solutions. Karen, for instance, states:

> Women have been excluded from the structure, hierarchy, and power system. If you are excluded like this you can have a different analysis and can be more critical [of how environmental change occurs] than if you are coming to these issues from within it [i.e., the power structure]. The very nature of that exclusion has allowed women and other particular groups of people to look at what is over there and see there is a problem and analyze and critique and do something about it.

Feminist beliefs that the "end is as important as the means" and that "all forms of oppression are connected and rooted in forms of hierarchy" highlight the need for more non-hierarchical, participatory, and consensus-building processes within the terrain of environmental change-making. As a Jewish woman, Michelle's environmental passion has always been embedded within a deep sensitivity to social oppressions. She states, "My influence in making the links between the environment and social justice has been my background which is that I am Jewish. My parents are both German Jews and they both survived the Holocaust. Out of that experience they taught me the very great importance of human rights and justice."

Growing up in a poor urban industrial area of England, Sue had no access to the most basic treasures of the natural world (such as oceans, lakes, forests, and clean air). Her firsthand experience of how poverty can set one apart from the natural environment informed her focus on social justice-environmentally blended advocacy. Shirley also indicates how she was attuned to injustice from a young age. She connects her father's disability and the racism her best friend experienced, as factors which inform her linking work. Shirley recalls:

> My father was disabled so I noticed injustice. You can't help but notice injustice and lack of tolerance. . . . There were also very few families of color in the town where I grew up. My best friend was East Indian. Just realizing how much she got picked on. . . . She fought racism in our town which was very white and racist and where everybody felt vulnerable if they should stray from the fold.

Blending her sensitivity to injustice on the one hand, and using her privilege as a white educated woman on the other, Shirley was clear about her focus on grassroots community activism. While technically adept, with a degree in engineering, Shirley indicates that she does not see herself as a "professional environmentalist." She states:

> I see too many professional environmentalists who are remote from their community and from popular movements. They see themselves as the expert. I don't want to be an expert. I want to be a grassroots community activist. My focus is on environmental, health, and economic issues. In my activism I make the links between those three issues from a community-grounded perspective.

Contributions to environmental change from minoritized constituencies were also raised in activist accounts. Speaking of the lack of ethnic diversity within the mainstream environmental movement, Ferris (1995) has stated, "Despite this fundamental commitment to biological diversity, there is very little racial or cultural diversity either in the employment spectrum of environmental groups or in their political or educational activities" (p. 70). Seager (1993b) gives some examples of the paucity of minoritized groups within key environmental organizations. She states:

> The exclusion of minorities from the environmental movement seems, too, to be deeply entrenched. At the beginning of 1990, the Audubon Society in the US had 3 minority staff members on staff, out of 315 (.9%); the Sierra Club could find only 1 minority staff person, out of 250 (.4%); the Wilderness Society had no minorities on its board of

172 Linking Activism

directors, and, in the work force of 130, only 4 in professional positions (3%); the Natural Resources Defence Council counted 5 minority staff members out of 140 (3.6%), while Friends of the Earth US had 5 of out 40 (12%) minority staffers, including secretaries. The record of minority representation in environmental groups in Britain, Canada, and throughout Europe is equally dismal. The whiteness of the green movement is not just a staffing problem. Minorities are underrepresented in the membership base of these organizations. The primary membership support for eco-establishment environmental organizations still comes largely from the white middle-class (pp. 181–182).

Shabecoff (1993) bluntly names environmental groups' sense of missed opportunity stating, "In reality, the environmentalists need the knowledge, talent, street smarts, practical experience, political energy, and militancy of angry outsiders from minority communities more than the minorities need the environmentalists" (p. 283).

In their linking accounts, many activists recounted powerful stories of their connection to the earth stemming from the spiritual-cultural beliefs of their community. Expressed in these narratives was both an ineffable sense of being connected to the natural world and to its ineffable worth to their lives. These narratives provide powerful messages on behalf of both human justice and environmental protection. Growing up in a Hindu household, the spiritual belief that all life is sacred and interconnected, was part of Nita's everyday life. As Nita recounts, in this lens human justice and respect for the environment are inseparable:

> These notions were part of my childhood growing up in a Hindu household. Spirituality is part of our everyday life and there are certain traditions and certain ways that are so much part of your analysis. Everything we do is so linked. We're all linked to each other. We're linked to the trees. We're linked to every object. Every action we take has some kind of sacredness. The notion of nonviolence towards living things is very important. Nonviolence is the practice of understanding the spirituality and divinity of everything that lives, and within this is the notion of environmental protection. So very early on that is what you are taught, that God is in everybody and is in every living thing and that the spirit world is all around you. God is not high in the sky away from you as depicted in Christianity. There is no broker between you and what God is considered. So if you believe that everything is sacred then you also believe that there should be justice.

Gail views herself as being intimately connected to the earth and spiritual realm. Gail speaks of the Eagle Bowl Wampum teaching of her people which relays that everything and everyone is interconnected. At the root of this connection, Gail asserts our responsibility to protect the earth. She states:

> I'm a woman, a mother. We are the eagle people here in North America, the Native people. We have an Eagle Bowl Wampum. Everything is in this bowl. We are all interconnected. There was a bead for every nation of Native people in North America representing that we are all connected. . . . Nothing is legal unless every man, woman, and child agrees across North America. If we started selling off the timbers up here that would definitely harm somebody somewhere. We don't have the right to do that. Or the waters, if we started to dump into Lake Erie that is going to hurt the people who need the water. It does not just affect our people, it affects non-Natives as well. That is what the non-Native community does not understand. The governments get so arrogant, greed I guess. It is the root of these problems. The three main sources of life are the earth, water, and air. Each and every one of us have a duty to protect these things.

First Nations beliefs in the power of the story and in the interconnectedness of all life challenges the segmented and professionalized approach of many presentations for environmental change. Irene recounts her awakening to the power of this First Nations approach within environmental forums. Referring to her involvement in hearings on nuclear fuel waste, she states:

> There were public hearings and there was a lot of intervention from First Nations. So I had the opportunity to see a number of aboriginal panel presentations and to be personally moved by their approach and affected by the tack they take on these issues. In many cases, it's like being awe-struck. In some cases they have a more emotional approach than environmental interveners and speak more from the heart. So it is more emotionally moving to hear their presentations.

Yuga recounts growing up in Africa before being forced by political unrest to leave in adulthood and enter Canada as a refugee. He narrates a powerful story of his early years in a village in Africa and the deep and inseparable intertwining of himself and his family and community with nature for their daily survival and nourishment. He states:

> In Africa I'm the first of several children who are alive. I'm mentioning this because my mother had 20 children. The first 5 died. This was somehow normal in the 1950s in Africa where children died for causes that are now preventable. I was the firstborn who is still alive. . . . In an African upbringing, you are very attached to nature. Sometimes children are born where the mother has gone to collect firewood or water several miles away. You could be born anywhere. I saw life and death early

on. As a firstborn child I was involved in looking after my siblings, looking after them so they don't fight, washing them, taking them to the bush. Where I come from, almost every family has at least two or three heads of cattle that need tending. There is a lot of land and grazing of cattle which is considered the responsibility of the boys. The grazing itself was a challenge. You are out for the whole day. You had to know where the best grazing lands are. You have to know where the drinking holes are. You have to know how to survive in terms of which foods are edible and what kinds of leaves you can chew in order to quench your thirst or clean your teeth.

In relaying these experiences, Yuga points to the racism and colonialism in North America that labeled African ecological practices as primitive. These are African practices that Canadians are now "inventing"—such as organic farming, recycling, and reduced meat consumption. He states:

> Protection from soil erosion, conservation, organic farming, recycling—these are things that are being "discovered" in Canada although we have been doing this in Africa for centuries. North Americans referred to our practices as primitive, speaking of us as peasants, subsistent farmers—all those negative labels. Canadians are now going towards organic foods and "discovering" red meat is high in cholesterol. We never ate meat and North Americans label African diets as having low nutritional value. Also, in Africa you don't use the word recycling, it is just done. Whether you get something from an old car tire and make it into a sandal. If you have too much clothing you give it to somebody, you don't say you are recycling it, you just give it, it is part of sharing.

Yuga encourages immigrants to share their culture and talents in Canada. He believes immigrants should share stories of their relationship to the land in their home country and to show how traditional ways of their home country are useful to Canada. This was also true for other activists. They encouraged their constituent members to voice and celebrate their complexly-aligned identities within environmental arenas.

CHALLENGING CONSTITUENT MEMBERS TO MOVE FORWARD ON ISSUES OF SUSTAINABILITY

Seeing not just strengths but also gaps in constituent-based ecological understandings and actions is another dimension of activists' linking work. In their passion to move their constituency forward on the issue of environmental sustainability, many activists named and confronted weaknesses in their sector. They were often insiders who stirred the pot, speaking up, and challenging the status quo within their constituency. For instance, Rick pressured the labor movement to move from considering environmental issues as a "soft issue" to a place where it is a "major serious issue with labor across the board." He was an upfront, vocal, and often unpopular spokesperson in his advocacy of radical environmental change and was not afraid to be critical of the labor sector's approach to environmental issues. Critical of the Canadian Auto Workers national position on transportation and its National Labour campaign on cancer prevention, Rick wanted the labor movement to embrace a strong policy of pollution prevention. He states:

> I am becoming much more critical of the CAW now than I was before, not local union activists but the national positions on things. One big argument I've had is their position on transportation. I'm not happy with what they're doing because they have not moved as far as they should. I'm also not happy with their big national cancer campaign in the plants. I think there is a lot more than just cancer in the workplace. The analysis should be to get those chemicals out of the plants, on pollution prevention, and putting the companies' noses to the wall forcing them to get rid of a lot of nasty hazardous chemicals they don't need to use any more. Instead of doing that, they have focused very narrowly on one issue, cancer.

Similarly, one activist's feminist analysis and connection to women's organizations are a source of strength that guides her work, but she struggles with the lack of connection to environmental health related illnesses within feminist groups. She states:

> In women's movements they talk about violence and poverty and health in terms of health care and cutbacks to health services. But rarely do they talk about primary prevention of environmentally linked diseases in the context of what they are talking about. In terms of people understanding that the chemicals, the pesticides, the radionuclides, this is part of the bigger picture of health.

The lack of environmental health awareness was an issue Gail struggled with in her First Nations community. In working to inform her community of the hazards of their drinking water (whose source is downstream from polluting chemical plants) she encountered a lot of apathy. Gail attributes this denial to the continued impacts of genocide on First Nations people. Sadly she indicates:

> It is still a genocide process. They have been trying to get rid of us for a long time. Our own people can't see it. A lot of them have been in poverty all their lives and all of a sudden they have these hundred thousand dollar

a year jobs for band councils. The hardest thing is having your work fall on deaf ears, dealing with people who don't seem to give a damn. It's heartbreaking. There are a lot of Native people who don't want to fight anymore. You can't really blame them. Maybe they have been so beaten down. They forget about coming generations. We call it "the faces beneath the earth that aren't born yet."

This theme of remembering one's socio-cultural roots and not getting "lost" in Western values is also raised by Yuga. He encourages new immigrants to not buy into Western materialistic values, stating:

We have brought values from Africa. We don't want our people who have come from traumatized places, who evidently come from the poorest places in the world, to adopt some of these materialistic ideas and tendencies that they find in North America of consuming too much. Particularly when your relatives back home do not have enough. So instead of buying things you don't need, why don't you at least send money and help your people. It is important to keep those kinds of sharing values.

By adopting a critically reflective stance to their constituents' environmental understandings and actions activists advocated for transformation within their own communities.

SUMMARY REFLECTIONS

Seven themes connected to activists' constituency-oriented linking efforts have been explored in this chapter. By looking at environmental change through the needs and perspectives of groups facing present and/or historical forms of social disempowerment, activists shifted and expanded the terrain of environmental discourse and practice. In their constituency-oriented efforts, activists brought forth issues of equity and justice to their environmental agency. They conveyed constituency-based insight and values to the field of environmental politics. They identified creative and effective ways to address environmental problems encountered in communities facing disempowerment. They pushed for more integrative social-ecological solutions.

In working for environmental change through aspects of their social locationality, activists brought valuable strengths and complexities of self into their environmental efforts. As constituency members, these activists have juggled the sorrows and strengths of their communities with their eyes focused on their communities' blended social-ecological empowerment. For activists who were not constituency members, their work as allies gave them an opportunity to express their complexly-aligned identities. This theme of alliance is taken up in the next chapter which explores activist efforts to build relationships and common cause across sectors.

Chapter Eight

Common Cause Linking Activism: Building Alliances between Environmental and Social Justice Sectors

Journal note: I received an e-mail from an activist friend this week. She knew it would brighten my day because it gave me another opportunity to celebrate the alliance building occurring across environmental and social justice movements. The e-mail advertised the following event:

> *Fighting Poverty and Pollution: The 2005 Low-Income Energy Network Conference—A gathering for anti-poverty, affordable housing and environmental advocates to share experiences and develop an action agenda on low-income energy issues. April 7, 2005; Toronto.*

Reading this e-mail also made me think back to the first time I attended a labor union meeting in my early 20s. I went as a representative of my local environmental group looking to forge alliances between our groups to jointly contest the proposed economic Free Trade Agreement. I was hoping we could co-host a community forum on the implications of Free Trade for workers and the environment. I still remember the sense of excitement and awkwardness I felt in planning this event, and in forming this alliance. What I remember most, however, was the lack of responsiveness by the majority of people in my own (environmental) group and in the labor group at that time. The real need or benefit of collaborative social change work was not seemingly apparent, and I remember feeling a bit isolated in taking this risk to reach across sectors.

Over the last 20 years, and over the course of this present study, these kinds of alliance building events are becoming increasingly prevalent in many Canadian communities. Links—between environmental groups and health organizations, poverty groups, anti-racist groups, affordable housing advocates, women's organizations, First Nation communities, organizations for new Canadians, labour unions, local community development groups—are occurring in varied shapes and forms. For myself, part of the excitement in becoming informed of these events has to do with imaging, what I have found to be, the often transformative journey many activists become engaged in when they embark on forms of alliance building and common cause work. In reflecting on the stories of activists in the study I would have to consider common cause building across sectors as the most difficult but potentially rewarding form of linking activist practice.

Stories of building relationships, dialogue, and alliances between environmental and social justice constituencies are another aspect of linking practice revealed in this study. At the center of this work are themes of engaging common cause and collective social change beyond existing sector/movement borders. In reaching through and beyond socially constructed divisions, expressions of unity across diversity and integrative social-ecological change are given priority and power in activist practice. The opportunities to engage complexly and multi-aligned aspects of self and community can be at their greatest within this form of linking work. On the one hand, in listening to activists' stories I could see how this form of linking work can be the ultimate gratification and reflection of their complexly-aligned identities. On the other hand, stepping out of, both the shelters of specialized spheres, and our theoretical, but not yet applied affinities, into connection-building and collaboration across sectors/communities can feel daunting. Here naive visions or ideals of collectivity can be shaken and replaced by the realization of the often arduous work required to create effective and meaningful forms of shared agency and empowerment.

This chapter discusses some of the barriers to embarking on common cause work recounted by activists and identifies some of the disappointments they encountered when doing it. Rewards of common cause building experienced by activists are provided, and some of the incentives supporting this work are outlined. The need for societal transformation to address the root causes of social and ecological problems, expressed by some activists, is described; and the issue of how to configure our alliances to allow both collectivity and autonomy is raised.

CHALLENGES TO BEGINNING THE PROCESS
OF ALLIANCE BUILDING

Numerous barriers impede activists from beginning to build alliances and common cause between environmental and social justice sectors. Some of the barriers to initiating common cause work relayed by activists include: the systemic compartmentalization of issues and sectors; the ignoring of negative social consequences of environmental protection measures; the insecurities of moving beyond familiar spheres; and the lack of relationship history between sectors.

The segmentation between environmental and social justice sectors has many facets. One aspect can be seen in activists' comments that environmental groups repeatedly miss opportunities to work collaboratively with other sectors that seek change on the same issue but from a different entry point. Encouraging the use of public transit without making the link to violence against women is one example of such missed opportunity. Women will often not use public transit at night because they are afraid to walk from the bus stop to their house. Lobbying with women's groups to reform transit policy, so that bus drivers would let women off as close to their homes as possible at night, would be working towards meeting women's need for safety and the need for greater use of public transit. Similarly, linking with social justice groups to jointly advocate free subway and bus tickets for the unemployed, would further support the creation of an equitable public transit system, helping enable unemployed workers in their ability to look for work. Shirley states, for instance:

> Transportation is an issue for everyone, but environmental groups are not looking at how unemployed workers are looking at transportation from a very different perspective where they can't afford subway tokens. Unemployed workers need support in asking the Toronto Transit Corporation (TTC) to provide people out of work with subway tokens to look for jobs. . . . This is what came out of the Unemployed Workers Council. One of their mandates is to get free transportation for people who are unemployed. It takes a lot of linking . . . and environmental groups [do not give energy to these concerns within] their [transportation] recommendations and work.

At the same time, Shirley asserts that getting beyond reactionary approaches so as to work collectively and proactively across sectors is particularly difficult within a system that channels us to respond in compartmentalized manners. She explains:

The fact that things are so compartmentalized has made it very difficult. The way our laws are set up. Where we fight Bill 160 and then we
are fighting Bill 142, but we can't get the two groups fighting these different but related Bills to fight together. I see the structures and the
ways that we are often forced into being reactionary . . . [rather than]
taking a proactive step and saying this is a part of this and a part of this
and a part of this, so when they target this area the circles complete and
you can see that it targets everything. Finding ways to be proactive and
seeing the connections before reacting is important.

When activists do take measures to work collaboratively across constituencies, there can be some personal uneasiness to maneuver. Speaking of
this discomfort and the motivation to work through it, one activist states:

I have come from a place of defining my community pretty much as the
environmental community, the concerned environmental public. I have
done an awful lot of organizing and campaign work through my work
and communication with environmental groups and the networks
within the environmental community. I know and trust and have established friendships through all the organizing I have done within the
environmental community. This sense of place combined with a feeling
of insecurity about branching out beyond this community have contributed to my lack of involvement with social justice sectors . . . [but] I
am motivated to figure out how we can work together. I do feel like it's
taking a risk and that it's going to be difficult. It has to be done very
sensitively because it's new ground and new people. But I feel ready
now whereas over the years I have lacked confidence to do that and to
some degree have lacked the recognition that such links were necessary.

When there is not a history of relationship between sectors, issues connecting spheres are less likely to be addressed collaboratively. This is particularly true if the impact of these issues is not immediate. Kathleen speaks to
the lack of time to build alliances and the challenges of "making links
stick" when there has been a lack of relationship between constituencies.
She states:

I am finding it really hard to keep the links and make them stick. It is
hard to continue those links because there is often not a history of relationship between us and both sectors are so involved in their regular
day to day stuff that it is really hard to expand and work together on
something that is new and integrated across sectors. For example, in
my work I have wanted to show how the development industry has
influenced government decisions in a direction which is harming the
environment and people who are poor. Removing curbs on urban
sprawl, removing rent controls, and affordable housing requirements

have all affected affordable housing and the environment. These changes make it easier to build housing for the middle class because this is where developers can make money. This agenda creates the need for housing activists and environmental activists to work together. But getting the time to work together is very difficult because housing activists are very busy and so am I.

This theme of being fully extended is echoed by one activist who expressed that, "we already all have our hands full." This sense of already being overwhelmed can greatly inhibit the forging of links and alliances. This activist states:

> Activists can only deal with so much at once, which may also explain why we often are not working together across social justice sectors. We already have our hands full. We are immersed in the work we are doing. . . . At the same time I think we can and should build alliances and coalitions because we're all working on much of the same root problems. It is so challenging when we are dealing with issues that are so huge and so complex. You have to make sure you do not bite off more than you can chew. And the effort required. . . . It is just so big that I know that is one of the barriers. It is just so big on top of everything else we do.

The realities of sector segmentation, feeling overwhelmed by the scope of one's current work, and not having a sense of relationship history with another sector are variables which dissuade activists from initiating or responding to forms of alliance building and common cause work.

RELATIONSHIP-BUILDING CHALLENGES

When activists do take up the opportunity to form alliances and common cause across sectors, another set of challenges are often confronted. Receiving token acts of solidarity is one challenge. Being offered verbal gestures of solidarity and support which fail to transpire in practice, or being used to simply further another's cause, are two forms of token solidarity. As a First Nations person, one activist, for instance, speaks to the lack of respect and genuine desire to build relationships with First Nations communities on the part of many environmental groups, particularly many larger environmental groups. The activist goes on to recount that many times, "We have had some initial meetings with big environmental groups and everybody throws around a lot of flowery phrases, yet when the time comes to do the work nobody seems to be ready to do that." Another activist has had similar experiences between southern and northern environmental groups, stating,

"We feel from time to time we are added onto things by southern environmental groups for the optics, not the substance. So that they can say, 'Look! We are so broad and speak for all environmental groups in Ontario.' Or, 'See we are sensitive to northern environmental groups.'" Recalling the "Days of Action" to protest provincial Conservative Government cuts, one activist recounts token acts of solidarity occurring:

> I just had an experience of working on the Days of Action where the relationship did not work between labor groups, community groups, and teachers' organizations. My assessment is that labor groups approached teachers and community groups to work with them, not for the substance of the work, but for the optics. Labor wanted the appearance, the media perspective and portrayal of them working more broadly, but did not want that for the substance. They didn't want their ideas to be broadened or detailed or filled out by the community and teachers' organizations. The result was that the event came off okay but the process was abysmal and the relationship between us is really damaged. It will be quite awhile before the community groups will work with those same players without having some definite insurances built into the process. People felt we were only there for the optics so that made it a very short-term relationship. It left hard feelings.

Becoming allied at more than a symbolic or superficial level can be messy and heated work. This may be another reason why some groups opt for token alliances. Divergences of experience and identity can create tensions obstructing collective action on common interests. Dowie (1996), for instance, contrasts the differences between environmental change rooted within a need for basic personal survival as compared to environmental change initiated through spiritual and recreation values and needs. He states:

> It will not be easy to reconcile the enormous differences, so deeply rooted in class, culture, and history, between environmentalists whose primary interests are wilderness and wildlife, and blue-collar environmentalists struggling for personal survival. Not only are their goals different, at times, but their style, philosophies, and worldview are so divergent, even conflicting, that they can barely communicate (Dowie, 1996, p. 170).

Diversity and differences between environmental groups and social justice organizations can make basic steps to connect difficult. Activists can get caught in mistrust, fear, guilt, and intimidation which can lead to paralysis in one's linking work. This was my sense of one activist who spoke of the desire to connect to First Nations and other minoritized communities. The activist stated:

I mean how do we relate to the Native community?! And that prospect is a little bit different because in a certain way we have to relate with them as a separate government. They are a separate government. On the other hand, they have not gotten their official status yet. Their worldview comes from a very deep spiritual feeling toward the earth which we may read and hear about but I am not convinced we understand. At least I don't . . . it's absolutely wonderful but I cannot say I understand it because I do not. As a white person, how can I?

So what do I have to tell them? I've got nothing to tell them but they have a lot to tell me. What right or arrogance can I possibly have to say I have something to tell them. So how do I relate to them or work with them? What skills do I have that I can give to them? The answer is that I think most environmentalists say, "Here we are. If you want to talk or chat or coordinate with us ask. We will do it." And then with other communities, like immigrant communities, how do you approach them? I do not know. I think we have to talk to them. A lot of the work that has to be done is very time consuming and slow and treading on territory we don't usually go into but I think this work is absolutely essential!

Another activist also spoke candidly of limitations in working through anger, mistrust, and stereotypes experienced between environmental and anti-poverty groups. The challenges this activist experienced led to moving away from linking work with anti-poverty groups. The activist shares:

Some of where my melancholy and anger comes from when we talk about social justice and working with other disenfranchised groups is that a part of me feels a sense of defeat. I feel weak. It feels like a short-coming in myself that I struggle with but have sort of come to terms with. I admit I cannot be all things to all people. I wish I was stronger and could go in there and struggle with anti-poverty groups and continue to go to their meetings and take their shit, their anger at me because they see me simply as some privileged white environmentalist, but I don't have it in me. I have a limited amount of energy. I am a sensitive person and susceptible to being dragged down. And that isn't ultimately the most populous format. I know that.

One of my real appreciations in hearing activists' stories was their ability to speak honestly of tensions and ambivalence they encountered in their attempts to build forms of alliance and common cause with (social justice) sectors. Many activists dealt with powerful emotions (both positive and painful/negative) related to their linking work. What was particularly interesting and valuable was the way in which activists were often capable of delving into complex emotional inner landscapes whereby their mixed emotions could blend, interest, and shape each other rather than be separated

into binary isolated places within themselves. The relationship between
activists' ability to navigate their complexly-aligned emotions/ inner landscapes and their capacity to stay complexly-aligned in their outer contexts
of activist work would seem central to meaningfully sustaining one's linking work.

BENEFITS OF COMMON CAUSE WORK

Challenging experiences can provide real rewards. While many activists
expressed the challenges of relationship and common cause work, many
also described the rewards. In fact, the taste of many activists' passion, per-
sistence, and depth of satisfaction in maneuvering across sector borders
could not be missed. Rick's unwavering passion for grassroots common
cause building (between local communities, labor, social justice, and environmental communities) shone across his interview with a bold tenacity.
Craig's sense of satisfaction in supporting a Chilean group in their struggle
against a Canadian company (proposing to build a natural gas pipeline
through their nature preserve) portrays the value of solidarity and alliance
work. Dorothy spoke of her networking (on health, environment, and
social justice) with women across geographical borders (national, international) with a tone of gratification and fulfillment. And like many activists
interviewed, Brennain situates her activism within the larger "fabric" of
social change which is, as she states, "tugging at the same cloth" (the global
patriarchal corporate agenda), affirming that she does not feel alone, but
experiences herself as part of a larger broad-based community of common
cause agency. Below are five examples of activists expressing the rewards of
relationship building and common cause work. In this first instance we see
the sense of personal empowerment Kathleen gained from a joint protest
between environmental and housing activists. It was an experience of comradery and common knowing across borders which surprised and inspired
Kathleen. Jointly protesting the provincial cuts that reduced affordable
housing and weakened green planning in Ontario, Kathleen shares:

> We held a funeral on the lawn of Queen's Park [to protest] the death of
> affordable housing and green planning. We came together, a whole
> bunch of housing activists and environmental groups. We signed on to
> a statement we wrote and then we held a mock funeral. We had a piper,
> tombstones, and so forth.
>   It was very rewarding to make contact with activists in a com-
> pletely different field and talk to them. I felt like I was talking to myself
> only doing another issue. It was wonderful! I experienced immediate
> connection with people. They knew the details of the issue they're

working on—affordable housing, that I don't know, and vice versa, but you immediately connect with people like that because we're so similar in terms of our outlook and our motivation. We both immediately understood each others' need to act and create strategies to work together without knowing the details of each others' issues. We just understood.

In a second example, Brennain describes a coalition that formed organically between environmental and First Nations organizations during a government hearing on timber management. Humbly but proudly she expresses the success of this interaction. Moreover, in effectively integrating the issues of these two sectors, and in developing a positive working relationship, an ongoing connection was formed (part of which involved being watchdogs on behalf of First Nations issues). Brennain recounts:

> In an environmental assessment of timber management we evolved into a coalition of environmental and First Nations organizations. We were northeastern Ontario-based groups and we were about 50/50 Native and environmental groups working in that timber hearing. The hearing was an environmental assessment to set timber management—meaning forest planning, policy and guidelines, rules and regulations, and so on. When we began we were mostly environmental groups working with one First Nations group. That then broadened so that we were working with two tribal councils and one treaty organization. It was a successful relationship which still lives on to this day. We managed to integrate Native concerns which was a living testimony to the ability we have to integrate environmental and First Nations concerns. First Nations concerns are sometimes environmental, but often economic. We developed policies and strategies in our approach to the minister of Natural Resources over several years that addressed these concerns.

Evolving into playing the role of watchdog, Brennain shares:

> As a result of this we were then able to play watchdog on how the provincial government consistently or inconsistently dealt with First Nations issues in a number of environmental assessments. What we have found is that the government will throw around the Aboriginal Rights language into the conversation when they are dealing with First Nations people and they will leave it out otherwise. So by having an alliance and relationship we are able to keep check on what agencies like Ontario Hydro and the Ministry of Natural Resources and so on, what level of consistency they had there and to call them on it.

Giving us more background to this successful coalition work, and the underlying principles that supported the effectiveness of this linking relationship,

Brennain speaks to the value of allowing relationships to start organically. She also speaks to the importance of fostering authentic relationships. She explains:

> The relationship with First Nations was an ongoing one and it developed somewhat organically. Having worked with one of the First Nations before on uranium issues, this person came into the discussion of the timber hearing and decided they would like to participate and then it went from that First Nations individual through their community, to the Tribal Council to the Union of Ontario Indians. And so it developed organically. And we just went ahead and did it. We didn't exploit it as an opportunity for media. We didn't put pressure on the relationship in that way. It was just an ongoing working relationship where we tried to understand and integrate and respect the common and the different interests of the two sets of communities. I think that allowed it to succeed. I think it is important in working with other communities, whether First Nations or labor groups, seniors organizations or poverty groups. If you consider us to be organized in constituencies and if you want to work with other constituencies, I think it is important that you do that for the substance of the work and not the optics of the work.

Helen's ability to embrace the work of dialogue across difference and seek areas of common ground provides a third example of activists' positive engagement with common cause work. In societal contexts where we are conditioned to avoid conflict, Helen's story illuminates the value of seeking dialogue and connection amidst adversity. When an outside environmental group received funding to conduct a project in her community on sustainable forestry and community economic viability, a project Helen supported, local suspicion and mistrust of the project was expressed by some community members. Helen shares what happened:

> There was a rumor that the township council was very upset about the project. So I called up a local reeve and asked him if this were true. And he said, "You bet we are!" And I asked him more about why. And he stayed on the phone for a hour and one half telling me why, in no uncertain terms, and laying out their strategy to deal with us. I really appreciated his honesty and willingness on a Sunday night to tell me what he thought of us and why. Part of the reason I got involved in this project is because I live here and the people are important to me and I am very fond of a lot of them. But, we have huge differences politically most of us. . . . Two local township councils went to one of the funders of our project and tried to get our funding taken away. There was a lively dialogue between some of the local councilors and some of us. We had meetings with the local council and ended up having a public

meeting that was well attended to express and deal with concerns over the project.

Indicating that their environmental and economic problems are often not in conflict, Helen speaks to the value of dialogue across difference, stating:

> I think it was a good example of dialogue across differences. Of talking about the ecological problems and the economic problems and how they have to be integrated, and talked through, and battled out if they are in conflict, but often we found they are *not* in conflict. But, if we can't talk about that stuff then it is not going to be good environmentally *or* economically. A lot of the local people felt we were trying to pull the wool over their eyes [i.e., caring about the trees but not the people]. There was a lot of mistrust and suspicion that we had to deal with.

Initiating the idea to collectively write an article on the events of the public meetings, Helen recounts her satisfaction in this collaborative effort between people who are usually on opposing sides. She continues:

> My treat after all this controversy and dialogue was when I spoke to one of the councilors about jointly writing up an article on the public meeting and what was discussed. I drafted it, the councilor vetted it and made some changes and then took it to another person from the other township, and the three of us signed the article that was put in the local newspaper. I just thought this was perfect! Writing this article together when previously we had written articles to the local newspaper on opposite sides of the issue.

Helen affirms that working across difference is a necessary reality of living in a small rural community. Unless "you are going to be a total hermit," she says, you have to work to find common ground with people. Helen welcomes living in a context that challenges her to embody a multi-aligned identity. Here she shares:

> I like living in a small rural community because you are really faced with this stuff on a daily basis. You have to work with people you disagree with. You have to talk and find common ground with people that are very different from yourself. In the city you can kind of wrap yourself in a cocoon where you are only talking to people who have a similar outlook on politics or on what is important. Here you cannot do that, unless you are going to be a total hermit. You are right in the midst of things. And I love it. It grounds me. It makes it real. If I can't talk to my neighbors about these things and learn from them and hopefully have them learn or think about something differently because of me, then why I am a communicator, writer, and environmentalist at all?

So this is where you really get down to brass tacks and say, "Is any of this workable or worthwhile?" And I do not mean that succeeding or failing on a given issue locally gives you the answer of whether you are doing okay or not. It just keeps things real. I love the challenge and the rewards and the warmth of finding the common ground with people that you really disagree with. In the city there would also be the differences of race. Here, except for the Native issue, which is the racial issue here, almost everyone is Caucasian, the difference between my worldview and theirs is in most cases quite large, and yet I am delighted when I find something we agree on.

For example, I wrote to the local papers about how provincial and federal downloading is hurting our local municipality in the tone of "How can they possibly be expected to cope with this downloading?" Our local politicians, most of whom I am in disagreement with on 90 percent of what they talk about, saw it as a gesture of solidarity and they tell me "I liked your letter." These are my political opponents! I like that. It means we can't write each other off. It means I know I have to listen if they are worried about an environmental proposal, and they may listen to me about what I think is important.

Brennain affirms this reality of the need to deal with difference. Within the context of her northern community she states:

One of the advantages of living in smaller communities is that there is no anonymity. You are accountable for everything you do and say and you have to work with a diversity of people unless you are going to work by yourself. . . . In fighting Toronto garbage we work with a man who is anti-Native and so forth. The meetings are very interesting because another woman works on Native solidarity issues. So these two people are sitting at the same table and we just sort of move along. This man will say something anti-Native and we tell him to talk about that when he is by himself and we will just carry on the meeting. You try to look for something in common and try to work based on that.

In a fourth example, Jack also depicts the intensity and rewards of relationship and alliance building between environmental and labor sectors. In this account his attempt to voice common ground with labor issues backfires. Instead of achieving solidarity, Jack faces the anger and mistrust of a labor representative. He recounts:

The job issue comes up a lot in toxics. It comes up all over the place. I was on a panel with policy makers about what to do about the phasing out of toxic chemicals. On the panel there was a very strong labor contingent, a very strong environmental contingent and very strong government and industry contingent. It was a very long day of discussions and I think, if successful, could further the policy of phase-outs. Towards the end of the day we were asked for summaries of why we should go ahead with a policy for the phase-out of persistent toxic chemicals and I gave three reasons.

The first two reasons were ecologically based. The third one, I stated, was because they used the chemicals in the plant and therefore worker protection was one of the reasons. Well, upon saying that, the labor representative got out of his chair and screamed, and I do not mean talked loudly, I mean screamed, at the arrogance of environmentalists to speak on behalf of labor. He made accusations of deceit and dishonesty indicating that in fact that is not what environmentalists say and said not to use labor as an excuse to further our own agenda.

Choosing to confront rather than avoid the real work of common cause building, Jack began a process of long-term dialogue with labor to resolve the tensions and miscommunications. Discovering the gaps in his own understanding of the issues, Jack shares:

After this event we began a dialogue around that contentious issue. It took a year and a half to resolve and it wasn't with the same players. We invited more labor people that knew about the issues and environmentalists. We brought in some grassroots labor groups and some big policy labor people. We found out the issue of most concern to workers was not that environmentalists were saying phase out chemicals. What they were ticked off at was the lack of accommodation to have workers at the decision-making table in deciding which chemicals would be phased out. They were also not clear about what mechanisms there would be for phase-out and were concerned that workers would be displaced unfairly. If they were displaced they wanted a fair accommodation plan over the long run.

In the end, a consensual alliance was found. He continues:

The conflict was reconciled at a very concrete level whereby we could agree that the environment has to be protected, that these chemicals should not be used, generated, or released but the process of identifying those chemicals, the process of phasing them out, the process of who decides, and the process of social considerations are first and foremost included in this whole process. And as environmentalists we never objected to that. I think if I could have been yelled at, I think I would have felt better if he yelled at me for not having thought through the role of the worker, rather than saying you used labor as an excuse. Because he is quite right. I had not thought through the role of the worker at that time.

Following these joint dialogues, Jack portrays how differently the labor-environmental dynamics played out as compared to a year and a half earlier. Describing another important forum where both labor and environmental contingents were present, he indicates:

> At another much bigger forum, a year and one half later, the two agendas (of environmentalists and the labor sector) were presented differently but coherently and consistently. We both used each other's language to further a certain goal. We [labor and environmentalists] each had implicit consent from the other to use the language we did. I could say worker safety and they could say environmental protection.

In a fifth example, Serren, too, shares the gratification of working to find areas of common ground. Initiating dialogue between her conservation organization and a rural forestry community, she felt the rewards of treading new territory. She states:

> One of the really exciting things that happened in the community we did the outreach in was that, before, whenever we worked in an area it would be with a small group of people very specifically thinking about environmental issues. But by the end of this project we had found common ground with a whole number of people who are in the forest industry. Not that we agreed on everything, but they were able to talk to us and we were able to talk to them and we were both able to see problems in the forest that we are concerned about. And we were able to see the connections between these problems and the future of the communities. Also in terms of eco-tourism stuff. [Before the project] we had never worked with any small tourist operators. People who are just sort of like "mom and pop" operations in the area. We've never really seen any common ground but as the project developed connections were made. We ended up pulling together eco-tourism workshops and we could really see where we came together.

As the previous examples have shown, numerous ingredients facilitated activists' common cause work, including, for instance, allowing connections between sectors to form organically as Brennain demonstrated; confronting rather than avoiding conflict as Helen and Jack did; living in contexts, such as small communities, which necessitate dialogue and collaboration across difference; possessing genuine interest in connecting across borders; and experiencing the rewards of comradery and of common interests, values, and approaches. The next section looks at three additional factors that fostered common cause linking work.

TURNING CHALLENGES INTO OPPORTUNITIES TO WORK COLLECTIVELY

Lack of resources, the increasing power of economic globalization, and the need to remain viable as environmental groups/movements were three challenges activists used as opportunities to express their multi-aligned identities through common cause efforts.

Resource constraints faced across social justice and environmental sectors can encourage sector boundary crossing. Dwayne states, for instance, that "The problem with us [First Nations groups] and with user groups [environmental groups] is that nobody has very much in the way of resources, so this prompts us to work together." Where organizational pressures distract activists from working across sectors, resource constraints can be the "gift" moving constituencies to cross borders.

Economic globalization comprised a second reason for activists to cross sector boundaries. In such a political-economic climate, areas of common ground between environmental and social justice sectors are increasingly apparent. The increasing expansion of corporate economic globalization, and its reflection in neo-liberal and neo-conservative governments in Ontario and Canada in general, have brought activists to link across sectors. Increasingly in touch with the similarity of problems faced between environmental and social justice communities, many activists acknowledged the need to jointly tackle these political and economic systems perceived as the source of their disenfranchisement. As Carol powerfully shares:

> The only good thing about this government in Ontario right now is the glimmer of hope that people are organizing and building alliances like we've never seen. I'm so motivated to do that because it just seems so essential. And it is empowering too. . . . Making these connections feels urgent now because of the onslaught of change from this Tory government and the globalization imperative that is happening and the impact this is having on the environmental and social issues.

The joining of groups across sectors (e.g., environmental, labor, poverty, housing, women's groups) to protest Conservative government cuts, in what became termed the Ontario "Days of Action," is an example of common cause collective resistance. Numerous activists interviewed participated in these Days of Action. Within this context, Shirley states, for instance, "All these groups getting together against this government has made us learn about each other and realize how much we have in common or at least expanded our view." With the slashing of both social and environmental spending and programs, many activists recognized their common interest in resisting these government actions and the corporate economic ideology they saw as underpinning these cuts. For instance, the similarity of environmental and health cuts was experienced firsthand by Kathleen. Comparing her own presentation with that of another presenter speaking from the health sector, she sees the echoing of disenfranchisement, stating:

> At a conference a presenter from the health sector put up an overhead summarizing his presentation. His summary on health care cuts was a summary of my presentation on environmental deregulation word for word! I then used his overhead for my presentation, and did not tell the audience. At the end of the presentation, I told the audience that this was not my overhead but was the overhead from the health care presentation clearly illustrating that the same approach is being applied across sectors, the same approach to eliminate public rights to information and protection, to cut government out of all kinds of public interest areas, and to privatize. You can summarize your own presentation by using a summary of what is happening in other sectors.

Witnessing these rollbacks brought home the lesson of being "too insular" and awakened in many activists the importance of building broader constituencies of resistance. Referring to the toppling of proposed provincial land use planning legislation, Kathleen asks herself whether the Ontario government could have toppled this legislation as easily if they (Ontario environmental groups) had created a broader constituency of support across social sectors instead of solely relying on the current network of environmental groups. Learning the lesson she describes as being "too insular," she states:

> What we achieved with the land use work, by four years of intense effort, I mean absolutely phenomenal effort by many people in the environmental movement across the province, was amazing and then we lost it all. It was devastating. It was a massive effort and yet it was wiped out so quickly. I'm still struggling with how what we did could have been so fragile and easily wiped out? We started from scratch organizing groups but we stayed insular. We did not have a relationship with other sectors mobilizing for reform. The lesson I take from this is that we were too insular. We were only working with ourselves (other environmentalists and environmental groups). We needed, and now what's needed even more urgently, is to build the broader coalition, the broader alliance of the *whole* movement—the social justice movement and placing the environment movement into that broader movement.

Ferris and Hahn-Baker (1995) affirm the importance of environmentalists working in collaborative partnerships with social justice-based groups/sectors if the viability of the environmental movement is to be maintained. They state:

> In partnership with environmental justice advocates, environmentalists can build upon the resources, strategies, and tactics in order to propel the environmental movement to the forefront of this nation's agenda. With mutual interests in environmental protection, advocates can work together for changes in both government and private sectors. . . . Because environmental justice activists target unequal control of pollution. . . . unfair employment, unequal access to jobs and jobs training, and inadequate housing and education opportunities, this struggle for environmental parity for all races is inextricably linked to an aggressive overall social justice agenda (p. 67).

Tonya also affirms this need to reach beyond one's sector. She argues that in socially tight times the environmental movement needs to be connected to social issues in order to show their relevancy and stay viable. Tonya states:

> As the enthusiasm of the late 80s and early 90s about the environmental movement dies off, those true blue environmentalists are looking to make the links in order to maintain the relevance of the issues in the public mind and in their work. . . . As individuals and groups we are needing to rationalize our work in the environmental movement. We are needing to do this in the face of a recession. We need to look at how are we viable given that people are being evicted from their homes. We need to be connecting with social justice issues and their organizations. . . . I think this linking work is one of the most important things happening to the movement.

In such a social climate, it may well be, as Faber (1998b) argues, that the very people who are being most exploited socially and environmentally, have the moral voice to put forward environmental change in a manner that white, middle-class sectors of the environmental movement cannot relay. Jack raises this very issue, stating:

> In the mid-1980s there was a view that the environmental groups were the vision of the future. . . . And I am not convinced it is environmental groups that are the agents of change in the future. The most dramatic and powerful presentation at a large environmental congress were made by labor groups because they made the links to economic and other social concerns. I suspect that if there were three press conferences to announce the problem with an Ontario river—one from Greenpeace, one from the Canadian Environmental Law Association,

and one from a Housing Co-op Group, my guess is that the latter one would get the most publicity . . . the most weight of power and influence. . . . I suggest the reason is the way they frame the argument. They have our children playing in the river not the children. . . . There is a backlash against environmental groups. Industry says to environmental groups you are just a bunch of people who are paid to say whatever you want. Environmental groups are deemed to be a special interest group. I suspect that the housing co-op would not be deemed a special interest and would receive more weight.

THE NEED FOR SOCIETAL TRANSFORMATION

Common cause work is, moreover, not just an expression of uniting around shared challenges, but also an expression of striving for more broadly defined visions of social transformation and change, of which ecological protection is but one component. For many activists efforts to build relationships and alliances are connected to more broadly defined hopes and visions. For some, this vision entails forging a radical grassroots movement that is local, provincial, national, and international in scope. It is a conceptualization of a movement of movements working together for socially just and ecologically sustainable communities. Moreover, as a movement it reflects the transformation of such hegemonic forces as global corporate capitalism, colonialism, and patriarchy—forces observed to be at the root of social and ecological injustice. Rick worked to engage such transformation. He spoke of his work running "a network that sends out communications to both social justice activists and environmental activists" in support of a critique of the global agenda and a call for social transformation. Lobbying for the creation of a collective grassroots resistance that empowers communities, workers and protects the environment, Rick states:

> I am part of a group working towards steering a larger social movement rather than just singling out individual corporations for problems. Steering a movement . . . with the overall analysis that the capitalist corporate system has to make necessary changes or as some of us would say, "has to go." . . . If we are going to get serious about environmental and social economic changes we have to look at the root cause of the problem. It's the corporate sector, the NAFTA,[1] the general agreement of tariffs and trade, the World Trade Organization and MAI.[2] . . . I advocate effective, fundamental social change steered by the common cause building across communities and sectors.

Struggling against the corporate paradigm of "community as commodity" in the hope of an alternative vision, a vision of citizen-empowered, just, and sustainable communities, Michelle passionately relays:

We need to embrace the aboriginal philosophy and practice of always considering the next seven generations. We need to embrace decentralized decision-making which focuses on maximum participation. We need to create prototypes for production with longevity in mind, not just build in obsolescence and short-term profitability. We need to educate our children with the values of caring for and sharing the earth's resources with everyone, not merely here in North America or amongst the privileged middle class. We need a fundamental paradigm away from commodification and towards meaningful interpersonal and social relationships which embrace our hearts, our souls, our physical beings as well as our heads. As environmentalists and social change agents we must break our addiction to control and forge a new democratic paradigm which promotes principles and practices of sustainability on all levels. It is of crucial importance that we are coming together as citizens, groups, communities, and countries to form movements to further this crucial and needed paradigm shift towards social justice and ecological sustainability.

Tonya highlights her desire to work together towards implementing aspects of her vision and not just become single-mindedly immersed in "fighting what the right wing has been doing." She states:

So many times on the left, we fight, we fight, we fight. We don't know what this vision is. For me this vision is much more about sustainability. Sustainable life styles, environmental sustainability, but also social sustainability in how we work with one another. So much of our energy has been going into fighting what the right wing has been doing. I want to be part of the creation of a new vision. That new vision is about community, about people cooperating and working together and about building an economic model for projects that we want to see happen.

Tonya's statement underscores the value of finding the means and method to start giving shape to collective vision for social justice and environmental sustainability.

FINDING THE APPROPRIATE FORM OF ALLIANCE

Assessing the specific form and level of collective resistance or vision-building is another aspect of reflection within common cause work. When is common cause work appropriate? What is meaningful and appropriate connection within a specific context—coalition work, establishing networks, alliances, solidarity? How much connection and consensus between organizations, sectors, and movements is effective? Which kinds of autonomy, boundaries, and differentiation of social action between groups/movements are important to maintain, and which are not? Several activists

spoke to these issues. For instance, Tonya relayed the importance of prag-
matics in determining whether linking work will be engaged. She states:

> Everybody believes in building the links in theory. I have so many oppor-
> tunities to build partnerships in my current work that I can tell you right
> now when a partnership isn't going to work or where there is an oppor-
> tunity for it to work. So much is based on pragmatism. If there isn't a
> reason for people to work together, if there isn't some mutual benefit, it
> just isn't a priority. I don't think any of us have the luxury of extra time
> to make something happen just because it would be nice. It doesn't mean
> partnerships don't happen. They do, but only where there is a reason or
> need of mutual self-interest or a common goal.

In deciding whether to grant a labor union's request for membership in
their environmental organization, one activist describes her organization
being faced with having to reflect on their organizational identity. They had
to ask themselves what kind of relationship and connection do they want
with other sectors? Sorting through these issues of identity and alliance
took months of emotional discernment and consideration. In the end, her
organization found a creative solution and became clearer on who they are
as an organization. She relays:

> I have been on the board of an environmental group for the past three
> years and have really enjoyed it. I am not the only one on the board
> making the links to race and gender issues. There is a lot of openness to
> one of us noticing something along these lines, and there is a lot of gen-
> erosity and solidarity. We don't always agree but we have really good
> discussions. No one says to someone else, "No, no, no don't be silly."
> We have dealt with some pretty tricky organizational political issues.
> Making the links with labor has been one of these areas. It has taken a
> fair bit of skillful maneuvering through various minefields.
>   One such minefield involved a large and fairly powerful group
> which wanted official linkages with our organization. This raised far-
> reaching questions around identity—for example, exactly what *is* an
> "environmental" group, anyway? Do they have to be "primarily" con-
> cerned with the environment? And around alliance-building, for exam-
> ple, if we alienate these folks, what repercussions will that have for our
> organization and for the movement as a whole? How can we maintain
> openness and dialogue with others, without risking the trust that is
> essential in our close-knit structure? Honoring difference is important,
> but what about when differences weaken our ability to remain clear
> and united around our core agenda as an organization?

She goes on to state:

So this request from the labor union presented quite a challenge. We spent a lot of time to work it out. There were widely differing opinions and strong feelings within our own organizations on what we should do, and things got pretty emotional. We took the time we needed. We met, consulted, communicated and discussed. After several months, some intuitive insights and inklings of a possible solution began to emerge. We were determined to talk until we agreed, at least on something all our members could live with. Any solution that made anyone feel like quitting the organization would not *be* a solution.

Their decision was to offer the union subscriber status but not membership status. This decision welcomed dialogue and collaboration but did not deny the philosophical differences between their organization and this particular union on environmental matters. This decision supported linking and connection, while at the same time did not pretend the level of connection and alliance was more that it was. The activist goes on to state:

So eventually we got one. In the process, we got a lot clearer ourselves on who we were and what our organization was for. We also learned the importance of alliances that respect solidarity with each other. Nor do our groups all have to have big overlapping memberships. In fact, we can sometimes be stronger and more effective by honoring our respective boundaries and then cooperating across them.

Embodying complexly-aligned identities means fostering healthy relationships. Healthy relationships allow for connection, autonomy, difference, and provide vehicles to enable exchange and collaboration in ways appropriate to each context. Irene's experience has led her to focus her common cause efforts more within the structure of networks than coalitions. For her, this former approach supports working together, but within a form that allows autonomy of movements. She explains:

I see a certain necessity to a sectoral approach to movements. When I first got involved in the disarmament area I had a vision of uniting the disarmament groups in the greater Toronto area. I got involved in the Toronto disarmament network. I was pretty naive politically at the time and thought well, there is nothing really that can stop this. It will be an incredible movement if we can just line up behind the same agenda. We could do amazing things. I spent a good chunk of time and energy trying to do that and came out learning that it does not matter what movement you are in, there are political splits and different approaches and it is very hard to unite people under one banner. I have come to recognize that it is probably important to just allow the different approaches to proceed. The important thing is to make sure there is at least some kind of linkages. So for me it is really important to define the difference between a coalition and a network. Coalition work involves signing on big time and agreeing on everything. Networking allows all the parts to be autonomous, which is what all the parts struggle to do in a coalition. Which is why coalition work is such a challenge. I see a need for coalitions but they don't last long. I think they are important for particular issues at a particular time but I don't see much purpose in reviving coalitions or keeping them going when what they really need to do is die off. This is why I have been involved in networks, because I think networks are really key to collective work and coalitions come and go as they are needed.

Morag also supports maintaining the integrity of movements, which enables a dynamic of working separately, but also together, when issues truly intersect. And within this context, she underscores the value of conflict and disagreement. She states:

> I have worked with a lot of different movements, some of which are social justice movements, like the human rights movement, and the environmental movement. Sometimes the issues intercept, not always. I think it is very important to maintain the integrity of the movement that you are working in by taking on board, when it is right and just to do so, the concerns of other movements and other organizations. But in actual fact, I don't necessarily think that homogeneity across a range of movements is a good thing. What you want, what you are struggling for and against becomes diluted with everything else. Working on different areas, there is a kind of dynamic that actually helps move the agenda along in a much more concrete, successful way than if we were all saying, "Well, this is an issue that impacts on this, this, and this, and if we work it all out with a consensus we'll come to some kind of reasonable understanding." In actual fact, that's not always the best thing. The best thing is to sometimes just slug it out and try to make the best of what you have by arguing through it. Dissent is not always a bad thing. I think there is political correctness out there that makes us think we should be afraid of that.

Brecher, Costello, and Smith (2000) argue "that people can indeed exercise power over globalization, but only by means of a solidarity that crosses the boundaries of nations, identities, and narrow interests" (p. x). To do this, these authors advocate a network structure. Specifically, they argue for "a coordinated social movement composed of relatively autonomous groups" that takes on a "network structure" which focuses on co-ordination, autonomy, and freedom as opposed to conformity (p. 86). Such conceptualization seems congruent with Irene's and Morag's views. In outlining the advantages and disadvantages of networks, Brecher, Costello, and Smith (2000) further argue, "networks require a high level of personal responsibility compared to conventional organizations" (p. 87). This enhancement of needed personal responsibility affirms the premise of this research that activists need to be in touch with their multi-aligned selves and not restrict their agency to organizationally defined identities.

In working to build alliances (whether with First Nations groups, workers, forestry communities, or housing activists) activists are engaged in a more integrative activist practice. In expressing their complexly-aligned identities by crossing segmented spaces, activists also stretch mainstream notions and practices of environmental advocacy prevalent in many environmental organizations. The significance given to "quiet activism" is one such example. Specifically, the skills of trust, empathy, respect, listening, and authenticity can be overlooked or under-valued within mainstream notions of activism. According to Si, these crucial behind-the-scenes relationship-building skills are hard to quantify. Explaining these different faces of activism, Si articulates:

> You have to build trust and empathy. Now, after being very actively involved for 10 years with the multicultural community, very actively, and 17 years of being really active in the women's center, I still do not have trust all the time. I always have to re-establish my trust and credibility. I have to make clear to them that I am on their side to an extent. That I am looking for win-win situations. So it takes a long time. . . . It comes back to what is your definition of activism. Some people think activism is only coming to the microphone and screaming at a protest, "No Justice, No Peace!" I like and do this kind of traditional male definition of activism. But activism is also developing the empathy and trust with the different sectors and this activism is less visible. . . . But someone who goes around and does a more quiet shifting and moving and developing of empathy is passed by. How do you quantify empathy? The other kind of activism you can say 872 people voted for Buzz Hargrove but no one can say 222 pounds of empathy have been cultivated by Si this year. Si has reached a critical mass empathy content. It is more diffuse.

Clearly, common cause work involves this kind of quiet activism to which Si refers. Kathleen affirms this view in her reflections that working across sectors takes courage and personal maturity. She shares:

> When I work on an issue I reach out to new people all the time in the environmental movement. But reaching out to social justice organizations involves a different kind of reaching out. It is about saying, "Here

is what I do. I don't understand the details of what you do, but I think we need to know more about what we do and examine whether we should be working together on some things." There will be direct conflicts to deal with in terms of potential economic or job costs of environmental objectives to address. There is the fear of being rejected and having one's work and concerns potentially trivialized or told it is not important, or less important than their concerns. It takes personal courage and maturity to do this kind of work with new sectors.

SUMMARY REFLECTIONS

The work of relationship and common cause building with social justice sectors reveals another aspect of linking practice. Here activists engaged in environmental protection by placing their efforts and concerns within larger social-political spheres. Most significantly, social and environmental cuts by the Ontario provincial government since 1995 demonstrated to activists the common roots of their struggle, and the need to act collectively in response to these measures. Program and ministry cuts, and deregulation measures, were not restricted to the environmental sector but hit the health, social program (e.g., women's organizations, social assistance programs), labor, and housing sectors as well. Moreover, most activists saw what was happening at a provincial level as a clear reflection of global economic trends which have framed social and ecological protections as barriers to free (borderless) trade, economic prosperity, and corporate control. These affronts have been bittersweet incentives illustrating the importance of common cause linking practices.

As discussed, not all activists required these external political forces to motivate their common cause work. Their community contexts acted as an inherent motivator to work across sectors. Activists located in smaller and/or rural communities pointed to the lack of anonymity in their communities and therefore the increased sense of accountability for one's words and actions. They spoke of the need to dialogue and work across differences to resolve environmental issues obviously connected to job and community economy issues. They cited the practical reality of needing each other as allies to mobilize effective social-ecological change for their communities. These aspects of noticeable community interdependence and interconnectedness expressed by rural and/or northern-based activists, supported them in engaging linking practice and in working from multi-aligned identities. And yet, as pragmatic as this form of linking practice can be perceived to be, given the realities or variables of specific contexts, many activists' accounts, such as Helen's, reveal that their linking practice is about more than effective environmental strategy. Many activists acted with courage and innovation to forge dialogue and alliances across terrains stemming from their sense of connection with other sectors. They were genuinely committed to finding more integrative social-ecological solutions. Activists' common cause work demonstrates the challenges and risks of building new alliances while simultaneously highlighting the rich personal and political rewards that can accrue from such efforts.

At the time of these interviews, the majority of activists appeared to be in the initial processes of this kind of cross-sector alliance, which stems in part from the timing or readiness of their environmental organizations to support such work, work which can be time and resource intensive without guaranteeing efficient, concrete, or positive organizational outcomes. While speaking of the importance of this work, Si remarked on its often seeming invisibility, astutely remarking, "How do you quantify cultivated empathy?" As a form of activist practice, linking work is grounded in this kind of cross-terrain relationship-building activity.

As activists bring their multi-aligned identities into their environmental work, and as outer pressures reveal the need for collaboration to effect social change, linking work and the skills it highlights (trust building, dialogue, empathy, respect, listening, dealing with difference) will become more valued and necessary within environmental change contexts. Consistent with Brecher, Costello, and Smith's (2000) view, the balance between autonomy and collaboration will continue to become an increasingly important theme for activists and their organizations.

Part Three
Linking Activism—Capacities, Approaches and Skills

Chapter Nine

The Journey: Bearing Witness, Questioning, Reflecting Critically and Holistically, and Demythologizing

Journal note: In portraying activists' linking work, I repeatedly found myself feeling such respect for what I saw as their capacity to bear witness. I also noticed that I kept coming back to this quality in activists' narratives for grounding and guidance. Like them, I too was engaged in the task of bearing witness–namely, to activist accounts. It was an endeavor that seemed to demand all of me, pulling me in varied directions at the same time, stretching and testing me in ways beyond traditional notions of "data analyzer" or "researcher." I was shocked at how deeply personal it felt to bear witness to their stories and realized that I was not just given openings to the activists' worlds but also to my own.

In reflecting on the meaning of bearing witness, an excerpt by Carol Lee Flinders seemed applicable. She states, "It has to do with slowing down enough to see what's before your eyes. As soon as people start taking time, the essential sacredness of life presses in on us. It's part of our society's diabolical plan that our time has been taken away from us, and so we only see the crazy fracturedness of things. A consumer culture needs people to be off balance, hungry, and frightened so they'll buy stuff. If we want it to be different, we can make that so." In slowing down to think about my own experience of bearing witness the following words and phrases came to mind—seeing holistically; seeing with an openness of heart, mind, soul; being attentive and receptive to self and surroundings; seeing inwardly and outwardly; looking with more than "routine" or "day to day" eyes; taking in what lies hidden or remains ignored; being embodied.

Reviewing my reflections I became aware of how much I treasured being with people or in contexts where I felt the freedom to bear witness and to share these experiences. I thought of environments which restricted my ability to bear witness. I reflected on situations which welcomed me to share some portions of what I witnessed while ignoring others. In this regard I realized my experience of activist movements was a messy one—there were areas of welcomed freedom and areas of experienced restriction.

While activist movements and social change discourses can support us to use and develop our abilities as change-makers, they can nevertheless impede us from becoming agents of integrative change. In adopting critical discourses which separate aspects of our social locationality (e.g., race, gender, class, sexual orientation) and contexts (e.g., housing, health, environment), activist movements perpetuate fragmented visions of self, agency, and social change. Activists can become oriented to view change from one particular lens, leaving complexities and issues, such as social-ecological links, behind.

In listening to their accounts I asked myself, how were activists able to push beyond the conceptual borders and boundaries of activist movements (e.g., environmental, feminist, anti-racist) to strive for more holistic change? What capacities, skills and/or approaches supported activists to link rather than fragment? How were activists able to be empowered by particular critical discourses (e.g., feminist, anti-racist) while remaining continually open to more inclusive, complex, and holistic understandings and responses to environmental challenges?

In partial response to these questions I can say that I witnessed activists become empowered in their linking efforts through their ability to embrace social change journeys that are rich in *bearing witness, questioning, reflecting critically and holistically and demythologizing.* As capacities/approaches/skills, these four qualities were constant intersecting themes across activist accounts. This chapter explores these intersecting themes through an exploration of activist narratives and asserts the importance of these themes in furthering integrative social change.

BEARING WITNESS TO THE COMPLEXITIES OF CONTEXTS

Without taking in the complexities of contexts, linking practice would remain pedestrian. This is because linking activism is nurtured by activists' capacity to attend to the webs of life around them. As a state of deeply attentive awareness, bearing witness opens activists to see the intricacies of the contexts around them. This is not an easy task.

There are numerous reasons why activists involved in environmental change may avoid bearing witness to social justice connections. As a form of holistic presence, bearing witness can require a level of attention and energy which activists do not feel ready to engage. Activists, for instance, may feel too focused in one area to expand their lens of attentiveness. Additionally problematic is the fact that dominant Western culture sanctions an ideology of detached rationality which serves to discourage the embodied presence (e.g., attentiveness of mind, emotion, spirit, body) of bearing witness.

Deeply attending to intersecting forms of oppression, moreover, is emotionally challenging. Witnessing people living in poverty in unsafe, polluted environments; seeing workers under pressure to pollute their bodies and their communities to earn a wage; watching economically vulnerable communities being paid to "house" the toxic waste of wealthier communities are hard realities to face.

Activists may also avoid bearing witness because they would experience discomfort in seeing the privilege they possess in relation to these linked injustices. As Karen states:

> I think there are a number of environmentalists that just work at the environmental level and don't take their analysis down to another level. A good example are those that are more conservationists, in that realm of conserving space. For them to truly integrate social justice into what they are doing would require them to totally reevaluate their own personal life and how they fit into the society and the community. Not everybody is prepared to do that. Some people do it at different stages of their lives and some never do it.

As Karen adds "In bringing social justice-environmental links down to a personal level you can face a lot of contradictions in your own life."

Bearing witness to intersecting oppressions highlights the complexity and scope of needed social change. In feeling overwhelmed by the need for societal transformation, activists may not feel prepared to take on the depth of personal, organizational or community change surrounding their environmental work. Si outlines the ramifications of bearing witness to social-ecological linkages within her own mining community, stating:

> If we stand up now and say we see what is going on here and we want change, there would be a lot of ramifications. If we want the mining company to take a fucking hike or pay more taxes so that money can be reinvested in the community in a truly sustainable re-greening there are going to be impacts. We might have to accept that this community would have to shrink because maybe this land base wasn't meant to

naturally sustain a population of 170,000, particularly at the level of four bedroom homes and eight strip malls. Then you would have to ask what would happen to all those people? That would be painful. There would be a re-shifting of our whole lifestyle to what is more sustainable. It may mean we would not be able to afford certain kinds of foods and have to grow vegetables locally. People would then become conscious of our soil and the fact we can't grow good potatoes because of the high acid content from the acid rain which is caused by the pollution from the super stack. So maybe we will have to stop the superstack so that we can grow good potatoes. Once you open up your consciousness one thing leads to another and another. It can be easier to stay with the blindness and distortion because the change needed is so vast.

Across a number of narratives I was taken aback by activists' capacity to witness the complex social-ecological challenges facing their community. How could they stand witnessing the multi-layered tensions that resided in their communities? How were they able to view their complex surroundings from an aliveness of emotion, intellect, spirit and body? Over time, why did they not become bitter or opt to intellectually categorize and simplify these situations to make them less gut-wrenching? Was it their capacity for bearing witness that allowed them, moreover, to recount these oppressive entanglements with such balanced threads of vulnerability and strength?

Cecilia's narrative reveals her ability to bear witness of the complexities of her context. Growing up in northern Ontario from a young age, Cecilia has remained attentive to the intersecting environmental, health, and jobs realities in her community, and to the impact of these realities on her own and others' lives around her. Witnessing these intersecting issues has meant being openhearted to many painful, difficult realities. She has witnessed children playing alongside the chemical pollutants of an aluminum plant which harm their lungs and other parts of their bodies. In one year, she witnessed eight workers who died in their thirties of lung cancer leaving their young children and partners behind.

Holding the web of complexities in her community, Cecilia bears witness to the sparse employment options that exist outside of their industry employer. She remains in touch with the high level of community fear, resistance, and anxiety to speak about the short and long-term human and ecological health impacts from their exposure to persistent industrial pollutants. Moreover, seeing the web of connections, her eyes are sensitized to the repeated avoidance and playing down of environmental health threats by industrial owners and shareholders. Making broader links, Cecilia sees the connection between the needed resolution of her community's social-ecological problems and the power imbalances between northern and southern Ontario which leave northern communities disempowered.

For Cecilia, bearing witness has meant accepting the truth that their community problems are complex ones. She believes that seemingly quick, simple, or easy solutions to their human and ecological health risks, such as simply closing the plant, are not realistic options. Both economically and socially, people's lives are deeply entwined in their community's industrial complex, making the task of addressing its ecological and social impacts sensitive and daunting. One excerpt demonstrating Cecilia's attentiveness to the complexity of issues in her community includes:

> I grew up in a community where you see such hardworking people die. These people do not have any less love or hope than anyone else. They do not have less to live for than anyone else. They have a lot to live for. Sometimes it feels overwhelming. It is hard to separate the issues when they are so integrated in your life. There are so many things that people do day to day. A lot of the issues are interconnected. They affect people in the community and it is hard to know where to start. It is hard to speak out against the company for instance. I do not think that you directly do that. . . . You do not want to appear anti-industry because you will just turn people off right away. There are some communities up north where mine tailings have affected the water system so much that the people cannot drink their own water. In that case people are actively speaking out. Whereas, here there are air pollutants and you can't actually say they have caused these respiratory problems because you can't see it and we are still being told we are smoking too much. . . . I think that the cause of our social and environmental problems are the same. I relate the problems in my community to issues of social justice. I believe the reason they can pollute and harm our health is because we are poor people. We do not have the power or the money to say, "No!" And that is why it hurts. It hurts us and the environment and I see it as a social justice issue first and then as an environmental issue.

Bearing the tension between these polarities and complexities of context takes courage and stamina. Continually attending to the relationships and dynamics between the varied dimensions of her community, Cecilia forges a holistic stance to understanding and responding to these challenges. It would certainly be easier for Cecilia to adopt a simplistic stance which sides either for jobs or for human and ecological health. In honoring and acting from this web of intersecting realities, Cecilia embraces her multi-aligned identity, and like many activists, she enters a lengthy process of question posing.

THE COURAGE TO QUESTION

When making connections across different terrains there is a lot of gathering and integrating to be done. The need to engage this work is certainly evident within our Western cultural context which habitually segments issues and sectors. Such compartmentalization means activists have many questions to ask in working to bridge social justice-ecological divisions. As Dorothy states, "It means asking questions all the time!" Activists got in touch with the complexities of their contexts and identities by embracing a continual journey of question asking. Across their accounts it was clear that questions acted like bridges to social justice-ecological relationships. Serving as a kind of daily "footwear," questions aided activists in crossing new terrain, sorting through complexities, unearthing gaps and missing links, and challenging assumptions. The constant process of questioning allowed them to ponder the social implications of environmental actions and to discern power dynamics. Activists explored how issues are framed, questioned how links cross local and global contexts, and explored alternatives which would address both areas of concern. Activists used questions to engage dialogue across sectors and were constantly posing questions which were not being asked.

What was apparent in activist accounts was their utilization of an array of different types of questions—critical questions, divergent questions, convergent questions, open questions, factual questions, evaluative questions, hypothetical questions, strategic questions, rhetorical questions, provocative and irreverent questions, questions of clarification and probing. In drawing from the richness of this questioning landscape, activists were better able to make the terrains of connections explicit. Invariably, activists acted as linking messengers through their advancing of questions.

Asking Questions Not Being Asked

Often activists posed questions which were not being vocalized or given priority by governments, organizations, the media, or their community. Activists asked questions such as, What will this environmental position mean for First Nations people? Why did they fly these big test bombers above our northern community? Why are environmental organizations not hiring people of color? Why do southern industries want to dump up by our beautiful northern lakes? How can environmentalists and labor unionists agree to publicly voice one another's interests? What causes pancreatic cancer in a 43-year-old woman? How can we envision sustainable forests and sustainable communities? Who is controlling this situation and in whose interests?

Shirley demonstrates this courage and skill of asking questions. Her questions examine issues of power and equity. Questioning the events of the toxic PVC fire in an Ontario community, Shirley asks, "Who controls the situation?" and "Who gets a say and who doesn't?" She goes on to say, "An incredible thing was when the community had their public meeting after the fire there were 16 police officers with billy clubs in the hallway. Such police presence questions whether democracy is taking place. Does everyone deserve environmental protection or just some? Does everyone have this right?" Looking at the research funded by officials following the crisis, Shirley argues that the wrong questions were being asked. She voices:

> Who gets to decide? Who gets access? Who gets to describe the problem and frame it and take it up as an issue? Who has the power to co-opt people's self-described problems? Who gets to frame the studies? The community residents who suffered the fire want their own study. They do not want another psychosocial study. They have been studied to death but not provided with the studies they want. These studies have not been asking the questions they want answers to. Instead, now, after the fire, a risk assessment study was funded which assesses risks rather than looking at community members' health and their actual lived experiences.

This mirrors what Di Chiro (1998) found in her interviews with women leaders within the U.S. environmental justice movement. These activists "argued that standard environmental health protocols ask the wrong questions or are not directed toward investigations that would provide relevant information to communities" (p. 125).[1]

Kathleen, too, was frustrated and disturbed to find crucial environmental health questions unexamined by medical research. Describing her soul-wrenching experience of watching her sister die of cancer, she found the lack of environmental health questions being asked weighed heavily on her. She saw her sister's death as a "suspicious homicide," a term coined by author Sandra Steingraber to refer to the countless premature deaths which cannot be explained by genetic or personal lifestyle factors. Kathleen shares:

> I heard about Meg's inoperable (and therefore terminal) cancer the night before I had to fly to Brazil. At only 43 years old, she was dying of a rare cancer that is on the increase in industrialized countries. I spent three months in semi-shock as the situation got steadily worse. Initial fleeting hopes quickly gave way to utter hopelessness and despair for Meg, as well as for everyone around her. Pain gave way to worse pain, pain like torture, more and more morphine, and ultimately for

Meg the soul pain of waiting to die, wanting to die, being afraid to die and grieving so much loss.

[During this time] I was reading a crucially important book called, *Living Downstream: An Ecologist Looks at Cancer and the Environment,* by Sandra Steingraber. She asks questions that I asked Meg's doctors. What causes pancreatic cancer in a 43-year-old woman? The oncologist did not know. Maybe genetic, maybe environmental factors. Nobody knows and I was assured that lots of research is occurring. Sandra asks about the gathering of basic data. So did I. Since these are diseases with long latency periods, do doctors collect information about occupational history, environmental history, any other information about chemical exposure? No. Is basic data collected to input to epidemiological studies and to perhaps find out cause and effect across a population? Not done. Do they analyze the affected tissues or other organs or tissues for chemical contamination? No. Maybe in teaching hospitals. There is no money for research.

Kathleen continues:

A few days after my discussion with the doctors, Meg's GP offered the information that in her shared practice with another physician she has five cases of pancreatic cancer. This is an incredibly rare cancer and typically only affects older men who are overweight and drink too much. It appears Meg is part of a cluster. The doctor also agreed that the basic data collection that I was suggesting would be possible and could be centrally coordinated using e-mail and/or internet.

Looking at the bigger picture, Kathleen relays:

So many people are affected by cancer . . . and we are not addressing the central question of whether our environmental contamination is the cause. . . . We are increasingly aware that environmental factors are involved, and yet there is entrenched power that refuses to accept such hypotheses or accept the findings when they do exist. . . . I agree with Sandra Steingraber's analysis that these deaths are suspicious homicides and should be treated as such, with great interest in gathering data to determine the cause of the disease. . . . And while, unlike other environmental justice issues, the increase in cancer in industrial countries is not always occurring along class lines, statistics from the U.S. definitely show a higher incidence of breast cancer in black women (and therefore often low income women) and there are probably lots of other examples as well.

The medical research focus on genetic and lifestyle factors to the exclusion of environmentally related contributors to or causes of illness is echoed by Novotny (1998) who states, "In particular, community activists have been critical of the tendency of traditional epidemiology to account for patterns of health problems in terms of lifestyle rather than community exposure to environmental hazards" (p. 142). With the prevalence of this kind of traditional epidemiological approach, Kathleen, similar to other activists, questions the basic assumptions and tenets of traditional scientific research. In their concern for social justice-ecologically blended problems, activists are discovering that many societal question-protocols bury these connections through their individualistic, specialized, and contextually narrow approach to social problems.

Being a messenger of questions is invaluable. Asking questions not being asked gives others the impetus and courage to ask their questions. Just as Sandra Steingraber's questions strengthened Kathleen's questioning voice, so did Kathleen's inquisitiveness give her sister's doctor incentive to pose these questions to other doctors. As initiators and innovators within their contexts, activists often began these kinds of question rippling effects pushing social justice-ecological linkages to greater attention and reflection.

Fear of Asking Questions and Superficial Linking Messages

Activists may refrain from asking questions which explore social justice-ecological links. They may be hesitant to ask because they expect, and feel others also expect, that they *should already know the answers*. Here, asking questions is not perceived as a skill of intelligence and caring so much as it is a means of revealing one's ignorance. Brennain speaks to this issue insightfully and candidly. She perceives a real hesitation on the part of many environmental activists to verbalize questions which explore social justice linkages. She states:

> People have to learn to ask questions. If someone has an instinctive feeling there is a link to a poverty issue in the environmental issue they are working on, because someone made a half remark to them that left them wondering, then they need to have the confidence to ask questions and to say to someone else, "I wonder if there is a link here and what do you think?" That is where we get stuck in the worst way! Somehow, we have an expectation that we should already know and if we should already know, then surely we are not going to go ask someone and reveal that we do not know. We need to get over that! Some people have complete comfort in asking questions but I think that many people do not.

Without the courage to ask questions activists become *superficial or token messengers* of social justice-ecological linkages. Their linking messages remain shallow and contrived because this question-asking process is essential to gaining meaningful understanding of these (social justice-ecological) relationships. Witnessing these superficial linking messages within environmental groups, Brennain goes on to state:

> A lot of time I see environmental groups trying to deal with First Nations so they say "And this proposal will not interfere with any land claim." This is their way of trying to acknowledge or grapple with the broad issue of First Nations people and their rights and needs. But what they need to do is first ask questions before they give answers. What will this mean for First Nations people? What do I need to think about in this? Once they do this they can figure out how to deal with the issue instead of giving a standard response like "All land claims should be settled promptly." Most First Nations issues in Ontario are not about land claims. They are mostly about land rights, economic and political rights, and rights to self-government and self-determination.

As elucidated, while activists may possess a general picture of specific social justice-ecological connections, they may lack more substantive knowledge necessary for a meaningful and informed response. Questions help activists move from general awareness of linkages to a more detailed knowledge of these relationships. Brennain makes this transition concrete with this example stating:

> We need to be able to ask questions. When we are thinking about making a proposal that cuts dioxin emissions by X percent, we need to say to labor, "Gee, how do you think this could work?" Rather than coming out with a pat phrase that says, "And there will be transitional funding and retraining." Well, maybe they do not want 700 workers being retrained as data entry operators. Maybe they want a way to figure out a different industrial process. The workers themselves would have a better idea about this, but we are not always so good at asking the questions.

Asking "Who will this Affect?"

Asking "Who will this affect?" moves environmental advocacy to the terrain of linking effort. In posing this question activists acknowledge their connection to the larger community and recognize that social contexts are embedded in inequities of power and control. One activist gives us an opening to explore this issue further. She argues that, compared to northern groups, southern groups are not having to ask the question "Who will this affect?." Describing her perceptions, using the example of an anti-MAI[2] campaign, she recounts:

> The energy in southern Ontario feels much more unbridled [than the north]. It is like you can do what you want and know there will be support. . . . It is easy to get people involved. You can say MAI in the south and many groups will get involved. In the south we do not care who we are going to run over in our campaign. We are just going to do it and the energy is there to do it.

In contrast, she articulates, a northern approach looks quite different. It is a grassroots approach of consultation, of acknowledged impacts, and of knowing the issues are connected. Asking, "Who does this affect?" acknowledges that one's goals exist within the broader scope of one's community's realities and needs. The activist goes on to explain:

> An anti-MAI campaign in the north would be different. If you say MAI in northern Ontario it is much more difficult. There are industries that will say to their employees, "This will hurt you because you will not have any jobs without MAI." To do an anti-MAI campaign in the north you would have to take a lot of other things into consideration before you went ahead. You would be asking, "Who does this affect?" There are these very preliminary questions that go through your mind. . . . Like who should we call about this to get their opinion? How do we get people involved if they want to be involved? How does this affect our community? . . . It makes sense to call people, like neighbors and friends to consult on what you should do. It is common sense because the issues and the complexities are in your face . . . and that is how you have to address issues. This approach . . . comes from people's ground up, direct experience with the issues.

From such a perspective, as this activist relates, change-efforts are naturally more process and time intensive. While more work, this activist contends this northern approach "is a good one." She asserts:

> The process is quite a bit longer but I think it is a good one. In the south when this type of approach is not followed we are leaving a lot of people out that will be affected. It is very easy to just run with a campaign if you don't know the people that are affected. It is easy to do that and it is hard to ask those questions. Southern environmental groups would need to ask northern groups, for instance, how do you feel about us coming into your community and blockading this road? Because the community has a vested interest they should be the first ones southern groups consult.

While the question, "Who does this affect?" promotes a linking perspective, certain contexts push the necessity of this inquiry more than others. As discussed earlier, small, rural, isolated, and/or single-industry dependent communities can conceptualize the process of consulting affected sectors as a basic social expectation. The interdependence, lack of anonymity, and need to work collectively to bring about community change would contribute to such a question-asking approach within these contexts. Environmental groups in large urban centers can more readily work in isolation and dislocation from the consequences of their advocacy work because they lack this closeness and interconnection of community fabric. How one's context fosters sensitivity or insensitivity to the question, "Who will be affected?" is something activists interested in equitable environmental change need to be aware of.

Question-Asking as an Effective Communication Approach

As linking work steers activists further into the complexities of issues, and into wider contact with other community sectors, the value of a question-asking approach becomes more accentuated. A messenger style of question-asking is valuable to linking work because it explores rather than assumes. Crossing terrain and building relationships from an answer-giving approach is often not the best way to foster connections across sectors. As discussed in previous chapters, many social change contexts are politically loaded environments where differences in privilege, discourse and approach create communication challenges across sectors. A question-posing messenger style can be advantageous in navigating across these terrains. In her environmental work with social justice sectors, Kathleen highlighted this question-posing attitude. She explains:

> I have come to realize that if you want to move forward on an issue you have to recognize your own strengths and limitations. You need to know what you can bring to an issue and also know what you don't. In order to address your limitations you need to be able to ask questions to those who have strengths in the areas that you don't. In my work with social justice sectors I do not go in there arrogantly telling them, "This is the problem or this is the answer." . . . I share with them what I see and know. I test out my ideas rather than coming from a closed and arrogant position of purporting to have all the answers to these concerns that jointly affect us.

As Kathleen alludes, in working towards more integrative change there needs to be an acknowledgement that often we (individually and collectively) are at a question-raising as opposed to answer-giving stage of linking work.

Knowing Who to Ask

Another linking challenge that Dorothy related is knowing *who* to pose your linking questions to. When concerns bridge specializations, disciplines, and sectors, it is not always obvious who is the best person to pose one's questions to. As Dorothy explains:

> Very often we're asking the right questions but to the wrong people. What [this] means is that you can't be at a health conference where the Minister of Health is talking about health without having the Minister of the Environment there to ask questions about what is causing our health to deteriorate. By the same token you can't have an environmental conference and have the Minister of the Environment do a fancy presentation without having the Minister of the Health there. You cannot segregate them. They have to be integrated. We might be asking lots of good questions but we may not be getting them to the right people.

It is also important to note that in some cases there may not be an existing body (i.e., institution) designated to answer our linking questions. For instance, there is no organization/governing body which specifically focuses on issues of environmental racism in Canada. As social justice-ecological linkages are taken seriously, new complexly-aligned organizations need to be formed to address these issues in a concerted way.

Being able to ask the *right questions* to the *right people* comes with forethought, time, and experience. Knowing the most effective questions to ask can be difficult. While asking questions off the top of our head begins to articulate our initial linking quandaries, it also takes skill to ask the questions which will lead to more integrative understandings of problems and their solutions.

CHALLENGING DIS-CONNECTION THROUGH CRITICAL-HOLISTIC REFLECTION AND DEMYTHOLOGIZING

Activists' approaches to questioning were intimately tied to their capacities to be critically and holistically reflective. In connecting social justice and environmental change, they realized the constant need to demythologize[3] and be critically reflective of many dominant assumptions, principles, and practices. For instance, within capitalist ideology the externalization (i.e., separation) of environmental and social costs within economic measures is accepted. There is a dominant narrative that asserts that economic globalization is inevitable. Assumptions exist that minoritized new immigrants do not care about environmental issues. There are fatalist attitudes that to earn a living means to accept health risks and impacts. There are suppositions that government-defined safety standards for pollution are safe. Presumptions are held that forms of violence (against people, animals, and nature) are distinct as opposed to intertwined.

Activists were engaged in contesting ideologies and practices of disconnection. They understood that issues and sectors cannot be ultimately separated because they exist in relation to one another. Their accounts reveal ways they challenged norms/values/approaches which construct forms of disconnection such as individualism, specialization, hierarchy, decontextualization, objectification, compartmentalization, competition and consumerism. Underpinning these critiques is the understanding that "[k]nowledge should be seen as tentative, provisional, open to critical scrutiny, modification and challenge, and needing to be shaped to meet different contexts and cultural situations" (Reid & O'Donoghue, 2001, p.8).

In explicitly acknowledging that understandings of environmental problems are socially and politically constructed (and should therefore be open to scrutiny), activists kept a critical perspective of the structures and processes of power at the forefront of their environmental analyses. Moreover, in situating their capacities of critical reflection within a holistic frame of reference, activists were able to develop incisive and timely linking analyses. Such a combined critical-holistic lens is central to the conceptualization of linking activism because of its power to simultaneously engage the need for integrative and socially just perspectives. For instance, activists challenged the lack of integrative analyses and attention to socially and ecologically viable solutions. Here, activists like Cecilia, Brennain, and Serren challenged "zero-sum" (i.e., win-lose) narratives of "either-or" choices, such as pitting economic strength against environmental health and protection. Instead they voiced calls for integrative solutions which are ecologically and economically compatible. Activists, moreover, challenged master narratives of the global economic imperative which exasperates social and ecological injustices. Attitudes that if your community does not want its waste it can simply pay another community to take it was also a dominant discourse challenged by many activists in their linking efforts. This section further examines the critically reflective and demythologizing approaches taken by activists within their linking work.

Telling Alternative Narratives: Challenging "Neat and Tidy" Narratives

Si's community economic development narrative (discussed previously) which made visible the issues of sexism, racism, and anthropocentrism (which were ignored by mainstream accounts) is one example of an alternative narrative.

Naming social-ecological costs that are denied or ignored is one form of critical inquiry and demythologizing work. Irene, similarly, engaged in this type of critical narrative re-storying. She contested myths propagated by politicians of the long-term economic viability, safety, and "tidiness" of nuclear energy facilities. These establishment-based narratives, Irene argues, have given communities with nuclear facilities a false sense of safety and environmental health, and a misperception of the long-term economic stability provided by these industries. She describes this mythology:

> When I started my nuclear awareness work in Durham region 10 to 15 years ago people were living under the assumptions that the nuclear plants will run for an indefinite future. Residents were under the impression that the nuclear waste will be shipped off somewhere because that is what they were told, and that eventually the plant can be demolished and carted off to some place and they will have a park where the nuclear plant was. The mythology around this is extensive in Durham region. Politicians have been living in this grand illusion which is an obscene way to lead a community. Politicians buy into this script becoming close-minded and short sighted and then residents buy into this and pretty soon it is a myth in the community. When in reality it is a known fact that nuclear plants run for 40 years and then shut down. The materials and the structures degrade because of the radiation fields, high pressures, high temperatures and wear and tear these facilities take.

Irene and her organization have worked hard to disrupt this narrative and to voice the likely reality of the situation. Irene vocalizes that these nuclear plants are not likely to be neatly packaged up and sent away. She asserts that their communities will likely be permanent nuclear fuel waste storage sites. She recounts:

> What we have been doing over the last ten years is to make it clear to the community, that in fact, it could become a permanent nuclear waste site. It could never really escape being the location where there is nuclear fuel waste stored. The demolition rubble from the reactors could be stored there indefinitely and guarded indefinitely. Through that kind of input into the community psyche we are hoping to burst this bubble in the community that says "Aren't they wonderful. They are going to clean it all up, vacuum it and put sod down!"
>
> The irony is that in the community they are building the water-front trail around the facility. So they are building this beautiful water-front trail and walkers have to deke around the back fence of both nuclear properties. There is something absurd about having a very beautiful waterfront trail and having to circumvent these two big nuclear facilities.

The common notion that it's okay to send what you don't want somewhere else is another narrative layer Irene contested. As already mentioned, dealing with one's waste by shipping it to another community, which promotes an out of sight, out of mind mentality, fosters inequitable "solutions" to environmental problems. Irene worked hard to show the ramifications of such myth-like attitudes, as was discussed in Chapter Six.

Challenging Lifestyle Narratives

Lifestyle narratives of health problems are also problematic for linking activists. These prevalent narratives place responsibility on individuals for their health problems while ignoring environmental factors, such as pollution, that cause illness. Shirley, Dorothy, and Cecilia challenged the pervasiveness of these consumer behavior-based messages. Shirley referred to Health Canada's targeting of First Nations people for their so-called over-consumption of fish (due to mercury poisoning risk) while failing to target the industrial polluters responsible (for dumping the mercury in the water in the first place). Calling such community outreach "propaganda," Shirley recounts:

> A recent Health Canada report reveals incredible statistics for mercury levels which could border on poisoning. In their message they only make the link to First Nations diet and lifestyle. But mercury does not come from wildlife. It comes from the industrial development of white persons. If there is a wish for clarity, it is very clearly industrial development. Looking at how it is framed in those ways and continues to be framed even when the source of the mercury is clear, the source of cancer is clear . . . is unbelievable . . . and we are still doing that.

In a similar vein, Shirley also recalls how breast cancer education fails to mention industrial development as a source of contaminants which are being linked to breast cancer. She continues:

> With the information around breast cancer the message is to watch your diet. They do not say watch for carcinogens in your diet because of industrial development. Or cut down on the use of industrial induced consumption or toxic chemicals. What they do is tell you to cut down on fat in your diet, have a regular mammogram. It is terrifying that they put all the emphasis on personal behavior and this is 1998 cancer research propaganda! They are not taking a larger societal view which looks at the larger consumptive and productive lives of people and addresses preventative measures. Many of the cancer awareness weeks, such as, breast cancer awareness month, are funded by Imperial Chemical Industries or Honda.

Cecilia challenges the discourse in her community that asserts that lung cancer is caused from smoking and not from the "black smoke that comes out of the industrial smoke stack behind your house." She states:

> I remember in our town they said that we have a high rate of lung cancer and respiratory problems. This is something that already happens a lot in southern Ontario, but in northern Ontario they say it is because we smoke so much. It is not because of the black smoke that comes out of the industrial smoke stack behind your house. People want to believe them. They want to believe that there is something that they can change about it personally rather than addressing the fact that their workplace is affecting their health. Their job is how they make their money and help their family survive. What option do they have?!

Lifestyle and other forms of "neat and tidy" narratives act like smoke-screens hiding harmful industrial practices and the larger political-economic structures which give license to such negative forms of ecological and human impact. Naming and contesting such dominant narratives relays an important aspect of activists' demythologizing work.

Claiming Multi-aligned Identities

Demythologizing the notion that individuals and communities do not deserve to claim the multiple dimensions that support wellness comprised another facet of linking work. There are attitudes, for instance, that people's lives are predominately economic rather than also centrally socially and geographically rooted; thereby, polluting industries can simply be shut down because workers can easily leave their families/communities and be "retrained" in other professions. Similar to other activists, Cecilia asserts the importance of claiming the value of our complexly-aligned identities (as individuals, families and communities). Within her own community she echoes Irene's sentiment of wanting to demythologize the simple solution sales pitch which slices and dices a community's well-being. She states:

> I really see the struggle between environment and social justice and jobs. It is so complex it is not easy to simply pinpoint the problem. Saying this is the problem and this is how we solve it. . . . It is a difficulty because the companies really come in and they try to buy communities. They say this is what we can offer you if our company moves here. The perfect example is the Nuclear Fuel-Waste Disposal concept. They are looking at northern communities to bury this radioactive waste. They are very good at selling this. They are willing to say we will pay you this amount of money to bury this waste on your land. It is not going to do anything to your community. It probably will provide a lot of jobs.

They know that is a problem in northern Ontario. They play all the right cards. Then the community 20 years down the road is suffering. They see it in health effects, in their children, in their overall quality of life.

I do not know exactly the place where we say this is where we have to attack the problem. Sometimes I just think that people need to know that they are worthy of these things, that they deserve all of these things and they do not have to compromise. But it is hard because there is a struggle to live every day, to make a living.

Utilizing Different Measures of Evidence

In order to challenge dominant tenets so that linking narratives can be fostered, activists need to conduct and advocate for new research. Many of these research endeavors involve gathering information, data, and experiences previously not examined together. This is what Serren and her forest conservation organization needed to do in order to foster dialogue and common interests with forested communities in Ontario. Forestry job losses were being blamed on forest protection measures, fuelling tensions between environmentalists and forestry workers/communities. Serren and her organization felt this message was untrue, but no research had been conducted to assess Ontario's situation. Taking on this investigative challenge Serren recounts:

> There's been a lot of talk about how protected areas in Ontario are responsible for the job losses in the forest industry. You can point to research in other provinces which challenges this notion, but when you do, other people say "You can't compare or apply there to here!" And to an extent this is true. There are many factors that are different between provinces. It is important to be able to have the facts which say, "This is what's going on here where we live." But no one had done the research in Ontario until we did. It was fairly clear from the investigation we did that this is not the case. Job losses are the result of technological change, rationalization in the forest industry and the declining wood supply because of the over-cutting that's been going on. We were able to document this from the research we did.

This finding mirrored research focusing on other Canadian and American locations. Foster (1998) states, for instance, that "[o]f all these factors affecting Northwest timber employment, automation has been the most important" (p. 203).

Lack of research on social justice-ecological links is a problem in Canada. Part of this challenge stems from the fact that moving from anecdotal reports to make empirically-based assertions at provincial or national levels is difficult. There is a lack of Canadian-based research that demonstrates, for example, that the economically disenfranchised face greater pollution levels. Kathleen gives us a sense of this Canadian problem, explaining:

> People working at the South Riverdale Community Centre in Toronto do not need to wait for any data. They know poor and minority persons are disproportionately affected by environmental problems. In the United States there are studies which show that, yes, most people who are poor live really close to dumps, to hazardous waste sites. In Canada, there are certain situations where we know that may be the case, particularly, in First Nations communities. For our organization to make these kinds of assertions at national or provincial levels we need research that shows that low income people are disproportionately affected by pollutant releases. For the most part, however, we do not have much empirical data. In fact, little data has even been collected that could be analyzed. For instance, we do not even measure lead levels in children living in old homes, especially children in poor families who do not have the money to upkeep the paint.

Kathleen went on to discuss a feasibility study, acknowledging that her environmental organization is at the initial stage of confronting such challenges. She indicates:

> Our organization is starting to get there. It is definitely a priority and we have made recommendations over the years about the need for such research but resources have been a problem. But we are finally at the stage of starting on a feasibility study looking at the national pollutant release inventory and socioeconomic information and being able to do some analysis of this information. So we are at the beginning of that, as you call, linking story. Over the next few years we will see the results of that analysis. And more than that, I should say that we are still in the stages of needing to figure out how to collect information to be able to get at some of these issues and questions. I mean, will traditional data collection approaches even get at the issues we are wanting to look at?

As Kathleen intimates, getting the facts on social justice-ecological relationships can be contentious, difficult work. Defining new measures of evidence is a second area of concern.

As intimated in Chapter Four, many activists disputed accepted definitions, boundaries, and validity attached to notions of "evidence," "fact," "standards of proof," "risk assessment." Current measurements and empirical instruments are repeatedly ill-suited to understand environmental health issues. Health impacts from environmental pollutants are often not immediate but found over the span of years or decades. Moreover, these health outcomes may be the result of a number of synergistically combined environmental contaminants, as well as being connected to additional non-environmentally related factors, such as genetic influences. Such multi-faceted complexities of etiology do not fit methodological approaches which look for one-to-one causal relationships, a research design which describes conventional medical research practice.

Additional factors impeding the visibility of connections between environmental well-being and human health also include: 1) the paucity of funding devoted to tackling the complexities of environmental health research; and 2) the continued emphasis on quantitative as opposed to qualitative measures of health. Commenting on these issues, Michelle implores:

> This kind of research is not being funded. Not only that, research focuses on quantitative measures of environmental and human health. It focuses on measuring the number of trees left in a forest as opposed to looking at the quality of forest diversity that remains. Similarly, health research looks at human health through measures such as age expectancy, which finds that people are living longer but does not look at the quality of life a person leads, such as whether they are surviving on numerous medications or are active and content with their physical, social, and emotional state of well-being.

Activists like Michelle, Dorothy, Shirley, Kathleen, and Nita worked to demythologize what Novotny (1998) calls "traditional epidemiology and conventional approaches to community health [which] frequently obscure the connection of physiological and sociological factors to the incidence of health disorders" (p. 141). Novotny explains:

> The work of traditional epidemiology and conventional conceptions of public health for the most part ignore what the Labor/Community Strategy Center refers to as the "unspoken categories" of class. Epidemiological research often *avoids disproportionate risks in workplace exposure* by low-income and working-class persons of color, particularly for working women. Much of the research in classic epidemiology, moreover, is limited to general or aggregate reviews of the incidence of health disorders and *ignores the disparate concentration of health and physiological disorders in particular localities.* Much of the existing health research in epidemiology, according to community activists, has been compromised since environmental hazards are studied under "normal" conditions that *do not take into account the factors that affect these chemicals when they are released or disposed of.* Where factories are densely clustered together in particular neighbourhoods,

local residents may have to contend with literally dozens of different chemicals [emphasis added] (1998, p. 141).

Contesting traditional epidemiology's specialized focus, its "overly cautious" approach to study results, and inability to address variables of race or class, Novotny (1998) continues:

> Popular epidemiology *challenges the decontextualized individualism of classic epidemiology* by focusing attention on the connections between workplaces and communities where the health and well-being of people are endangered. Popular epidemiology is therefore interested in the connections between environmental, occupational, and residential health disorders that might not otherwise be evident in traditional epidemiology. Too often, a tendency towards *specialization results in researchers only studying one aspect* of these health disorders in relative isolation from other factors. . . . Much of the work of traditional epidemiology also *tends to be overly cautious and tentative in its findings*. Through a focus on methodological factors, this research often places many qualifications on its findings rather than coming to conclusions about the health effects. Further, in traditional epidemiology and approaches to public health, according to Nancy Krieger and Mary Bassett, "existing analytic techniques *cannot address phenomena like class relations or racial oppression* which cannot be expressed as numbers" [emphasis added] (p. 143).

In exposing the assumptions and limitations of traditional epidemiology, linking activists, similar to activists in the U.S. environmental justice movement, were messengers of what has been termed "popular epidemiology." Novotny (1998) succinctly describes popular epidemiology as:

> an empowering approach to health that places squarely in the foreground the knowledge that community residents, labor unionists and others have of the health and environmental problems resident to their communities and workplaces. The work of popular epidemiology is largely based on the assumption that broad-based political organizing is fundamental to solving the health problems of the workplace, community, and environment (p. 140).

Such analysis and action described in popular epidemiology is congruent with linking activist practice. Activists interviewed saw environmental problems within the complexity of their contexts and advocated a preventative and precautionary approach to research findings which would allow concrete and proactive steps to be taken. Moreover, many activists interviewed, like Dorothy, Kathleen, and Nita, brought adversely affected citizens together to discuss their environmental problems, and to strategize effective personal and political solutions.

SUMMARY REFLECTIONS

This chapter explored ways activists embarked on journeys of bearing witness, questioning, critical-holistic reflection and demythologizing. These intersecting themes were powerful navigators of activists' efforts to strive for socially just environmental change. It is important to note how activists used these capacities/approaches/skills both as bridges to cross socially constructed boundaries and as looms to weave more holistic analyses and practices. It is also significant that linking practices stretched activists in these areas. Their capacities/approaches/skills of bearing witness, questioning, critical-holistic reflection and demythologizing were developed, deepened and expanded through the practice of linking activism. Such experiences of unfoldment may be limited within activisms that are fragmented (e.g., specialized) rather than integrally-focused. For instance, activists can become oriented to ask questions in ways that simply reconstruct rather than challenge or expand a particular viewpoint (e.g., whether feminist, anti-racist or environmental). How these and other capacities/approaches/skills of change-making become restricted and/or empowered across different activisms is an area of needed investigation.

Chapter Ten

More on the Journey: Translation, Trust Building, Hope, and Emergence

Journal note: One of my favourite ecological places is a local wetland which is nestled within the ecosystem of the Niagara Escarpment and accompanying Bruce Trail. In the many hours I have spent in this lovely piece of the earth I have never ceased to be amazed by the many layers of movement that surround me in the ponds, meadow, swampland, streams, edging forests, and sky above. Movements of the red-winged blackbird, chickadee and dragon fly; motions from worms, frogs, salmon, beaver and water spiders; tassels of wind-blown water lilies, cattails, woody plants, and a plethora of other water loving vegetation and trees. Across these layers of life there is an emergent complexity of movement that is bold and subtle; lyrical and staccato; patterned and chaotic, to say nothing of the many forms of motion I have yet to recognize or name.

Linking activism can be seen as a site of dynamic movement. There is the movement between the social and ecological and between the personal and political. There are the moving intersections betweens forms of oppression (e.g., race, class, gender) and between forms of linking practice (e.g., common cause, constituency-based, democratic rights of information and participation). There is the movement between linkages at local, national and international levels. There is the dance of shifts and change that occur in activist linking practices across time and differing involvements. There is the interplay of movement between the array of capacities, approaches and skills used by activists to empower their linking work. And so on.

It can be hard to imagine feeling empowered to navigate effectively such complex, ever-emergent landscapes. Like my favorite local wetland, the project of linking activism can simply feel like a journey of attempting the undoable because of the moving complexity of learning and experiencing that is involved. How do you "capture" (via sense-making) this complex moving landscape when wholeness resides in motion, and "capture" requires creating artificial forms of stillness? Moreover, how do you live meaningfully and express one's agency amidst the undoable?

Since the inception of this study these dilemmas are something I have pondered at length—not so much as problems to solve but more as valuable kinds of riddles to keep living amidst. Activist accounts can be seen to offer a variety of responses to these questions—having a sense of trust and hope, being a kind of shape-shifter (i.e., translator), and embracing a worldview of change and flux are possible responses.

In listening to activists' stories it was readily apparent that linking activism is a journey that calls forth the importance of translation, trust building, hope, and emergence. This chapter examines ways activists made linking messages accessible through a variety of methods of translation. For instance, in order to foster the visibility of linkages, activists often deciphered expert messages for citizens who found the information inaccessible. Additionally, in dealing with complex, heavy issues, activists developed strategies to avoid becoming simply overwhelming or bad news messengers. I argue that in being effective translators, activists experienced empowerment as linking messengers.

The importance of building trust and maintaining hope were also powerful themes across activist stories. Because linking practice is rooted in bridging issues and sectors establishing trust is pivotal. This form of "quiet activism" needs greater priority in social movements if integrative change is to occur within communities. Similarly, maintaining hope was essential to activists' sense of sanity, self-care and sustainability as change agents. Seeing themselves as part of the broad scale movements for social justice played an important role in nurturing activists' sense of hope.

The theme of emergence was also found in activist accounts. In engaging a journey of emergence activists acknowledged that they live in constantly changing social-ecological contexts and thereby need forms of agency which are creatively responsive to these evolving, dynamic movements. One of the central ways activists articulated this viewpoint was through their rejection of "neat and tidy formulas" or "cook book recipes" of linking practice. Instead, their accounts emphasized the centrality of being flexible and responsive to the specific needs and variables of each context. This chapter further explores the themes of translation, trust building, hope, and emergence with respect to linking activist practice.

FORMS OF TRANSLATION WHICH HELP LINKING MESSAGES BE HEARD

Deciphering "Expert" Messages

Making "expert" information accessible comprised a key area of translation work for many activists. Expert, professional, and power-holder discourses are habitually difficult to understand, and activists repeatedly acted as translators of these messages, facts, and figures for concerned citizens wanting to be able to relate what they heard to their own lives. Concerned citizens want to know, for instance, "What does this mean that the air quality is 'x'? When a government official says this amount of lead in my soil is acceptable, what are they saying to me? If the filter lining for the proposed dump in my community is made out of this material, how can I evaluate this? How does this measure of potential risk relate to the health of my family, community, and the ecosystem around me?"

Kathleen recalls an example of working with issues of lead contamination in a disadvantaged urban neighborhood in the early years of her activism. Her account depicts the kinds of translation work she engaged on behalf of the residents affected. Kathleen recalls:

> Working with a community dealing with lead contamination from a lead smelter in their neighborhood in the 1980s was when I started to really make the links between environmental protection and social justice. The lead contamination was a huge children's health risk potentially exposing kids to irreversible brain and central nervous system damage. This community was so clearly impacted because of being disadvantaged in various ways. It was a poor neighborhood, predominately of Portuguese and Chinese ethnicity. The community was politically disenfranchised. There was an apathy, lack of understanding, and discrimination by power holders of this low-income ethnically diverse community. All of these standard issues of why disadvantaged communities get disproportionately impacted by environmental problems brought the linkages right in front of me in black and white.
>
> The community wanted to know all about the regulatory framework that they were dealing with, the specifics of the plant, a detailed report of the health effects, the nature of the contamination in their community. They really needed this because the information that was accessible through the ministry which they tried to access came out in dribs and drabs. Information received did not make sense. There was no context given making it hard to know whether you need to be concerned or not. The information was technical and inaccessible. . . . My

colleague and I digested all this information for them into a form that they could understand. We had regular meetings with them and set up a Lead Committee to explain what was going on.

Kathleen's analysis depicts the obstacles facing this community and reveals the kinds of information in need of translation (i.e., fragmented information about regulations, standard practices, and reports) to enable social justice-ecological links to be deciphered by residents.

Trying to Avoid Being Overwhelming or Bad News Messengers

Many linking messages can easily become too complex or depressing to hear. This calls on another dimension of translation skill. How can linking messages be more inclusive and holistic without confusing and overwhelming people? How can intersecting oppressions be voiced in ways that foster dialogue, agency, and empowerment rather than cause people to shut down, become immobilized and disheartened? These are questions activists struggled to address.

Kathleen refers to this challenge of wanting to convey social-ecological complexities in a manner that resonates and empowers audiences. Striving to convey the connections between environmental deregulation, social program cutbacks and corporate economic globalization without overwhelming citizens, she states:

> A major focus of my work deals with the challenge of conveying the interconnectedness of the issues, the underlying causes of the issues, and doing it in a way that really resonates with people and motivates them to do something. . . . It is a rediscovery of lateral thinking . . . of coming up with analyses and perspectives on these issues that enable me to talk about that complexity in a way that is understandable and in a way that draws the links between it all. Both dealing with the big picture stuff and conveying this big picture and then figuring out a way to take off manageable chunks that people can deal with.

Presenting "big pictures" manageably so as not to confuse or inundate audiences challenges activists to prioritize, organize, and synthesize their message well. Michelle recounts the need for such skills, stating:

> It is always a balancing act to present the whole picture without getting engrossed in the complexity of details. This means one has to make priorities well and synthesize information. This then requires being able to present a message which makes clear those priorities

within the broader, complex whole while not losing the whole or losing the audience.

In addition to these strategies outlined by Michelle, activists discussed ways they helped themselves and audiences keep a healthy sense of perspective when being confronted with far-reaching, challenging realities. For instance, Dorothy offers clear advice acknowledging the need to promote personal sustainability. She tells audiences to use holistic or "big picture" messages in ways that help give understanding and agency to their lives. While individuals cannot "do it all," they can, Dorothy asserts, stay aware of these larger realities, frame their work within larger pictures, and take action on this broader information as it crosses their current work. As a messenger of larger, socially critical messages, Dorothy asserts this balance stating:

> I think it needs to be said upfront, "Look, there's a big picture." You can only work on what you're doing, but you need to know that the other things are happening so that you can deal with them when the call comes. Or, as you talk about this, you are also aware of that. Taking it apart and working with a piece of it but seeing the whole is the way we need to do it. Too much happens where people take it apart and don't put in the whole picture. . . . We need to look at big pictures and we need to look at small pictures and we need to work in both ways. This is why we do these workshops so that people can start from where they are and then they can go back and work in their groups in ways that are good for them. There is no one way, as we know.

Karen speaks to this theme of keeping perspective amidst the array of social justice-ecological challenges. She highlights the importance of being patient and accepting that our lives are littered with contradictions that need to be tackled over time. She states:

> There are a lot of contradictions in our society and in living in our society. You have to be patient in working through them. You can't expect to deal with it all at once. I think a lot of people beat themselves up trying to do it all now. They say everything I do from now on will make sense and there will be no contradictions. But this is impossible. The closest is if you opt out of society and completely exist on your own, going out to the backwoods or whatever.

Stating that linking attempts may *not be* as involved or overwhelming as one imagines is another dimension of translation engaged by many activists. Cecilia gives us an example indicating if you are part of a southern environmental group that wants to do something on northern mining problems, check out your intentions with people affected by mine tailings. She states this is not about "doing it all," indicating:

> If a [southern] environmental group wanted to do something on [northern] mining, for instance, the first place people should start is with calling up that mining community and talking to those affected by mine tailings. And then, asking them, if and where you can help. They may say, we need help lobbying Queen's Park and that is where you can help. And sometimes it is about providing support. It is not necessarily being there on the front line with people but about making that connection, saying that you are supportive and that you are there if they need you to be. It is that kind of relationship.

Brennain adds further texture to this picture of personal sustainability, stating:

> You have to have some sense of the long haul and the whole person to sustain yourself. In the present tense you have to assess what is available to you in any given moment, in any given day and then take that action. You also have to have some confidence that you will make another decision tomorrow and another decision the next day. And that there are millions of other people also doing that so not everything is up to you. It is always a struggle between having a sense of personal responsibility but not a sense of personal irreplaceability. No big changes ever happen because of only one person. But no big changes happen without many people being that one person who was part of it.

Acknowledging that our messages or actions will never be perfect integrations of social and ecological needs is also central to communicating effectively. One activist spoke to activists' fear of taking a verbal stance on race issues for fear of not getting the message just right. Speaking of sentiment within her environmental organization the activist states:

> There was real hesitancy to talk about what our position was or whether we should be doing something as an organization to address racism. What I saw was fear of saying something wrong, essentially fear of not being perfect. There was the fear of not having an entire analysis that was correct, and even that there was some sort of analysis that was correct and that we should have it before we do or say something. It stopped people from expressing themselves or coming forward. We were almost getting into a position of not doing anything for fear that we may not be quite right or perfect.

While desires to be integrative, sensitive, and non-oppressive in our linking work are crucial, Tonya is blunt about the need to be realistic. She asserts the fact that one's efforts are unlikely to "please everyone," nor is it possible to know "what all the implications of an action [are]." Holding onto the principle of being respectful, Tonya states:

> I know that nothing I do is going to be perfect and I know that nothing I do is going to please everybody. But I seek only to enter partnerships where everybody can be respected. I don't think it is worth entering a partnership where everybody cannot leave with respect. . . . I try to make sure what we do is well planned and we try to look at what the implications of an action are. . . . I don't think you can know what all the implications of an action you take are going to be. You try to make it as good for as many people as possible.

Opposing social injustices connected to environmental problems does not mean thinking you have to do it all. Whether being awoken to the effects of economic globalization or wanting to support communities facing environmental injustices, effective linking messengers help us to frame our linking concerns in ways that work *both* for ourselves and for those we are wanting to support. In this sense, effective linking activists are pragmatic visionaries. They reach out and up while remaining grounded. They see the larger pictures. They possess hopes and aspirations for transformation at many levels. And yet, they work from the here and now of their situations.

Readiness to Hear: Navigating Fine Lines

As intimated in previous chapters, activists often struggled with the heavy and painful content of the issues before them. They prided themselves on being informed, accurate, and truthful, and yet many possessed a strong activist and pedagogical commitment to empowerment. Navigating this balance is tricky. Strategies used by activists to address this need for balance included, for instance: *starting from where people are; readiness and use of good timing; using creativity and humor; being accurate yet sensitive; and being critical without cutting off lines of communication.*

In her northern community, Cecilia believes in starting from where people are. She frames the opening and broadening discourse on why people get sick in their single-industry community within a respectful and gentle approach. She states:

> It really depends on the situation. You have to suss out the situation and see how open people are to hearing certain information. You just kind of roll with the community and with their readiness to accept. We used to do regular inserts in the paper and say this is what we are doing

to improve water quality in the lakes and then, as people call in who are interested, we provide them with more information. If the people are interested in knowing more than the propaganda story then we do have that information too and we are able to give it to them. I think that awareness takes a long time and needs to be built up fairly slowly. When someone talks about their neighbor getting sick we might ask how they see that [why do they think that happened?] and then we might offer other reasons [such as pollution from the steel plant] leaving it with them to think about . . . but we let the person decide.

The themes of readiness and good timing are picked up in detail by Si. She outlines some of its nuances. Embarking on cross-pollinator efforts thoughtfully, she reflects:

With each conversation and interaction, thinking about the person's readiness is part of the figuring out. If you tell someone something that you know, in advance, they are not ready to hear, then you are just pissing into the wind. You are wasting your energy. You also may be giving them a very negative experience that they resent, and as a result, they close you off. Future opportunities are then ruined. If I overwhelm them, they will avoid me and not want to talk to me. But maybe, if I keep talking to them and build more trust, maybe the next month at our meeting I can tell them a smaller piece that they are ready to absorb and help them identify one or two small things they could do which they would feel good about and help them become more integrated in their work. Then, the next month, I could say more and keep building on that slowly over time.

Making verbal advances paced by one's assessment of listener readiness is sensitive, respectful, and strategic. But such an approach can also be driven from a place of arrogance and paternalism—from a position of "*I* know what is best for you!" This pitfall is easier to fall into when the relationship between activists and their audience is lacking and/or when activists have not critically examined their own areas of privilege.

Balancing what and how much to say is a regular challenge for activists wanting to be effective translators of linking messengers. It is reasonable to assume that activists will learn, in part, simply by trial and error. Irene experienced this learning curve. She witnessed the panic pregnant women can face when learning of the potential fetal risk from nuclear plant pollution in their community. This was information she and her group had shared with citizens. Reframing their message (after such experiences) to be more sensitive to these fears, Irene recalls:

It is a hard line to walk. On the one hand, you want to tell people there is an increased risk of cancer and birth defects in our community because of the pollution coming from the nuclear plant. You also want to tell people that these risks could be taken away but the solutions cost money and they don't want to incur such costs. On the other hand, you want to say these levels of risk are low. They are considered acceptable by regulators and government, but we do not necessarily believe the risks are as low as they say they are. We think it is unjustified for the industry to continue polluting when we know these are carcinogenic materials. We pride ourselves on being 100% accurate in what we say ... [and yet] we have become more sensitive in trying not to scare people, particularly students and pregnant women who have at times been deeply affected by this information. So we link nuclear issues to human health issues but we are not as graphic about it as we were when we started out. We make more generalized statements ... rather than saying our kids can die of cancer.

Linking work often brings activists to critical views of specific social movements (whether the labor, environmental or feminist movement etc.). Social movements often have far to go in their journey towards more integrative goals and practices. How does one balance honest critique with the need to keep open communication across movements? Rick talks about the challenge of this balance. "Walking a thin line" between environmental movement politics and labor politics, he explains:

Sometimes people say, "You haven't been critical enough of the corporate sector in your own community." Keeping in mind that some of the biggest national polluters are the same ones in this community. We haven't been as critical. We've been trying to be critical, but at the same time keep in mind that we want to maintain open communications and effective networks with the rank and file in the labor leadership. It has not always been easy. I've walked a very thin line for many years, very cognizant of [the need to challenge unions on issues of corporate control and environmental issues] ... and [critical of] environmentalists about the politics of the labor movement. Not necessarily do both understand what those politics are about or what they are trying to do. I can be critical of both, I can also be very commending of both.

Cecilia speaks to the same underlying struggle. How can industry be challenged without ostracizing the labor union or community members? A direct confrontational approach, she expressed, was not a realistic option if they wanted to be heard. She recalls:

It is hard to speak out against the large steel plant. I do not think you can directly do that. One thing we did was work with the union. We invited them to a lot of workshops we had. We had a lot of air quality workshops. We invited them to talk at these workshops. We tried to involve them to come to some of the events we had. We did not actually speak out against the industry. We knew we had to do a lot of general public education in terms of the issues and getting out information. We tried to do this in a way that was not too political. . . . You do not want to appear too anti-industry because you will just turn people off right away.

Humor can be a great vehicle to navigate the heaviness of linking work. Using humor as a medium to get across her message, Kathleen states, "Part of the way I have started raising these [linking] issues is by beginning my presentations with cartoons. A picture paints a thousand words and it makes people laugh because this is all often incredibly depressing stuff. So it has to be fun as well." Moreover, as noted, several activists, such as Serren, Nita, Dorothy, strove to work amidst translation challenges with the creative energy of humor, film, theater, and storytelling.

Being Bold Messengers

Possessing a style of presentation that is question-asking, sensitive, fun, and starting from where people are, is a means of approaching the contentiousness of working across issues and terrains. Few activists, however, presented themselves strictly as sensitive messengers. They were also bold in their border-crossings and boundary-breaking change efforts. They were messengers who were, at times, bluntly critical of or angry about, attitudes and actions they saw within sectors, government, communities and industries. They spoke like a "meme warrior" depicted in Kalle Lasn's (2000) book, *Culture Jam*. Lasn states:

> This may not be nice, it may not be considerate, it may not even be rational—but damn it, I'm going to do it anyway because it feels right. . . . You act. You thrust yourself forward and intervene. And then you hang loose and deal with whatever comes. In that moment of decision, in that leap into the unknown, you come to life. Your interior world is suddenly vivid. You're like a cat on the prowl: alive, alert and still a little wild (p. 129).

Being a critical "linking warrior" as a sector-insider offers disadvantages and advantages. As an insider to both labor and environmental movements, Rick may possess good insight into how far to be critical of either movement without closing channels of communication. Placing blood, sweat and tears into both movements, Rick may be perceived as earning his entitlement to speak out, even if his message is perceived as too radical or sharp. His critique may also receive greater consideration simply because he is an insider. An outsider with the same comments may be quickly silenced and attacked. As a critical insider, however, Rick has also experienced being ostracized by colleagues. Because of his challenging views, he stated, some labor representatives see him as a "crackpot."

NAVIGATING ISSUES OF TRUST AND BELONGING AS A BRIDGE-BUILDER

Trust was a central ingredient underlying activists' success in building relationships and alliances across sectors. Activist accounts of building common cause, discussed in Chapter Eight, elucidated this fact. Here Brennain fostered trust by letting linkages develop organically with First Nation groups; Kathleen's recognition of shared values and approaches with housing activists created a trust building climate; and Helen and Jack took the time and initiative to build dialogue and understanding with groups which initially received them with suspicion. Additional approaches discussed in this book also relate to the issue of trust building—approaches such as not using an arrogant or preachy tone in communicating with others, and being respectful to the needs and realities of each context.

Navigating issues of trust and belonging as a bridge-builder is complex. Linking activism highlights the need to understand this complexity more fully. Raising suspicion by being a bridge-builder comprises one theme to explore. In her bridging work between residents in her northeastern community and southern environmentalists, Helen recalls an experience of supporting the interests of both groups. In doing so, she experienced being suspect to both constituencies. She states:

> I went on a hike once with a group of what I would call "pure" environmentalists, and found myself vehemently defending the local people and natives. The purists were saying to me "Why are the local people being so obtuse about this park proposal? It would be good for them." And I was defending the local people, saying, "Well, they worry about their lifestyle and economy, all their kids have pretty much left the area because there are no jobs. So of course they are worried. Locally, I am defending the views of environmentalists from the city. So I appear to be on one side when I am with one group, and the other side when I am with the other group. So with things like that I sometimes end up being seen as the enemy to both sides in a way.

Rick alludes to the exertion activists can experience in bridging across issues and sectors, stating:

> Sometimes it was like trying to straddle a small creek. You had one foot on one side and one on the other. Constantly trying to mesh the two

issues and being one person with a lot of both labor and community activists at the same table. We were doing CAW environment work, labor council environment work and community environment work.

Claiming messier identities and alliances can paradoxically enough make some activists feel without a "home." It is the experience of *not quite* fitting here or there. Si shares such experience, soberly stating:

> What is painful about all my cross-pollinating and linking work is that in lots of ways I am very alone because I am in a different place than most people I meet—anti-racist, anti-classist, anti-sexist, anti-killing of animals, anti-raping of nature, anti-homophobia. If you are trying to be conscious, empathic, and respectful on all those fronts at the same time, not taking turns, but *at the same time,* not selling out one ally when you are with another ally, it seems to mean you will be alone.

Si's statement offers the insight that the challenge is not just in trying to *expand our sense of connectedness and relationality to others.* The pain and frustration of living in divisive, disconnecting contexts can be equally or even more difficult.

MAINTAINING HOPE AND APPRECIATION

Activists treasured spaces where their multi-aligned selves were accepted, celebrated, and shared with others. These places/spaces/moments supported activists in their ability to be personally sustainable in their work. Yuga and Linda spoke of how personally significant it felt to be part of grassroots organizations that blended, in one case, race and the environment, and in the other case, gender and the environment, respectively. They commented on how these contexts honored significant aspects of who they are. Dorothy celebrates the web of women across the world working for social justice and environmental health. You can see the meaningfulness she attributes to being a part of this larger circle. Dorothy states:

> Understanding the issues and world understanding that we are part of a big circle of people all over the world doing this work. . . . We need to have the energy not to burn out by understanding that we are part of a web, and women talk about webs and circles. One needs to go to international conferences once in a while to see this. . . . The Kingston Conference was one such conference, the Breast Cancer Conference was a world conference. I was in Rio for the United Nations Conference on the Environment and Development in 1992. I was in Beijing for the Women's Conference. We are doing all this stuff in concert with so many other people. . . . I was in Nairobi for the UN Women's conference as well

in 1985. . . . That is why I think our national and international links are really important as well. It's the mentoring. It's the not feeling alone. It's working in groups. It's the kind camaraderie and joyfulness and playfulness and fun that we have to have with each other. You know when you are in a workshop with good people and something funny happens and everybody laughs. It is such a nice relief. We did that yesterday. We had moments of great laughter and fun even though the issues were deadly serious and half the women had breast cancer.

This kind of optimism and positive focus were common qualities found among many activists' linking stories. Brennain's reflections also illuminate this empowering attitude. Focusing on the good moments and company, Brennain draws on the advantages of working from an integrative perspective. She states:

Partly you have some good moments along the way. Partly you have some good company along the way. Partly because what are you going to do, not do this work? That does not seem like a very viable option. Partly because of the fact that I work on a lot of different things. The downside is that my focus is split and all over the map. In my work I am generally an inch deep and a mile wide and that is a disadvantage. But it is also an advantage because you can't feel the defeat anywhere too deeply or for too long because you always have something else that is different and demanding that needs to be taken care of. I think it is just the reality of working regionally and of trying to have an integrated or connected perspective. A lot of issues come your way . . . but I have found an advantage within it that assists in my ability to sustain myself.

In seeing themselves connected to the larger community of change-makers, activists supported a capacity-building approach. That is to say, they acknowledged the value of each movement's contribution to social change while appreciating the value of their own efforts within the tapestry of these global social movements.

EMERGENCE: HONOURING COMPLEXITY AND CHANGE IN SELF, OTHERS AND CONTEXT

There is no formula to linking activism. Rather, linking work resides in the ever-shifting richness and complexity of our interconnected experiences with self, others and context. Henry James articulates this sense of complex emergence beautifully, stating "[e]xperience is never limited, and it is never complete; it is an immense sensibility, a kind of huge spider-web of the finest silken threads suspended in the chamber of consciousness, and catching every air-borne particle in its tissue." Capacities, approaches and skills which keep activists mindful of these rich realities are invaluable to linking activist practice. As shown throughout this book, activists' linking efforts were often met in the moment and in the complexities these moments held. How-to formulas of activist practice cannot guarantee these moments will be met effectively. The journey of capacities/approaches/skills discussed here, and in other chapters, supports activists in maintaining a reflexive practice which navigates the balance between developing a linking plan or approach, while at the same time enabling responsiveness to the dynamics of the moment. This sense of balance and flexibility is exemplified beautifully by Karen. Speaking first of having a plan of approach, she states:

> Certainly, I know if I go into a council meeting and I know I'm coming at something from a very different point of view and I know there are some very hostile people in the room to my particular point of view I need to be grounded in the position I have on that issue. I have to be able to stand up and say something or to push it. If I have not done the conscious work of understanding my values and analysis I won't get up and speak. I will censor myself. I have to consciously sit down and say my position on this, is because of this, which relates back to all these other links. In doing this I can go out with confidence and speak for it and push it.

Simultaneously, Karen articulates an approach that is constantly being open to new ideas and points of view. She adds:

> I think it is important to be open. I know things have come at me from left field that I had not thought about, or conceived of, which really turned my understanding of something around quite significantly. It's not just another thing that I have to tack on to what I think, rather it integrates but in way that can shift the whole thing.

Conceptualizing linking activism as a journey that is honoring to self, others, and context while simultaneously acknowledging the need for forms of personal and collective revision, expansion, integration, and transformation allows activists to embrace a journey of both definition and openness. Here activists can experience a sense of resonance and connection to different critical discourses, while simultaneously knowing that no single ideological or philosophical perspective can ultimately capture or fully speak for the complexities of their experiences and identities. Karen says it this way:

> I didn't go out reading and saying this analysis is where I fit. I was moving where I wanted to move reading different things. Some of the eco-feminist

analysis resonated with me. So did some of the social ecology analysis as well. I don't call myself an eco-feminist, however, a lot of what I do resonates with a lot of the writings in the eco-feminist field. I wouldn't call myself a social ecologist yet I resonate with a lot of the readings that are there. I think labels are limiting. Even in a political spectrum, the left-right dialogue I find limiting as well. It limits creativity if you start to get pigeonholed into one area. You need flexibility. None of these philosophies are finished. There are people discussing them. There is a lot of debate. They evolve. There are eco-feminist thinkers who have moved over into social ecology because they find it works better for them. There is a lot of moving around. New ways keep coming in.

When activists identified themselves as feminist, community activist or environmentalist they focused on the potential capacity within these identity frames to embrace both ecological and social justice terrains. They focused on the open spaces within these identifications to make connections across social justice and ecological terrains. While over half of the activists seemed to feel that their work was not best captured under the title "environmentalist" because the term was repeatedly understood and used in narrow ways (referring only to nature and not people), Craig found space for his multi-aligned identity within this term. He states:

> I am an environmentalist first and foremost. I have a pretty strong biology background and in my mind the planet is a closed system and everything is clearly interdependent. The social interdependence is just as important as the ecological. The linkages are so important. I have linked out further than what you would call strictly environmental within the environmental movement itself into the world of the Inuit.

In contrast, Brennain does not self-describe as an environmentalist even though others see her as one. Community activist and feminist are identifications she feels are more representative of who she is. She explains:

> My organization was created in 1988. Before that I would have considered myself more of a peace activist than an environmental activist. What is consistent though is that I was always a community activist. I probably would not have described myself as an environmental activist or an environmentalist until 1988 and that was due to the Wise Use movement and their call to keep environmentalists out of northern Ontario, and I knew they were talking about me so I said, "Oh, I must be an environmentalist!"
>
> Even now "environmentalist" is not generally how I self-describe. I would call myself a community activist or community organizer. I work on issues that are broader than the societal definition of environmentalist. And in part because "community activist" is a

more appropriate descriptor. It is a less restrictive descriptor. Socially, environmentalists are expected to deal with pollution and parks and a fairly narrow band of issues. Perhaps I should adopt the descriptor of "environmentalist" and work to broaden the concept, but I just think why bother. Sometimes language just isn't working. Then you have to decide in every instance to try and rework the term or just use a new term. For me the language of being called an environmentalist doesn't particularly work. . . . So not taking the term in this case feels positive. I don't correct people if they call me an environmentalist. I will usually say I am a community organizer and that I work on environmental issues. I find I am more comfortable with that than with being called an environmentalist.

Brennain goes on to state:

Sometimes you hear women say "I believe in women's equality but I am not a feminist." They do not want to use the language of feminist or feminism because it has a negative social connotation. I have always been frustrated by that. I have always felt take the word. It is *our* word. Occupy it. Feminist and feminism is a positive and progressive word.

When I say that I do not want to be called an environmentalist it is because I would like to be called something that is broader. I would like to be called something that says more about where and how I work than the term environmentalist does. . . . I would like to see more permeable dividers between sets of concerns—between environmental concerns, community concerns, First Nations concerns and so on. If you self-describe as a community activist then when you are working on environmental issues you are either addressing it from a human community perspective or a natural community perspective, or a combination of those. As a community activist I am an activist for the natural community as well as the human community.

Si embraces this breadth of self-definition, but instead uses multiple descriptors, simultaneously stating, "I am a Feminist, capital F, anti-racist, anti-classist, grassroots, Buddhist, vegan, nature caring, social worker, therapist, northern, middle class but imprinted as working class recycled white trash. This is how I could best be described." In social contexts embedded in divisions and boundaries, activists' ability to make room for their multi-aligned selves is vital. The diverse and creative ways activists weave these spaces of complex self-identification is in keeping with the textured quality of linking work. Moreover, in claiming their complexly and multi-aligned identities activists give view to the ever-shifting richness and complexity of our interconnected experiences with self, others and context.

SUMMARY REFLECTIONS

This chapter explored how activists incorporated the capacities/approaches/ skills of translation, trust-building, hope and emergence in their linking efforts. These themes reside like brightly colored tangled threads across activists' accounts. As valuable themes of linking practice, we have yet to fully appreciate or examine how they empower activists to be ever responsive to the complexities and change within their social-ecological contexts. This study provides impetus for further exploration.

Chapter Eleven
The Unending Journey

Journal Note: This past summer I was off the hydro grid enjoying cottage life with close friends in Byng Inlet, which is located on the mouth of the Magnetawan River near the top of Georgian Bay. We stayed in an 80-year-old cottage which used to be a fishing lodge called the Loraine Club. Sitting on a point, the cottage overlooks a fantastic tapestry of Group of Seven rocks, pines, and water. It was like a grand ecological quilt of bold and hardy Amazon country, fearless in its diversity, beauty, and interconnectedness. It was a landscape unabashedly complexly-aligned in its identities. I couldn't help thinking that in their celebration of diversity and interconnectedness, linking activists portray this kind of complex and vibrant beauty.

Through the eyes of 30 Ontario activists, this research has examined the linking of environmental work with issues of social justice. As a complex and multi-dimensional form of social change agency, the portrayal of linking activism is a narrative that is not easily contained. In particular, this work has given view to a wide span and locationality of combined social justice-ecological struggles (see Table 1). Across this range of linking issues, four broad forms of linking practice were discussed (Chapters Five through Eight). Personal, socioeconomic, and cultural factors shaping activists' linking efforts were outlined. A collection of linking skills and strategies was explored. Opportunities and barriers encountered by activists were described. These aspects of linking work have been given view, moreover, through the narrative interplay of academic discourse, activist accounts, and my own personal voice as researcher and activist.

Table 1: Definitions of Social Justice & Sites of Linking Struggle Depicted Across Activists' Linking Accounts

Ways of Framing Social Justice within the Context of Environmental Change-Making	Sites of Linking Struggle
1. Need to protect our *environmental health*	1. Individual level
2. Need to preserve and expand *the right to know information* affecting our environment	2. Organizational level
3. Need to preserve and expand the *right to participate* in government decisions affecting our environment	3. Community level (local to international
4. Need to address forms of *social discrimination and oppression* (sexism, racism, classism, ageism, etc.) embedded within environmental problems and "solutions"	4. Government level (municipal, provincial, federal)
5. Need to stop the *contamination of and encroaching on First Nations lands*	5. Sector level
6. Need to contest the harmful social-ecological *impacts of economic globalization*	6. Movement level
7. Need to address *geographical political-economic disparities* which lead to the inequitable control over environmental problems and implemented 'solutions'	
8. Need for there to be a *connection between culture and the environment*	
9. Need for *just transition for workers* who become jobless because of environmental reforms (e.g., forestry or chemical workers)	
10. Need to preserve *human biological survival and nonhuman species survival*	

This chapter outlines some of the central themes across the intersecting layers mentioned above, offering one among many possible patterns of closing reflections. Within this broad thematic discussion, the concepts "linking activism" and "multi or complexly identity" are revisited and recommendations for further investigation are discussed.

MULTIPLE MOTIVATORS OF LINKING PRACTICE

Activists' linking efforts were catalyzed by a range of interrelated factors. Specifically, eight variables creating a dynamic of opportunity for more integrative or holistic forms of social agency can be articulated. First and foremost, activists' linking work was motivated by their increasing awareness of environmental inequities at local and global levels. Secondly, this awareness was further activated by their desire to contest economic globalization, a paradigm they saw as accommodating and further perpetuating environmental injustices. A third factor motivating their linking efforts was the expressed need to build alliances across communities, sectors, and social justice movements in order to challenge these global hegemonic political-economic forces and expand their connectedness to broader notions of community. A fourth factor influencing activists' linking work relates to the need for organizational survival. With the persistent withdrawal of government funding supports, and the increasing challenge to receive public and media exposure, nonprofit environmental organizations increasingly need to be responsive to local communities if they are to be viewed as relevant to these communities. For many activists, this meant the need to create shifts in organizational structures, processes, and environmental priorities to better represent the social-cultural needs and diversities of communities.

Pressure from social groups and actors (such as labor unions, women's groups, and anti-racist activists) to address forms of environmental discrimination has been a fifth variable motivating activists' efforts to address social justice issues. A sixth instructive factor is activists' desire for long-term solutions to environmental problems and their realization that without addressing social equity issues their environmental gains would be only short-term.

A seventh motivating variable constitutes activists' increasing consciousness of the complexity and intersectionality of our social and ecological worlds and of the value, thereby, of engaging in more holistic and integrative approaches to social change. What was additionally clear, comprising an eighth factor across many activists' accounts, was their desire to embrace rather than disengage their complexly-aligned identities in their activism.

RESPONDING TO THE "CRISIS OF PERCEPTION"

Connected to these eight motivating factors outlined above lies the central theme of perception and the supposition articulated by Albert Einstein that "You cannot solve a problem with the same thinking that created it." In striving to link social justice to environmental advocacy, activists engaged the societal "crisis of perception" which is further explored by Capra (1996). He states:

> The more we study the major problems of our time, the more we come to realize that they cannot be understood in isolation. They are systemic problems, which means they are interconnected and interdependent. . . . Ultimately these problems must be seen as just different facets of one single crisis, which is largely a crisis of perception. It derives from the fact that most of us, and especially our large social institutions, subscribe to the concepts of an outdated worldview, a perception of reality inadequate for dealing with our . . . globally interconnected world. There are solutions to the major problems of our time . . . [b]ut they require a radical shift in our perceptions, our thinking, our values. And indeed, we are now at the beginning of such a fundamental change in worldview in science and society (pp. 3–4).

By conceptualizing and acting on more integrative and complex views of environmental problems and solutions, linking activists took up this struggle towards "a radical shift in our perceptions, our thinking, [and] our values." Through their linking work, these activists contested the cultural reproduction of hegemonic ideologies rooted in reductionist and unjust social and ecological relations. We see the movement and tensions they both catalyzed and encountered while acting from a perceptual lens which acknowledges the intersection of oppressions and the need to engage environmental change from such complex social intersectionality. This kind of, what we could call, more "holistic justice" work demonstrates activists' contribution to a broader vision which "invites us to be a little more whole, a little less fragmented, in our work, our lives, our destiny (Wilber, 2000, p. xii).

Concepts like "integrative" or "integral," "holistic" or "holons," "complexity," "ecological," "systems" or "transformative" are terms being used by many theorists and practitioners to articulate this perceptual shift (Wilber, 2000; O'Sullivan 2002; O'Murchu, 1995; Davis, Sumara, & Luce-Kapler, 2000; Capra, 1996). This shift marks the journey towards a view of all living forms, both human and non-human, as interconnected and embedded within an ever-unfolding process of meaningful relationality and co-creation. In the context of exploring the meaning and implications of such a perceptual shift in consciousness, O'Sullivan, Morrell, and O'Connor (2002)

offer one depiction of what this may involve via their description of transformative learning. They state:

> Transformative learning involves experiencing a deep, structural shift
> in the basic premises of thought, feelings, and actions. It is a shift of
> consciousness that dramatically and permanently alters our way of
> being in the world. Such a shift involves our understanding of ourselves
> and our self-locations; our relationships with other humans and with
> the natural world; our understanding of relations of power in inter-
> locking structures of class, race and gender; our body-awareness, our
> visions of alternative approaches to living; and our sense of possibilities
> for social justice and peace and personal joy (pp. xvii).

The concepts of linking activism and multi or complexly-aligned identity
have been used to *invite* this transformational view of self and world into
our understandings and practice of environmental change making. In doing
so, our perceptions of environmental activism, and of agency, more generally, become deeply complicated and open to many layers of re-conceptual-
ization and re-negotiation. For instance, environmental change mottos
expand to capture human diversity in addition to ecological diversity. The
environmental principle to "think globally, act locally" becomes enlarged
to designate the need to act locally, not just on ecological problems, but
against the broader social discriminations within these landscapes. The perception that if enough environmental protection measures are instituted
(whether in the form of policies, laws, or lifestyle change), then these
changes will reach down to protect those who are most socially and ecologically vulnerable (a form of trickle-down environmentalism) becomes
deeply contested.

This research has taken up the need for a fundamental shift in societal
perception. Each chapter demonstrates ways activists have worked to re-con-
ceptualize and re-negotiate forms of environmental agency so that social justice issues are engaged, not ignored. In theoretical terms, activists' linking
efforts contested reductionistic assumptions embedded in 1) how environmental problems and solutions are defined; 2) who is included or excluded in environmental decision-making; 3) who defines environmental impact; 4) what
the skills and boundaries of the environmental change maker are; and 5) how
activists' identities engaged in environmental change are conceptualized.

In practical terms, activists worked to better understand the social costs
and benefits of their environmental initiatives. They were increasingly cognizant of the webs of broader relationships intersecting their ecological work.
Their stories revealed they held broad-based rather than narrow understandings of social justice. Their stories served to transform traditional notions of

environmentalism by their growing capacity to examine environmental issues through the lens of labor, class, race, and gender. They showed effort to connect beyond the environmental sector to social justice sectors and local communities. They expressed the need for fundamental social change and their desire to contest economic globalization. They took on roles of community builder, catalyst, and innovator within their organizational and community contexts. They demonstrated courage to witness the complex array of enfolding relationships across social and ecological worlds, and moreover, to grapple with the complexities and creative tensions of working across socially constructed boundaries so that these interplays of connections, intersections, and diversities could be taken up within the landscape of political struggle.

LINKING ACTIVISM: A DYNAMIC, MULTI-DIMENSIONAL, MESSY JOURNEY

In examining the factors that prompt linking practice, and in positioning linking work within the current paradigm shift towards holism, we are still in search of more effective narrative forms to depict this complex journey (as depicted in Chapter Three). The specific goal is to elicit a continually textured and rich account of activists' linking work. This requires more sophisticated and complexly-aligned narrative frames. These narrative frames require an expanded flexibility and openness to the multi-dimensionalities, movements, incongruities, and tensions of activists' linking experiences as they engage in the layered societal landscapes in which they find themselves. In looking across activists' linking experiences there are two broad thematic patterns which particularly highlight these multi-dimensionalities of linking practice. These themes include the interplay of both the breadth and movement of linking experiences and of the pitfalls and promise of linking work.

The Breadth and Movement of Linking Activism

Building on their recognition that we are not only in this environmental challenge together but also in it differently, activists sought to respond to varied forms of environmental discrimination. Locationalities of gender, class, race, geographical location, age, citizenship, and issues of health, culture, species survival, and political-economic control were given view as they intersected with an array of environmental issues such as garbage and toxic waste siting issues, pesticide use, chemical production, forestry protection, indoor and outdoor air pollution, land use planning of public lands, control of water resources and water pollution, energy use, and species protection.

Within this breadth of linkages, some individuals gave priority to the varied social justice dimensions within a specific environmental issue area. Irene is an example of this. In her anti-nuclear activism, for instance, she worked to underscore the centrality of the public's right to know about nuclear incidents. She facilitated community awareness of the justice implications of sending radioactive waste to economically vulnerable communities, and served as a supportive ally to First Nations and other marginalized communities confronting nuclear contamination. Other activists, such as Brennain and Dorothy, engaged in a range of environmental involvements and confronted varied social justice issues within these different engagements.

Importantly, activists did not just frame environmental discriminations within the context of pollution and waste siting issues, which have been the focus of the U.S environmental justice movement,[1] but considered a breadth of social injustices created through the use and distribution of public land and resources. Recall Karen who spoke of the impacts of water privatization on economically vulnerable citizens; Kathleen who initiated a joint protest with housing activists regarding impacts of land use planning reforms on the construction and availability of affordable housing; and Brennain's and Dwayne's groups who worked as allies in the Ontario government Lands for Life provincial review process to voice values of social and ecological health and contest the increasing commodification of people, the land, and communities by corporate interests. This research has brought to light natural resource and policy discriminations that go beyond the realm of toxic issues as a result of a research methodology which positioned activists to define social justice-ecological linkages for themselves and through the formulation of a broad-based construct of linking activism.

It is not only this breadth of linkages within an activist's environmental efforts that is important to note, but also the flow and movement between these efforts. In recognizing the ways an activist flows between different linking acts, both within and across different environmental involvements, we can begin to notice the expanding complexity and intricacy of an individual's social change agency. We can observe ways their strands of movement foster an interweaving between linking acts, energizing integrative (social-ecological) transformation at both the personal and societal level. Moreover, it is only through honoring the activist's threads and tapestries of linking effort that the extent and significance of linking activism and its contribution to societal transformation will be fully appreciated.

In order to achieve this complex focus of observation and understanding, the study of social change agency needs to increasingly move away from reductionist and mechanistic approaches which hone in on a specific piece of expressed agency (whether that be a specific initiative or type of linkage or aspect of self). There is a need for more holistic research approaches which engage in the rich, multi-dimensioned messiness of an individual's agency (e.g., across different linkages, environmental involvements, aspects of self, times, and locations) so that articulated meanings of social change will be informed by such personal, social, and ecological complexity. From their own contexts of study, both Payne (2000) and Selby (2002) raise this need for greater attention to the complexities of environmental agency and social change. As a global environmental educator, Selby (2002) states:

> We need to see entities—ourselves, nonhuman animals, rocks, nation-states, political grouping—not first and foremost as objects but primarily as processes or dances. Phenomena (people, other-than-human life-forms, places, countries) at this level are coevolving manifestations of a multileveled and multidimensional dance of internal and external relationships (p. 83).

Selby goes on to state:

> Our approaches to [environmental] change have been wedded to mechanism. We have opted for restricted change focuses (e.g., developing a global or environmental pack or program for a specific grade and school subject . . .) when our ecological understanding tells us that change is about strength/resilience through diverse yet connected initiatives, coalitions, and partnerships and dynamic and synergistic interplays between different change initiatives. Change, in short, has to be holistic to be effective (p. 90).

In his study of "young, adult, undergraduate outdoor/environmental educators," Payne (2000) observes the need for researchers to examine lives in ways which are less simplifying of individuals' complex realities and behaviors. Referring to individuals he interviewed, he states:

> Their uncertainty, optimism, confusion, ambivalence or apathy presses for an educational response that has researchers acknowledge that an individual's (or researcher's) attempts to make meaning of his/her life are not as simple or straightforward as measuring certain dispositions, evaluating certain experiences or assessing particular interventions, listening only to what they say, or pre-emptively positing a unified, coherent identity for such selves. Something additional, more encompassing is needed. Hence, this weave of conceptual and empirical insight aims to capture some of the complexity of studying and revealing embodied identities. Of particular interest is the exploration of identity with the 'continuity of experience' (Payne, 1997, 1999a, b). Here, the construction of 'unifying'

> narrative concepts of selfhood developed through incorporating different experiences of others, environments, times, places and spaces may help us more clearly see human agency and identity as something that is for, with, neutral or against the environment, self and others (pp. 70–71).

As researchers, this perceptual shift takes us to a needed exploration of ecological theory, complexity theory, and chaos theory as frameworks for new forms of social science research. Such endeavors would support a fuller examination of the layers, patterns, and incongruities of identity and agency and their interplays of spontaneity, adaptation, uncertainty, intentionality, ebb and flow, and more. This is starting to happen. Landsman (2001) provides an example of the application of the fractal metaphor (stemming from chaos theory) to understandings of the liberation of Palestinian women. This study of linking activism clearly points to the need for such kinds of exploratory investigations.

Two additional points are worth noting in this discussion. First, while social and ecological injustices catalyze movement between forms of linking practice,[2] dominant reductionist paradigms simultaneously work to restrain this flow by not having in place the priorities, structures, resources, or processes to empower integrative practices. Amidst these challenges, activists creatively propelled a varied array of covert and explicit linking movements. They, for instance, navigated through crevices and open spaces within governments, organizations, communities, and themselves, so that linkages could be nurtured. These openings often offered opportunities for small rather than large scale linking projects. In many ways, activists' linking work is *not* best depicted by images of construction workers building thick sturdy bridges across social and ecological divisions with precisely engineered blueprints and heavy industrial materials (i.e., resources). A more fitting image would be that of Charlotte the spider in E. B. White's children's story, *Charlotte's Web*. Like Charlotte, activists spun numerous small threads across different doorways to foster greater social-ecological connections. And like a web, activists' strands of effort were apparent in some cases and not in others, strong in some cases and fragile in others. In these actions, they were often quiet catalysts engaged in the challenging and lengthy processes of trust-building across divisions, or engaged in information gathering and research which would, over time, allow for the creation of more permanent structures and processes of social justice-ecological integration within organizations, communities, and government processes.

Second, forms of linking breadth and movement support activists' development and maturation as more integrative change makers. Linking experience moved initially limited understandings of social justice-ecological connections and practices to more sophisticated ones. For instance, activists' critique of social-structural forces was continually being deepened; understandings of environmental discriminations as they manifest across local to global levels were developed; the movement from arm-chair alliances within marginalized communities to forms of actual engagement within communities shifted activists' thinking and actions; linking experiences increasingly expanded activists' conceptualization and sense of resonance with their environmental work as part of a larger social change community; and across experiences, activists became more adept at communicating the complexities of environmental problems as they intersected within different social sector spheres.

The breadth and movement across activists' linking expressions raise numerous questions worthy of future research: How does this integrative approach at an individual level inform theory of collective social change? How can the identification of different expressions of linking practice assist activists to identify gaps and limitations within their current activist work? Does the breadth and movement across activists' linking activism foster greater personal empowerment, and in turn, does this process energize further linking practice?

The Promise(s) and Pitfalls of Linking Activism

As a form of agency, linking activism is full of promise(s) and pitfalls. In examining activists' stories, the messiness of the potential and challenges were given view. We witnessed the often experienced enormity of challenge confronting activists in their attempts to effect more integrative social-ecological change, while also viewing the ways in which their linking efforts affected change, for instance, within environmental campaigns, organizational structures, government processes and within the consciousness of communities. These complexities call on the need for narrative forms which are flexible enough to give voice to activists' yearnings and efforts to foster socially just environmental change, while also acknowledging the dynamic tensions, nuances, contradictions, and ambivalence that are encountered in such efforts. For instance, in the challenges of environmental work, there can be a tension between wanting to be awake to the intersections of social oppression and their implications and on the other hand, and a desire at times to be asleep to these complexities on the other. Activists reveal that bearing witness to forms of environmental discrimination is disturbing. Similarly, challenging the relations of power that fuel these injustices is daunting. Linking work positions the individual to become aware of varied forms of injustice. This can make integrative forms of agency all the more intense and difficult to engage in. The "dynamics of denial, despair and grief" (O'Sullivan, 2002) which are the result of taking in an array of injustices can be daunting. O'Sullivan's (2002) articulation of the steps in moving through this process of denial, despair, and grief is one that is very relevant to linking activism and the kinds of inner work it demands of the activist. He states:

> Denial is a defense mechanism that prevents us from being overwhelmed by the deeply problematic nature of our times. But in order to solve problems, it is necessary to come out of denial. Despair will be one of the major difficulties. . . . Without the development of a critical understanding and creative vision, despair has the capacity to overwhelm. Finally, grieving is a necessary ingredient. . . . The sense of loss at the personal, communal, and planetary level . . . demands a grieving process at profound levels (p. 5).

The theory and practice of integrative activism needs to take this landscape of psychological challenges into account. Supporting change-makers to successfully navigate these challenges is crucial, yet these themes often lie unaddressed both in activist research and the therapeutic professions.

Ambivalence towards linking work can also be experienced in navigating the interplay of challenge and promise. In certain instances, activists experienced their linking acts as ripe for engagement, whereas in other efforts they were strewn with difficulty. Throughout this work, for example there were accounts which portrayed linking work in positive, productive, and satisfying terms. Some of the factors imbuing promise within activists' linking efforts include contexts in which environmental discrimination is highly visible in the political arena, situations where connections are made organically, and organizations in which combined environment-social justice mandates have been established. Other factors which supported the promise of activists' efforts included the availability of time and resources, the history of relationship between issues, organizations and sectors, and the ability to forge win-win solutions between environmental and social justice concerns. Of equal importance were those individual expressions that cannot be easily weighted or counted—like Si's stated "222 pounds of empathy work" cultivated over a year; like Helen's commitment to finding forms of connection across difference in her community; like Michelle's honesty in acknowledging the importance of her own personal growth work in being an effective agent of social change; and like Nita's ability to deeply value the linking work she did, even when her efforts went largely unseen by others. Moreover, activists' conceptual and/or actual experience of being part of a larger international/global movement for social justice

and ecological change relayed the promise of linking work. This research
affirms the growing chorus of assertions within activist literatures of the
impact and importance of such anti-globalization solidarity work. Miles
(2002) provides one such example reflecting tenors found in this research.
She states:

> Celebration of solidarity in diversity is characteristic of the many centers
> of visionary opposition to corporate capitalism. These groups are affirm-
> ing their own value and identity as well as their connection to others,
> seeking their own good as well as the good of all; selectively building on
> and honouring traditional culture and contributions while welcoming
> change; articulating new senses of self and others and of possible futures
> grounded in the value of all of life. And they are doing this against the
> hegemonic antilife worldview backed by the fast-increasing power of
> patriarchal capital in collusion with the state (p. 30).

This research provides narratives of promise, affirming the kinds of social
change narratives outlined by Miles (2002), while also offering new narratives for political reflection and action resulting from the breath and complexity of scope undertaken in this investigation of activism.

This research has also documented the ways in which linking efforts
are strewn with challenges. The multi-layered social justice-ecological dis-
connections within the dominant culture, communities, and activist movements confronted by activists in their linking work cannot be
underestimated. As articulated by innumerable authors (for example,
Naples, 2002; O'Sullivan, 2002; Hall, 2002; Clover, 2002), there are powerful hegemonic ideological and structural forces at play. None of the
activists interviewed were naive about this fact. They knew that articulating
the reality of these hegemonic forces was pivotal, but also challenging.
Miles' (2002) articulation of these hegemonic forces is again a reminder of
the backdrop against which linking work must take place, regardless of the
level of struggle (i.e., local, provincial, nation, international) engaged in by
the activist. She states:

> All notion of communal life and values and government responsibility
> outside the support of economic "growth" is fast disappearing. Con-
> trols on the pursuit of profit in the name of social priorities such as
> equity, security, cultural integrity, labor rights, and environmental pro-
> tection are losing legitimacy and are being progressively removed. As
> Vandana Shiva (1997:22) has noted, "we are seeing the replacement of
> government and state planning by corporate strategic planning and the
> establishment of global corporate rule." Free Trade agreements such as
> the North American Free Trade Act (NAFTA) and the Free Trade Act

of the Americas (FTAA) and international agreements such as the General Agreement of Trade in Services (GATS) and Trade Related Aspects on Intellectual Property Rights (TRIPS) are being negotiated without democratic scrutiny, debate, or agreement and forced on less powerful nations by the more powerful. The world is being opened not to free trade with a level playing field but to unfettered trade by transnational corporations. Not only goods but also services and capital are now traded "freely," regardless of cost to communities or environments (Barlow, 1996). Governments are not free to withdraw from these agreements once they have signed (pp. 24–25).

Succinctly articulated by Hall (2002), such "forms and practices" of economic globalization are being sold by its powerful proponents not only as "inevitable," but moreover, as a "Utopian vision" for our world community.

It is not merely the strength and scope of hegemonic economic forces that can cause ambivalence towards the potential and promise of linking activism; it is equally the divisions and forms of mistrust and discomfort across progressive social change movements which contribute to this challenge. While the promotion of diversity is an articulated agenda across progressive social movements, these movements fall short of embodying these principles. Maxwell (2002) articulates one example of these challenges, stating:

> Most neo-Marxists have little time for spirituality; many radical feminists are concerned almost exclusively with deconstructing patriarchal hegemonies and view any transcendental spirituality with suspicion; deep ecologists like George Sessions (1995) have little good to say about Gaia theorists like James Lovelock (1990); and so on (p. 19).

As articulated by activists like Rick, there are challenges of language and discourse across different movements and sectors, and also genuine ideological and strategic differences at play. One of the richest aspects of this research were those very stories where activists invested in the effort and courage to confront these differences so that understanding could be developed. Helen, Serren, Cecilia, and Jack, for instance, provided some of these powerful accounts.

Facing ridicule or attack, lacking the necessary time and resources, and needing to invest tremendous effort to forge small changes are also fuel for mixed emotions towards linking work. Other dissuasions affecting activists include linking experiences in which activists were positioned in such a way that they repeatedly felt overwhelmed, vulnerable, or misunderstood. Similarly, being torn in different directions, facing inner doubts and self-judgments, confronting failures and burnout, and frequently being unrecognized for one's linking efforts, fostered similar unease. Ambivalence stemming from these dynamic tensions should not be surprising given this messy coinciding of pitfalls and promise. These emotional complexities of linking work need to be integrated into accounts of efforts toward holistic practice. Research needs to give attention to these landscapes of ambivalence and examine strategies activists use to navigate these challenges.

THE CONCEPT OF LINKING ACTIVISM

Wilber (2000) argues that, "A good theory is . . . not a fixed or final theory, simply one that has served its purpose if it helps you get to a better one" (p. xiii). The concepts of linking activism and complex or multi-aligned identity have been created with such a view in mind. As constructs they have provided new perspectives on environmental change practice for the activists involved in this research.

The concept of linking activism gives recognition to the integrated connections of our social and ecological worlds. As a construct, it has prioritized the actual experiences of activists, providing much needed hands-on views of linking work, while simultaneously offering new areas of theoretical reflection. As an inclusive rather than exclusive concept, linking activism has given visibility to a wide breadth of linkages, demonstrating both the reality of these connections and the ways these myriad of intersections inform activist work. It is as process-oriented as it is content-focused, making a clear assertion that the *how* of integrative practice is as central as the *subject* or *what* of linking work. The concept of linking activism also inherently breaks away from reductionist models which offer narrow understandings of self and agency.

At an individual and pragmatic level, the concept of linking activism is intended to empower activists to honor, explore, and expand their linking work. At a theoretical level, this concept is intended to expand the lens with which we understand activist practice. At a political level, this concept is intended to push the act of connecting across socially constructed divisions towards the center rather than the periphery of political change. Using the concept of linking activism, this research has supported the documentation of blended social justice-ecological practices, facilitated the investigation of movement between linking efforts, and encouraged more holistic narratives of activist practice to be written.

Would Activists Define Themselves as Linking Activists?

The concept of linking activism was developed through this research. Activists interviewed did not refer to themselves as linking activists. Rather, activists' blended social-ecological work was embodied in terms such as community activist, activist, feminist, environmental health activist, environmentalist, or in the combining of an assortment of terms, such as "anti-racist," "feminist," "anti-homophobic," etc. Whether activists identify their activism as linking activism, in addition to their current identifications, is a personal decision that I conjecture would vary among them. This decision will be influenced by the extent to which they feel linking activism is a term that is consistent with what they do and how they conceptualize their activism. Some, such as Morag and Doug, may state that linking activism depicts a proportion of their work while others, including Dorothy, Shirley or Brennain, may express it as a central defining feature of their activism.

THE NOTION OF MULTI OR COMPLEXLY-ALIGNED IDENTITY

As stated in Chapter One, the concept "multi or complexly-aligned identity" has been used to highlight three aspects of activists' linking accounts, namely, to make visible the dynamic between personal and social change, to acknowledge activists' multiple alliances and social locationalities, and to give view to understandings of self which acknowledge our complex relationality and connectedness to one another and the natural world.

In an increasingly global market culture which commodifies and homogenizes notions of identity and self, giving voice and affirmation to the above three aspects of activists' identity is vital. Payne (2000) argues, for instance, that while we have more control with which to shape our identities in postmodern culture, postmodern options of identity are in fact narrowly defined. He states, "Identities increasingly are selected, shaped and played out in this more abstract or virtual scenario of individualized 'choice' and 'opportunity' (or precarious lack of) in a technologically-driven commodity culture" (Payne, 2000, p. 75). A central question to ask, as researchers, is how do we access and give visibility to individuals' multi-dimensioned and aligned identities, to their blended inner and outer worlds, and to their capacities of relationality with others and the natural world?

In an initial response to this question, I maintain that we need conceptual frameworks that embody a number of assertions. One assertion includes the acknowledgement that activists are engaged in *a continual process of unfolding and maturation* as change makers. This means that integrative practices involve messy, dynamic processes of honoring, revising, integrating, expanding, and transforming aspects of self amidst one's outer efforts for social change. A second assertion is the *valuing of empowerment and strengths-based models of the individual.* These models remind us of our human potential and capacity for goodness and right action, and are thereby able to highlight activist strengths and desires to connect to others across social and ecological landscapes. Empowerment models also support our capacity for hope. Within empowerment frameworks personal and collective limitations are not denied, but are seen as opportunities for growth and change, and are situated with the broader discourse of an individual's abilities, strength, and potential.

Supporting activists to *start from where they are* comprises a third assertion. This orients activists to their own unique biographies and contexts, and to the available inner and outer resources which can motivate and support linking work. A fourth assertion recognizes the *importance of inner grounding within activist pr*actice. Inner grounding reflects the activists' ability to embody their social and ecological experiences and forms of knowing in ways which empower their efforts as social change makers.

The study of linking activism and notions of complexly multi-aligned identity is central to the creation of socially just and ecologically viable communities. This is particularly true in an era of increasing neo-conservative governments, global economic expansion, and deepening forms of social and ecological injustice.

Notes

NOTES TO CHAPTER ONE

1. See for instance, Agnew, 1996; Athanasiou, 1996; Bannerji, 1995; Belenky, Clinchy, Goldberger, & Tarule, 1986; Bishop, 1994; Borysenko, 1996; Brecher, Costello, & Smith, 2000; Briggs & Peat, 1999; Bullard, 1993a; Calliste & Dei, 2000; Capra, 1996; Chomsky, 2000; Cruden, 1995; Dei, 1996; Fine, Weis, Powell, & Wong, 1997; Forest, 2000; Franklin, 1990; Gaard, 1998; Gilligan, 1982; Gilligan, Lyons, & Hanmer, 1990; Goldberger, Tarule, Clinchy, & Belenky, 1996; Gomes & Kanner, 1995; Gottfried, 1996; Grewal & Kaplan, 1997; Griffiths & Campbell, 1989; Hill Collins, 1998; hooks, 1990; hooks, 2000; Jhappan, 1996; Johnson, 1989; Jordan, 1997; Kohn, 1990; Lerner, 1986, 1993; Macy, 1991; Merchant, 1983 and 1992; Miller & Stiver, 1997; Miller & Scholnick, 2000; Naess, 1989; Naples, 1998; Naples & Desai, 2002; Noske, 1997; O'Sullivan, 1999; Paleczny, 2000; Pike & Selby, 1999; Plumwood, 1994; Razack, 1998; Seager, 1993b; Seed, Macy, Fleming, & Naess, 1988; Shaikh, 2000; Sjoo, 1999; Spretnak, 1997; Starhawk, 1987; Surrey, 1985; Warren, 1994.

NOTES TO CHAPTER TWO

1. I am using the term marginalized community or constituency to mean a group that historically or presently has relatively less access to power and resources in relation to the dominant social group.
2. I am using Adkin's (1998) distinction between traditional social movements and NSMs, NSMs referring to "movements that mobilized in the late 1960s around such issues as sexual equality and freedom, civil liberties, anti-racism, peace, ecology, health, and international solidarity with anti-imperialist and democratic struggles in the Third World. The NSMs are distinguished from the "traditional" social movement, the labour movement . . . [and] earlier women's, peace, environmental and human rights/anti-slavery movements of the nineteenth and early twentieth centuries" (p. 1).

3. Initially the construct of "sustainable development," coined in the Brundtland Report, embraced the centrality of equity and justice within environmental change. With current movements for sustainable development, some have held onto the centrality of these values, while others have not. Regardless, this Report stirred North American social justice-ecological connections.

4. Women living in the Love Canal community in the United States began making the connection between illnesses in their children, miscarriages among them, and toxins leaking up through their basements and backyards. Lois Gibbs, a mother and key leader in this fight to get these hazards acknowledged and addressed, spearheaded with others a national Citizens Clearinghouse for Hazardous Waste, to support other communities and organizations fighting the same health and ecological injustices. This work has led to the mobilization of a movement across the United States against toxics, and has forged powerful links between environmental and health issues.

5. In 1989 the first anthology on ecofeminism was published, *Healing the Wounds*, following Francoise d'Eaubonne's coining of the term in 1974 in her book *Le feminism ou la mort*. Within ecofeminism there has been an expansion, and reframing, of the feminist movement, to embrace and tackle the destruction of nature, and the ways the degradation of nature and the oppression of women in male-dominated societies are interwoven. Ecofeminism, has also been a place within which women could voice their connection to the earth, claiming this relationship as a vital and powerful one in their lives—thereby, dismissing the patriarchal lie that women and nature are connected to one another by virtue of their mutual inferiority to men. Since this publication, there have been over 20 books and anthologies on ecofeminism and a vast number of journal articles. A movement has grown in Canada, United States, and countries abroad to link human and nonhuman oppression with action and discussion to fight these interlocking injustices (see Batt, 1999; Biehl, 1991; Calliste & Dei, 2000; Cuomo, 1998; Diamond & Orenstein, 1990; Gaard, 1998; Gibbs, 1997; Gomes & Kanner, 1995; Griffin, 1995; Kaplan, 1997; Macy, 1991, 1992, 2000; Mellor, 1992; Merchant, 1983; Plant, 1989; Sandilands, 1999; Seager, 1993; Shiva 1997, 1991, 1989; Spretnak, 1997; Starhawk, 1987; Sturgeon, 1997; Warren, 1997).

6. A specific landfill siting, a research study, and a national conference summit are central landmarks in the political awakening to the linkages between race and the environment in the United States and the rise to fight the injustices embedded within these linkages. In 1982, the predominately poor, African-American Warren County in North Carolina was chosen for a proposed PCB landfill site. The county was selected not for its ecological suitability but for its constituents' perceived powerlessness to resist the proposal. Opposition and protests to this siting fuelled the creation of an environmental justice movement in the United States stemming from the desire to stop environmental racism.

Further evidence of such racism was confirmed in the 1987 study *Toxic Wastes and Race*, which was initiated by a national civil rights organization,

The United Church of Christ Commission for Racial Justice. The study expanded the documentation of such injustices across the United States and identified areas of racial discrimination in environmental policy making, and regulatory and legal enforcement operations that target communities of color for toxic waste disposal and pollution industries (Chavis, 1993).
7. This debate also refers to issues of "job blackmail" (see Kazis & Grossman, 1991).

NOTES TO CHAPTER FOUR

1. For instance, Dowie (1995) quotes Charles Lee of the United Church of Christ's Special Project on Toxic Injustice who states: "When you use the word 'equity' it suggests that if we all share the problem it's OK" (p. 157). For environmental justice groups terms like "equity" are seen as soft terms used to avoid the truth of racism and injustice. Dowie (1995), for instance, recounts the story the U.S. EPA's use of the term "equity" not "justice" in a report on environmental equity stating, " The word *equity* was carefully chosen to avoid the hostile repercussions and reactions that agency feared would be evoked by *racism* and *injustice*. . . . [Minority environmentalists were] incensed by the use of *equity* and the avoidance of the word *justice* throughout the report "(pp. 156- 157).

NOTES TO CHAPTER FIVE

1. Media release from the Canadian Environmental Law Association, February 22, 1999, titled, "Ontario Hydro Should Be Subject to the *Freedom of Information Act* Say Environmental and Energy Watchdog Groups."
2. *114957 Canada Ltee (Spraytech, Societe d'arrosage) v. Hudson (Town) Supreme Court Decision,* June 28, 2001: 2001 SCC 40. File No.: 26937.

NOTES TO CHAPTER SIX

1. Specific questions would have to be asked to provide a coherent evaluation of Ontario environmental organizations with respect to social justice linkages. Specific questions pertaining to a group's mission statement, policies, structure, values, and practices would have needed explicit formulation for activists' response.
2. Within the U.S literature, many large mainstream U.S. environmental organizations have been seen to epitomize how social justice and equity gets left out of environmental activism and yet, these gaps are also present in environmental groups/environmental movements more generally.
3. See Adkin & Alpaugh, 1988; Adkin, 1998; Athanasiou, 1996; Boswell, 1992; Bryant, 1990, 1995; Carothers, 1990; Commoner, 1989; Dowie, 1996; Faber, 1998a, 1998b; Faber & O'Connor, 1993; Feagan, 1994; Field, 1998; Gardner, 1992; Genge, 1994; Gray, 1992a, 1992b; Harris, 1999; Jordan & Snow, 1991; Kaulbars, 1992; Levenstein & Wooding, 1998; Mann, 1993; Ostertag, 1991; Paehlke, 1993; Sale, 1993; Schrecker, 1995; Seager, 1993a; Shabecoff, 1993; Surman, 1993.

NOTES TO CHAPTER SEVEN

1. In Chapter Two, the example of economically vulnerable communities having financial incentives waved at them to "house" hazardous waste was given. Additional evidence that environmental reforms can have adverse impacts on socially oppressed and marginalized groups and communities can be explored. Field (1998) cites examples of U.S. environmental policy initiatives which have increased the burden of environmental pollutants in poor and minority communities. Speaking of environmental laws passed in the 1970s, Field (1998) states that they have, in part, facilitated:

   > pollution itself becom[ing] a movable commodity . . . capital increasingly mov[ing] pollution from the point of production across state and national borders to communities that possess less political power to resist being the dumping grounds for this "foreign" waste (p. 93).

   American and Canadian companies have sought to move business across national boundaries where environmental and social/worker standards are lower, and resources are cheaper.
       Traditional environmental regulatory approaches have also been connected to environmental injustice as they have enabled "cost-effective reforms" to replace "across-the-board compliance." The *Clean Air Act* in the United States is such an example. Within this Act, companies are allowed to buy and sell permits to pollute from one another which has increased cases of distributional injustice of pollution. Faber (1998a) cites an example of this environmental injustice stating, the:

   > commodification of pollution (which can be bought and sold on the stock market), . . . has allowed enterprises such as the Tennessee Valley Authority (TVA) to exceed federal limitations on sulfur dioxide and other toxic emissions in older facilities, mostly in the poor working class communities of color in the South (p. 35).

NOTES TO CHAPTER EIGHT

1. North American Free Trade Agreement—"An agreement effective January 1, 1994, reducing barriers to trade and investment between Canada, Mexico, and the US, and providing protection for corporations' investment and "intellectual property." (Brecher et al., 2000, p.124)
2. Multilateral Agreement on Investments—"A proposed treaty that would limit governments' ability to regulate foreign investment" (Brecher et al., 2000, p.124).

NOTES TO CHAPTER NINE

1. Research focus and protocol is further discussed in the subsequent section on demythologizing. Here the differences between traditional and popular epidemiology are explored.
2. Multilateral Agreement on Investments (MAI)
3. The literary and representational forms of myths themselves, however, are not being criticized.

NOTES TO CHAPTER ELEVEN

1. The lack of attention to natural resource-based environmental injustices in the United States is starting to be addressed as Torre (2002) articulates in Mutz, Bryner, & Kennedy (2002) stating:

    > This book moves the inquiry of [environmental justice] issues into a new direction. It takes the insights of the environmental justice movement out of the urban or rural southern setting, where the focus has been on toxic issues and locates them in the natural resources realm and at the level of policy (p. xxi).

2. We saw, for example, how the election of the Ontario Conservative government in 1995 moved some activists into new and expanded areas of alliance building to contest regressive government measures and priorities.

References

Adkin, L., & Alpaugh, C. (1988). Labour, ecology, and the politics of convergence. In F. Cunningham, S. Findlay, M. Kadar, A. Lennon, & E. Silva (Eds.), *Social movements/social change: The politics and practice of organizing* (pp. 48–73). Toronto: Between the Lines.

Adkin, L. E. (1998). *Politics of sustainable development: Citizens, unions and the corporations.* Montreal: Black Rose Books.

Agnew, V. (1996). *Resisting discrimination: Women from Asia, Africa, and the Caribbean and the women's movement in Canada.* Toronto: University of Toronto Press.

Alcasid, J. P., Chaudhuri, N., Miller, M., & Petrie, S. (1997). *Hidden exposure: A practical guide to creating a healthy environment for you and your children.* Toronto: South Riverdale Community Health Centre.

Alcoff, L., & Potter, E. (Eds.). (1993). *Feminist epistemologies.* New York: Routledge.

Appendini, K. (1999). "From where have all the flowers comes" women workers in Mexico's non-traditional markets. In D. Barndt (Ed.), *Women working the NAFTA food chain* (pp. 128–139). Toronto: Second Story Press.

Armstrong, L. (1999). *Proceeding from the March 26 & 27, 1999 workshop on primary cancer prevention: everyday carcinogens.* Paper presented at the Everyday Carcinogens: Stopping Cancer Before It Starts, McMaster University, Hamilton, ON.

Arnstein, S.R. (1969). A ladder of citizen participation. *American Institute of Planning Journal, 35,* 216–224.

Athanasiou, T. (1996). *Divided planet: The ecology of rich and poor.* Boston: Little, Brown and Company.

Bannerji, H. (1995). *Thinking through: Essays on feminism, marxism and anti-racism.* Toronto: Women's Press.

Bantjes, R., & Trussler, T. (1999). Feminism and the grass roots: Women and environmentalism in Nova Scotia, 1980–1983. *Canadian Review of Sociology and Anthropology, 36*(2), 179–198.

Bateson, M. C. (1990). *Composing a life: Life as a work in progress—The improvisations of five extraordinary women.* New York: A Plume Book.

Batt, S. (1994). *Patient no more: The politics of breast cancer.* Charlottetown, PEI: Gynergy Books.

Batt, S. (1999). Politicizing cancer. In M. Wyman (Ed.), *Sweeping the earth: Women taking action for a healthy planet* (pp. 113–120). Charlottetown, PEI: Gynergy Books.

Belenky, M. F., Clinchy, B. M., Goldberger, N. R., & Tarule, J. M. (1986). *Women's ways of knowing: The development of self, voice, and mind.* New York: Basic Books.

Bell, L. A. (1997). Theoretical foundations for social justice education. In M. Adams, L. A. Bell, & P. Griffin (Eds.), *Teaching for diversity and social Justice* (pp. 1–29). New York: Routledge.

Bernstein, M. (1997). Celebrations and suppressions: The strategic uses of identity by the lesbian and gay movement. *AJS, 103*(3), 531–65.

Biehl, J. (1991). *Finding our way: Rethinking ecofeminist politics.* Montreal: Black Rose Books.

Bishop, A. (1994). *Becoming an ally: Breaking the cycle of oppression.* Halifax, NS: Fernwood Publishing.

Bolen, J. S. (1984). *Goddesses in every woman: A new psychology of women.* New York: Harper Perennial.

Borysenko, J. (1996). *A woman's book of life.* New York: Riverhead Books.

Boswell, R. (1992, September 16). In Praise of Reconciliation and Three-Pitch. *CEN Bulletin.*

Brecher, J., Costello, T., & Smith, B. (2000). *Globalization from below: The power of solidarity.* Cambridge, MA: South End Press.

Briggs, J., & Peat, F. D. (1999). *Seven life lessons of chaos: Timeless wisdom from the science of change.* New York: Harper Collins.

Brophy, J. (1999). *Proceeding from the March 26 & 27, 1999 workshop on primary cancer prevention: Everyday carcinogens.* Paper presented at the Everyday Carcinogens: Stopping Cancer Before It Starts, McMaster University, Hamilton, ON.

Bruner, J (1985). Narrative and paradigmatic modes of thought. In E. Eisner (Ed.), *Learning and teaching the ways of knowing* (pp. 97–115). Chicago: NSSE.

Bryant, B. (1990). *Environmental advocacy: Concepts, issues and dilemmas.* Ann Arbor, MI: Caddo Gap Press.

Bryant, B. (Ed.). (1995). *Environmental justice: Issues, policies, and solutions.* Washington, DC: Island Press.

Bullard, R. D. (Ed.). (1993a). *Confronting environmental racism: Voices from the grassroots.* Boston: South End Press.

Bullard, R. D. (1993b). Anatomy of environmental racism. In R. Hofrichter (Ed.), *Toxic struggles: The theory and practice of environmental justice* (pp. 25–35). Gabriola Island, BC: New Society Publishers.

Bullard, R. D. (1993c). Anatomy of environmental racism and the environmental justice movement. In R. D. Bullard (Ed.), *Confronting environmental racism: Voices from the grassroots.* Boston: South End Press.

Calliste, A., & Dei, G. J. S. (Eds.). (2000). *Anti-racist feminism: Critical race and gender studies.* Halifax, NS: Fernwood Publishing.

Canadian Environmental Law Association (1999). *The lands for life proposals: A preliminary analysis by the Canadian Environmental Law Association* (No. 373). Toronto: Canadian Environmental Law Association.

Canadian Environmental Law Association (1999). *Presentation to the standing committee on the administration of justice* (November 19). Toronto: Standing Committee on the Administration of Justice.

Capra, F. (1996). *The web of life: A new scientific understanding of living systems.* Toronto: Anchor Books.

Carothers, A. (1990, July/August). Towards a new environmentalism. *GREENPEACE,* p. 2.

Carter, K. (1993). The place of story in the study of teaching and teacher Education. *Educational Researcher, 22*(1), 5–12.

Chase, S. (1995). Taking narrative seriously: Consequences for method and theory in interview studies. In R. Josselson & A. Lieblich (Eds.), *The narrative study of lives* (Vol. 3, pp. 1–26). London: Sage.

Chavez, C. (1993). Farm workers at risk. In R. Hofrichter (Ed.), *Toxic struggles: The theory and practice of environmental justice* (pp. 163–170). Gabriola Island, BC: New Society Publishers.

Chivian, E., McCally, M., Hu, H., & Haines, A. (Eds.). (1994). *Critical condition: Human health and the environment.* London: MIT Press.

Chomsky, N. (2000). *Chomsky on miseducation.* London: Rowman & Littlefield.

Clover, D. E. (2002). Toward transformative learning: Ecological perspective for adult education. In E. O'Sullivan, A. Morrell, & M. A. O'Connor (Eds.), *Expanding the boundaries of transformative learning* (pp. 159–172). New York: Palgrave.

Cogswell, D. (1996). *Chomsky.* New York: Writers and Readers Publishing.

Colborn, T., Dumanoski, D., & Myers, J. P. (1997). *Our stolen future: Are we threatening our fertility, intelligence, and survival? A scientific detective story.* New York: Plume Book.

Coles, R. (1989). *The call of stories: Teaching and the moral imagination.* Boston: Houghton Mifflin.

Collin, R., & Harris, W. (1993). Race and waste in two Virginia communities. In R. Bullard (Ed.), *Confronting environmental racism: Voices from the grassroots* (pp. 93–106). Boston: South End Press.

Commoner, B. (1989, September/October). Why we have failed. GREENPEACE, pp. 12–13.

Connelly, F. M., & Clandidin, D. J. (1990). Stories of experience and narrative inquiry. *Educational Researcher, 19*(5), 2–14.

Cooper, K. (1998). Trashing environmental protection: Ontario's four-part strategy. In L. Ricciutelli, J. Larkin, & E. O'Neill (Eds.), *Confronting the cuts* (pp. 77–82). Toronto: Inanna Publications and Education Inc.

Cooper, K., Vanderlinden, L., McClenaghan, T., Keenan, K., Khatter, K., Muldoon, P., & Abelsohn, A. (2000). *Children's health project: Environmental standard setting and children's health.* Toronto: Canadian Environmental Law Association Ontario College of Family Physicians.

Creed, D., & Scully, M . (2000). Songs of ourselves: Employees' deployment of social identity in workplace encounters, *Journal of Management Inquiry, 9*(4), 391–412.

Cruden, L. (1995). *Coyote's council fire: Contemporary shamans on race, gender and community.* Rochester, VT: Destiny Books.

Cuomo, C. J. (1998). *Feminism and ecological communities*. New York: Routledge.

Davis, B., Sumara, D., & Luce-Kapler, R. (2000). *Engaging minds: Learning and teaching in a complex world*. Mahwah, NJ: Lawrence Erlbaum Associates.

Dei, G. (1996). *Anti-racism education: Theory and practice*. Halifax, NS: Fernwood Publishing.

Denzin, N. K. (1989). *Interpretive interactionism* (Vol. 16). Newbury Park, CA: Sage.

Desai, S. (1996). Common issues, common understandings. In C. E. James (Ed.), *Perspectives on racism and the human services sector: A case for change* (pp. 246–252). Toronto: University Press of Toronto.

Diamond, I., & Orenstein, G. (Eds.). (1990). *Reweaving the world: The emergence of ecofeminism*. San Fransciso: Sierra Club Books.

Di Chiro, G. (1998). Environmental justice from the grassroots: Reflections on history, gender and expertise. In D. Faber (Ed.), *The struggle for ecological democracy: Environmental justice movements in the United States*. New York: Guilford Press.

Dijkstra, B. (1986). *Idols of perversity: Fantasies of feminine evil in fin-de-Siecle culture*. New York: Oxford University Press.

Dowie, M. (1996). *Losing ground: American environmentalism at the close of the twentieth century*. Cambridge, MA: MIT Press.

Eckersley, R. (1992). *Environmentalism and political theory: Toward an ecocentric approach*. Albany, NY: SUNY Press.

Eisner, E. W. (1991). *The enlightened eye: Qualitative inquiry and the enhancement of educational practice*. New York: Macmillan.

Environmental and Occupational Working Groups. (2000). *Preventing cancer from environmental and occupational factors: A strategy for the City of Toronto*. Toronto: Toronto Cancer Prevention Coalition.

Estrin, D., & Swaigen, J. (1993). *Environment on trial* (3rd ed.). Toronto: Emond Montgomery Publications.

Faber, D. (1998a). The political ecology of American capitalism: New challenges for the environmental justice movement. In D. Faber (Ed.), *The struggle for ecological democracy: environmental justice movements in the United States* (pp. 27–59). New York: The Guildford Press.

Faber, D (1998b). The struggle for ecological democracy: Environmental justice. *The struggle for ecological democracy: environmental justice movements in the United States* (pp. 1–26). New York: The Guildford Press.

Faber, D. (Ed.). (1998c). *The struggle for ecological democracy: Environmental justice movements in the United States*. New York: The Guildford Press.

Faber, D., & O'Connor, J. (1993). Capitalism and the crisis of environmentalism. In R. Hofrichter (Ed.), *Toxic struggles: The theory and practice of environmental justice* (pp. 12–24). Gabriola Island, BC: New Society Publishers.

Feagan, R. (1994). Expanding worldviews: Social movement backgrounds bring a deeper analysis to the environmental movement. *Alternatives*, 20(2), pp. 26–31.

Ferris, D., & Hahn-Baker, D. (1995). Environmentalists and environmental justice policy. In B. Bryant (Ed.), *Environmental justice: Issues, policies, and solutions* (pp. 66–75). Washington, D.C.: Island Press.

Field, R. C. (1998). Risk and justice: Capitalist production and the environment. In D. Faber (Ed.), *The struggle for ecological democracy: Environmental justice movements in the United States* (pp. 81–103). New York: The Guildford Press.

Fine, M., Weis, L., Powell, L. C., & Wong, L. M. (Eds.). (1997). *Off white: Readings on race, power, and society.* New York: Routledge.

Flinders, C. L. (1998). *At the root of this longing: Reconciling a spiritual hunger and a feminist thirst.* New York: Harper Collins.

Forest, O. S. (2000). *Dreaming the council ways.* York Beach, ME: Samuel Weiser.

Foster, J.B. (1998). The limits of environmentalism without class: Lessons for the ancient forest struggle in the Pacific Northwest. In D. Faber (Ed.), *The struggle for ecological democracy: Environmental justice movements in the United States* (pp. 188–217). New York: The Guildford Press.

Franklin, U. (1990). *The real world of technology.* Concord, ON: House of Anansi Press.

Fulford, R. (1999). *The triumph of the narrative: Storytelling in the age of mass culture.* Toronto: House of Anansi Press.

Gaard, G. (1998). *Ecological politics: Ecofeminists and the greens.* Philadelphia: Temple University Press.

Gadamer, H. G. (1975). *Truth and method.* New York: Seabury.

Gadamer, H. G. (1976). *Philosophical hermeneutics.* Berkeley: University of California Press.

Gancher, D. (1993). Preface. In A. Wallace (Ed.), *Eco-Heroes: Twelve tales of environmental victory.* San Francisco: Mercury House.

Gardner, J. E. (1993). Environmental non-government organizations (ENGOs) and sustainable development. In S. Lerner (Ed.), *Environmental stewardship: Studies in active earthkeeping.* Waterloo, ON: Department of Geography, University of Waterloo.

Gardner, M. (1992). *Environmental advocacy and social equity: Case study of the a community in crisis.* Unpublished thesis. University of Toronto, Toronto, ON.

Gardner, M. (1993). *The importance of public participation funding: A study of non-litigation funding for the proposed Ontario Environmental Bill of Rights.* Toronto: Ontario Environment Network.

Genge, C. (1994). Paul Watson's Eco Terror. *NOW Magazine.*

Gibbs, L.M. (1997). *Dying from dioxin: A citizen's guide to reclaiming our health and rebuilding democracy.* Montreal: Black Rose Books.

Gilligan, C. (1982). *In a different voice: Psychological theory and women's development.* Cambridge, MA: Harvard University Press.

Gilligan, C., Lyons, N. P., & Hanmer, T. J. (Eds.). (1990). *Making connections: The relational worlds of adolescent girls at Emma Willard school.* Cambridge, MA: Harvard University Press.

Gitlin, A., Siegel, M., & Boru, K. (1989). The politics of method: From leftist ethnography to educative research. *Qualitative Studies in Education, 2*(3), 237–253.

Glesne, C., & Peshkin, A. (1992). *Becoming qualitative researchers: An introduction.* White Plains, NY: Longman.

Goldberger, N., Tarule, J., Clinchy, B., & Belenky, M. (Eds.). (1996). *Knowledge, difference, and power: Essays inspired by women's ways of knowing.* New York: Basic Books.

Goldman, B. (1993, December). Not just prosperity: Achieving sustainability with environmental justice. *National Wildlife Federation.*

Gomes, M. E., & Kanner, A. D. (1995). The rape of the well-maidens: Feminist psychology and the environmental crisis. In L. R. Brown, M. E. Gomes, & A. D. Kanner (Eds.), *Ecopsychology: Restoring the earth, healing the mind* (pp. 111–121). San Francisco: Sierra Club Books.

Gottfried, H. (1996). *Feminism and social change: Bridging theory and practice.* Chicago: University of Illinois Press.

Gottlieb, R. (1993). *Forcing the spring: The transformation of the American environmental movement.* Washington: Island Press.

Gray, S. (1992a, November/December). Democracy, jobs and the environment. *Canadian Dimension,* pp. 17–20.

Gray, S. (1992b, June). Double exposure: The environment as a worker's issue. *Our Times,* pp. 27–30.

Greed, C. (1990). The professional and the personal: A study of women quantity surveyors. In L. Stanley (Ed.), *Feminist praxis: Research, theory, and epistemology in feminist sociology* (pp. 145–158). New York: Routledge.

Grewal, I., & Kaplan, C. (Eds.). (1997). *Scattered hegemonies: Postmodernity and transnational feminist practices.* Minneapolis: University of Minnesota Press.

Griffin, S. (1995). *The eros of everyday life: Essays on ecology, gender and society.* New York: Anchor Book.

Griffiths, L., & Campbell, M. (1989). *The book of Jessica: A theatrical transformation.* Toronto: The Coach House Press.

Guzman, M. B. (1996). *Women reshaping human rights: How extraordinary activists are changing the world.* Wilmington, DE: Scholarly Resources Inc.

Hall, B. L. (2002). The right to a new utopia: Adult learning and the changing world of work in an era of global capitalism. In E. O'Sullivan, A. Morrell, & M. A. O'Connor (Eds.), *Expanding the boundaries of transformative learning* (pp. 35–46). New York: Palgrave.

Harding, S. (1987a). Conclusion: Epistemological questions. In S. Harding (Ed.), *Feminism and methodology* (pp. 181–190). Bloomington: Indiana University Press.

Harding, S. (Ed.). (1987b). *Feminism and methodology.* Bloomington: Indiana University Press.

Harris, H. (1999). *Rainbow dancer.* Prince George, BC: Caitlin Press.

Henderson, H. (1999). *Beyond globalization: Shaping a sustainable global economy.* West Hartford: Kumarian Press.

Heyward, C. (1989). *Touching our strength: The erotic as power and the love of God.* New York: Harper San Francisco.

Hill Collins, P. (1998). *Fighting words: Black women and the search for justice.* Minneapolis: University of Minnesota Press.

Hofrichter, R. (Ed.). (1993). *Toxic struggles: The theory and practice of environmental justice.* Gabriola Island, BC: New Society Publishers.

hooks, b. (1990). *Yearning: race, gender, and cultural politics.* Toronto: Between the Lines.

hooks, b. (2000). *Feminism is for everyone: Passionate politics.* Cambridge, MA: South End Press.

Hunt, D. E. (1987). *Beginning with ourselves.* Toronto: OISE Press.

Hunt, D. E. (1992). *The Renewal of Personal Energy.* Toronto: OISE Press.

Husserl, E. (1965). *Phenomenology and the crisis of philosophy.* New York: Harper Torchbooks.

Jacob, E. (1987). Qualitative research traditions: A review. *Review of Educational Research, 57*(1), 1–50.

Jhappan, R. (1996). Post-modern and gender essentialism or a post-mortem of scholarship. *Studies in Political Economy, 51,* 15–63.

Johnson, A. (1996). Towards an equitable, efficient, and effective human service system. In C. E. James (Ed.), *Perspectives on racism and the human services sector: A case for change* (pp. 209–221). Toronto: University Press of Toronto.

Johnson, S. (1989). *Wild Fire: Igniting the she/volution.* Albuquerque, NM: Wildfire Books.

Jordan, C., & Snow, D. (1991). Diversification, minorities, and the mainstream environmental movement. In D. Snow (Ed.), *Voices from the environmental movement: Perspectives for a new era* (Vol. 71). Washington, DC: Island Press.

Jordan, J. V. (Ed.). (1997). *Women's growth in diversity: More writings from the Stone Center.* New York: Guilford Press.

Jordan, J. (1995). *Relational awareness: Transforming disconnection.* Work in Progress, No. 76. Wellesley, MA; Stone Centre Working Paper Series.

Kaplan, T. (1997). *Crazy for democracy: Women in grassroots movements.* New York: Routledge.

Kaulbars, M. (1992, April). The movement that never was. *Canadian Environmental Network, 2*(3), 2.

Kazis, R., & Grossman, R. (1991). *Fear at work: Job blackmail, labor and the environment.* Gabriola Island. B.C.: New Society Publishers.

King, T. (2003). *The truth about our stories.* Toronto: House of Anansi Press.

Kirby, S., & McKenna, K. (1989). *Methods from the margins: Experience, research, social change.* Toronto: Garamond Press.

Kohn, A. (1990). *The brighter side of human nature: Altruism and empathy in everyday life.* New York: Basic Books.

Krauss, C. (1993). Blue-collar women and toxic-waste protests: The process of politicization. In R. Hofrichter (Ed.), *Toxic struggles: The theory and practice of environmental justice* (pp. 107–117). Gabriola Island, BC: New Society Publishers.

Labonte, R. (1986, March). On the brink. *New Internationalist,* pp. 21–22.

Landsman (2001). Toward a fractal metaphor for liberation of Palestinian women. *Radical Psychology, 2,* (1). Retrieved September 25, 2003, from www.radpsynet.org.

Lasn, K. (2000). *Culture jam: How to reverse America's suicidal consumer binge— And why we must.* New York: Harper Collins.

Lather, P. (1992). Critical frames in educational research: Feminist and post-structural perspectives. *Theory into Practice, 31*(2), 87–99.

Lavelle, M., & Coyle, M. (1992, September 21). Unequal protection. *National Law Journal.*

Lavelle, M., & Coyle, M. A. (1993). Unequal protection: The racial divide in environmental law. In R. Hofrichter (Ed.), *Toxic struggles: The theory and practice of environmental justice* (pp. 136–143). Gabriola Island, BC: New Society Publishers.

Lee, C. (1993). Beyond toxic wastes and race. In R. Bullard (Ed.), *Confronting environmental racism: Voices from the grassroots* (pp. 41–52). Boston: South End Press.

Legault, L., Baldini, T., Beland, D. P., Bayh, S., Murphy, F., & Chamberlin, A. (1998). *Ninth biennial report on the Great Lakes water quality.* Ottawa: International Joint Commission.

Lerner, G. (1986). *The creation of patriarchy.* Toronto: Oxford University Press.

Lerner, G. (1993). *The creation of feminist consciousness.* New York: Oxford University Press.

Levenstein, C., & Wooding, J. (1998). Dying for a living: Workers, production, and the environment. In D. Faber (Ed.), *The struggle for ecological democracy: Environmental justice movements in the United States* (pp. 60–80). New York: The Guildford Press.

Lincoln, Y. S., & Guba, E. G. (1985). *Naturalistic inquiry.* Beverly Hills, CA: Sage.

Lindgren, R. (1999, January-March). The right to participate. *Intervenor, 24* (1), 5–8.

Lynn, H. (1999). Women's Environment Network. In M. Wyman (Ed.), *Sweeping the Earth: Women taking action for a healthy planet* (pp. 272–280). Charlottetown, PEI: Gynergy Books.

MacFarlane, D. (1999, July). Monte's gift. *Toronto Life,* pp. 89–93.

MacKinnon, L. (1998, March 19). The politics of garbage. *The National Magazine.*

Macy, J. (1991). *World as lover, world as self.* Berkeley, CA: Parallax Press.

Macy, J. (1992, Winter). *The Institute for Deep Ecology Education Newsletter,* p. 3.

Macy, J. (2000). *Widening circles.* Gabriola Island, BC: New Society Publishers.

Macy, J., & Brown, M. Y. (1998). *Coming back to life: Practices to reconnect our lives, our world.* BC, Canada: New Society Publishers.

Mann, E. (1993). Labor's environmental agenda in the new corporate climate. In R. Hofrichter (Ed.), *Toxic struggles: The theory and practice of environmental justice* (pp. 179–185). Gabriola Island, BC: New Society Publishers.

Marino, D. (1997). *Wild garden: Art, education, and the culture of resistance.* Toronto: Between the Lines.

Martinez-Salazar, E. (1999). The "poisoning" of indigenous migrant women workers and children: From deadly colonialism to toxic globalization. In D. Barndt (Ed.), *Women working the NAFTA food chain* (pp. 99–112). Toronto: Second Story Press.

Maxwell, M. (2002). What is curriculum anyway? In E. O'Sullivan, A. Morrell, & M. A. O'Connor (Eds.), *Expanding the boundaries of transformative learning* (pp. 13–22). New York: Palgrave.

Maynes, C. (1989). *Public consultation: A citizens handbook*. Guelph: Ontario Environment Network.

McQuaig, L. (1998). *The cult of impotence: Selling the myth of powerlessness in the global economy*. Toronto: Penguin Books.

Mellor, M. (1992). *Breaking the boundaries: Towards a feminist green socialism*. London: Virago Press.

Merchant, C. (1983). *The death of nature: Women, ecology and the scientific revolution*. San Francisco: Harper & Row.

Merchant, C. (1992). *Radical ecology: The search for a livable world*. New York: Routledge.

Milani, B. (2000). *Designing the green economy: The postindustrial alternative to corporate globalization*. Oxford: Rowman & Littlefield.

Milbrath, L. (1984). *Environmentalists: Vanguard for a new society*. Albany, NY: SUNY Press.

Miles, A. (2002). Feminist perspectives on globalization and integrative transformative learning. In E. O'Sullivan, A. Morrell, & M. A. O'Connor (Eds.), *Expanding the boundaries of transformative learning* (pp. 23–33). New York: Palgrave.

Miller, A. (1995). *Recommendations for the primary prevention of cancer*. Toronto: Report of the Ontario Task Force on the Primary Prevention of Cancer.

Miller, J. B., & Stiver, I. P. (1997). *The healing connection: How women form relationships in therapy and in life*. Boston: Beacon Press.

Miller, P. H., & Scholnick, E. K. (Eds.). (2000). *Toward a feminist developmental psychology*. New York: Routledge.

Minors, A. (1996). From uni-versity to poly-versity: Organizations in transition to anti-racism. In C. E. James (Ed.), *Perspectives on racism and the human services sector: A case for change* (pp. 196–208). Toronto: University Press of Toronto.

Moore, R., & Head, L. (1993). Acknowledging the past, confronting the present. In R. Hofrichter (Ed.), *Toxic struggles: The theory and practice of environmental justice* (pp. 118–127). Gabriola Island, BC: New Society Publishers.

Morrel, A., & O'Connor, M. (2002). Introduction. In E. O'Sullivan, A. Morrell, & M. A. O'Connor (Eds.), *Expanding the boundaries of transformative learning* (pp. xv-xx). New York: Palgrave.

Morss, J. R. (1996). *Growing Critical: Alternatives to developmental psychology*. London: Routledge.

Moses, M. (1993). Farm workers and pesticides. In R. Bullard (Ed.), *Confronting environmental racism: Voices from the grassroots* (pp. 161–178). Boston: South End Press.

Moustakas, C. (1990). *Heuristic research: Design, methodology, and applications*. Newbury Park, CA: Sage.

Muldoon, P., & Winfield, M. (1999). *Democracy and environmental accountability in Ontario*. Toronto: Canadian Environmental Law Association.

Mutz, K. M., Bryner, G. C., & Kenney, D. S. (Eds.). (2002). *Justice and natural resources: Concepts, strategies, and applications*. Washington, DC: Island Press.

Naess, A. (1989). *Ecology, community and lifestyle: Outline of ecosophy* (David Rothenberg, Trans.). Cambridge, MA: Cambridge University Press.

Naples, N. A. (1998). *Grassroots warriors: Activist mothering, community work, and the war on poverty.* New York: Routledge.

Naples, N. A. (2002). Changing the terms: Community activism, globalization, and the dilemmas of transnational feminist praxis. In N. A. Naples & M. Desai (Eds.), *Women's activism and globalization* (pp. 3–14). New York: Routledge.

Naples, N. A., & Desai, M. (2002). *Women's activism and globalization: Linking local struggles and transnational politics.* New York: Routledge.

Nelson, L. (1990). The place of women in polluted places. In I. Diamond & G. F. Orenstein (Eds.), *Reweaving the world: The emergence of ecofeminism* (pp. 173–188). San Francisco: Sierra Club Books.

Noble, C. (1993). Work: The most dangerous environment. In R. Hofrichter (Ed.), *Toxic struggles: The theory and practice of environmental justice* (pp. 171–178). Gabriola Island, BC: New Society Publishers.

Noddings, N. (1991). Stories in dialogue: Caring and interpersonal reasoning. In C. Witherell & N. Noddings (Eds.), *Stories lives tell: Narrative and dialogue in education* (pp. 157–170). New York: Teachers College Press.

Noffke, S. (1991). *Knowledge, voice, and values: Issues of validity in research with teachers.* Paper presented at the Spencer Hall Invitational Conference on Understanding Teacher Development in Context, London, ON.

Noske, B. (1997). *Beyond boundaries: Humans and animals.* Montreal: Black Rose Books.

Novogrodsky, C. (1996). The anti-racist cast of mind. In C. E. James (Ed.), *Perspectives on racism and the human services sector: A case for change* (pp. 187–195). Toronto: University Press of Toronto.

Novotny, P. (1998). Popular epidemiology and the struggle for community health in the environmental justice movement. In D. Faber (Ed.), *The struggle for ecological democracy: Environmental justice movements in the United States* (pp. 137–158). New York: The Guildford Press.

Oakley, A. (1981). Interviewing women: A contradiction in terms. In H. R. Roberts (Ed.), *Doing feminist research* (pp. 30–61). Boston: Routledge and Kegan Paul.

O'Donoghue, M., & Reid, A. (2001, September). *Rethinking policy and practice in teacher education.* Paper presented to the Australian Teacher Education Association conference, Melbourne.

Olson, D. R. (1990). Thinking about narrative. In B. K. Britton & A. D. Pellegrini (Eds.), *Narrative thought and narrative language* (pp. 99–112). Hillsdale, NJ: Lawrence Erlbaum Associates.

O'Murchu, D. (1995). *Our world in transition: Making sense of a changing world.* New York: The Crossroad Publishing Company.

Ostertag, B. (1991, March/April). Greenpeace takes over the world. *Mother Jones,* p. 32.

O'Sullivan, E. (1999). *Transformative learning: Educational vision for the 21st Century.* Toronto: University of Toronto Press.

O'Sullivan, E. (2002). The project and vision of transformative education: Integral transformative learning. In E. O'Sullivan, A. Morrell, & M. A. O'Connor (Eds.), *Expanding the boundaries of transformative learning* (pp. 1–12). New York: Palgrave.

O'Sullivan, E., Morrell, A., & O'Connor, M. (Eds.). (2002). *Expanding the boundaries of transformative learning*. New York: Palgrave.

Paehlke, R. (1993). *Environmentalism and the future of progressive politics*. New Haven, CT: Yale University Press.

Paleczny, B. (2000). *Clothed in integrity: Weaving just cultural relations and the garment industry*. Waterloo, ON: Wilfrid Laurier University Press.

Payne, (2000). Identity and environmental education. *Environmental Educational Research,* 7(1), 67–88.

Pearson, C. (1998). *The hero within: Six archetypes we live by*. San Francisco: Harper San Francisco.

Peavy, Vance R. (1998). *SocioDynamic counselling: A constructivist perspective*. Victoria, BC: Trafford.

Pike, G., & Selby, D. (1988). *Global teacher, global learner*. London: Hodder & Stoughton.

Pike, G., & Selby, D. (1999). *The global classroom 1*. Toronto: Pippin.

Plant, J. (Ed.). (1989). *Healing the wounds: The promise of ecofeminism*. Philadelphia: New Society Publishers.

Plischke, H. (1997, July 10). Feds agree to study health of natives near waste plant. *Edmonton Journal*.

Plumwood, V. (1994). Ecosocial feminism as a general theory of oppression. In C. Merchant (Ed.), *Ecology* (pp. 207–234). Atlantic Highlands, NJ: Humanities Press.

Polkinghorne, D. E. (1988). *Narrative knowing and the human sciences*. Albany: State University of New York.

Rappaport, J. (1995). Empowerment meets narrative: Listening to stories and creating settings. *American Journal of Community Psychology,* 23(5), 795–807.

Razack, S. H. (1998). *Looking white people in the eye*. Toronto: University of Toronto Press.

Reason, P., & Marshall, J. (1987). Research as personal process. In D. Boud & V. Griffin (Eds.), *Appreciating adults learning: From the learner's perspective*. London: Kagan Page Press.

Reinharz, S. (1983). Experiential analysis: A contribution to feminist research. In G. Bowles & R. D. Klein (Eds.), *Theories of women's studies* (pp. 163–191). London: RK Press.

Reinharz, S. (1992). *Feminist methods in social research*. New York: Oxford University Press.

Ricciutelli, L., Larkin, J., & O'Neill, E. (Eds.). (1998). *Confronting the cuts*. Toronto: Inanna Publications and Education Inc.

Rice, B., & Weinberg, J. (1994). *A case study in sunsetting chlorine chemistry: Perchloroethylene in the dry cleaning industry*. Toronto: Pollution Probe.

Richardson, M., Sherman, J., & Gismondi, M. (1993). *Winning back the words: Confronting experts in an environment public hearing*. Toronto: Garamond Press.

Riessman, C. K. (1993). *Narrative analysis* (Vol. 30). Newbury Park, CA: Sage.

Sale, K. (1993). *The green revolution: The American environmental movement, 1962–1992*. New York: Hill and Wang.

Sandilands, C. (1999). *The good-natured feminist: Ecofeminism and the quest for democracy*. Minneapolis: University of Minnesota Press.

Schrecker, T. (1995). Environmentalism and the politics of invisibility. In M. D. Mehta & E. Ouellet (Eds.), *Environmental sociology: Theory and practice* (pp. 203–218). Toronto: Captus Press.

Schwartz, S., & Chance, G. W. (1999). Children first: Environmental contaminant protection policy needs to be rewritten to reflect the needs of our most vulnerable citizens. *Alternatives, 25*(3), 20–25.

Seager, J. (1993a). Creating a culture of destruction: Gender, militarism, and the environment. In R. Hofrichter (Ed.), *Toxic struggles: The theory and practice of environmental justice* (pp. 58–66). Gabriola Island, BC: New Society Publishers.

Seager, J. (1993b). *Earth follies: Coming to feminist terms with the global environmental crisis.* New York: Routledge.

Seed, J., Macy, J., Fleming, P., & Naess, A. (1988). *Thinking like a mountain: Toward a council of all beings.* Philadelphia: New Society Publishers.

Seidman, I. E. (1991). Interviewing as qualitative research. New York: Teachers College Press.

Selby, D. (2002). The signature of the whole: Radical interconnectedness and its implications for global and environmental education. In E. O'Sullivan, A. Morrell, and M. A. O'Connor (Eds.), *Expanding the boundaries of transformative learning* (pp. 77–93). New York: Palgrave.

Shabecoff, P. (1993). *A fierce green fire.* New York: Hill and Wang.

Shaikh, S. S. (2000). Conceptualizing linked social and ecological injustice. *Environments: A Journal of Interdisciplinary Studies, 28*(2), 77–88.

Shiva, V. (1997). *Biopiracy: The plunder of nature and knowledge.* Boston: South End Press.

Shiva, V. (1991). *The violence of the green revolution: Third world agriculture, ecology, and politics.* New Jersey: Zed Books.

Shiva, V. (1989). *Staying alive: Women, ecology and development.* London: Zed Books.

Shrybman, S. (1987, January). Poverty and pollution. *Canadian Environmental Law Association*, pp. 1–28.

Sjoo, M. (1999). *Return of the dark/light mother or new age armegeddon?* Austin, TX: Plain View Press.

Small, F. (2000, November). Environmental activism—A social justice issue. *The Hamilton Unitarian, 51*(10), 15.

Smith, C. (1997). Comparing traditional therapies with narrative approaches. In C. Smith & D. Nylund (Eds.), *Narrative therapies with children and adolescents* (pp. 1–52). New York: Guilford Press.

Smith, J. K. (1983). Quantitative versus qualitative research: An attempt to clarify the issue. *Educational Researcher, 12*(3), 6–13.

Spretnak, C. (1997). *The resurgence of the real: Body, nature, and place in the hypermodern world.* Don Mills, ON: Addison-Wesley.

Stanley, L., & Wise, S. (1990). Method, methodology and epistemology in feminist research processes. In L. Stanley (Ed.), *Feminist praxis: Research, theory and epistemology in feminist sociology* (pp. 20–62). New York: Routledge.

Starhawk. (1987). *Truth or dare: Encounters with power, authority, and mystery.* San Francisco: Harper San Francisco.

Steingraber, S. (1997). *Living downstream: An ecologist looks at cancer and the environment*. Don Mills, ON: Addison-Wesley.

Strauss, A.L. (1987). *Qualitative analysis for social scientists*. Cambridge, MA: Cambridge University Press.

Sturgeon, N. (1997). *Ecofeminist natures: Race, gender, feminist theory and political action*. Routledge: New York.

Sullivan, E. (1990). *Critical psychology and pedagogy: Interpretation of the personal world*. Toronto: OISE Press.

Surman, M. (1993, Spring). Interview with Eric Mann—Auto-free: Revolution or reaction? *Trans-Mission: Politics, Culture and Sustainable Transportation*, pp. 18–21.

Surrey, J. L. (1985). *The "self-in-relation": A theory of women's development*. Work in Progress, No. 13. Wellesley, MA: Stone Centre Working Paper Series.

Swenarchuk, M. (1997). *CELA Brief No.314, Submission from the Canadian Environmental Law Association to the Ontario Legal Aid Review*. Toronto: Canadian Environmental Law Association.

Swenarchuk, M., & Muldoon, P. (1996). *In defence of environmental regulation*. Toronto, ON: Canadian Environmental Law Association.

Szasz, A. (Ed.). (1994). *EcoPopulism: Toxic waste and the movement for environmental justice*. Minneapolis: University of Minnesota Press.

Taylor, D. E. (1993). Environmentalism and the politics of inclusion. In R. Bullard (Ed.), *Confronting environmental racism: Voices from the grassroots*. Boston: South End Press.

Tindall, D., & Begoray, N. (1993). Old growth defenders: The battle for the Carmanah Valley. In S. Lerner (Ed.), *Environmental stewardship: Studies in active earthkeeping* (pp. 297–322). Waterloo, ON: Department of Geography, University of Waterloo.

Torre, G. (2002). Foreward. In K. M. Mutz, G. C. Bryner, & D. S. Kenny (Eds.), *Justice and natural resources: Concepts, Strategies, and Applications* (pp. xxi-xxviii). Washington, DC: Island Press.

United Church of Christ Commission for Racial Justice. (1987). *Toxic wastes and race in the United States, A national report on the racial and socio-economic characteristics of communities with hazardous waste sites*. New York: United Church of Christ.

vanManen, M. (1990). *Researching lived experience: Human science for an action sensitive pedagogy*. London, ON: The Althouse Press.

Wallace, A. (1993). *Eco-heroes: Twelve tales of environmental victory*. San Francisco: Mercury House.

Warren, K. (1994). Toward an ecofeminist peace politics. In K. Warren (Ed.), *Ecological Feminism* (pp. 179–199). London: Routledge.

Warren, K. J. (Ed.). (1997). *Ecofeminism: Women, culture, nature*. Bloomington: Indiana University Press.

Weedon, C. (1987). *Feminist practice & poststructuralist theory*. Oxford: Basil Blackwell.

Wernette, D. R., & Nieves, L. A. (1992). Breathing polluted air: Minorities are disproportionately exposed. *EPA Journal, 18*, 16–17

Wilber, K. (2000) *A theory of everything: An integral vision for business, politics, science and spirituality.* Boston: Shambhala.

Woodman, M. (1982). *Addiction to perfection: The still unravished bride.* Toronto: Inner City Books.

Wright, B. H., & Bullard, R. (1993). The effects of occupational injury, illness, and disease on the health status of Black Americans. In R. Hofrichter (Ed.), *Toxic struggles: The theory and practice of environmental justice* (pp. 153–162). Gabriola Island, BC: New Society Publishers.

Zimmerman, M.A. (2000). Empowerment theory: Psychological, organizational, and community levels of analysis. In J. Rappaport & E. Seidman (Eds.), *Handbook of community psychology* (pp. 43–64). New York: Kluwer Academic Plenum Publishers.

Index